THE WILL TO VIOLENCE

THE WILL TO VIOLENCE

The Politics of Personal Behaviour

Susanne Kappeler

Polity Press

Copyright © Susanne Kappeler 1995
The right of Susanne Kappeler to be identified as author of this work has been
asserted in accordance with the Copyright, Designs and Patents Act 1988.

First published in the United Kingdom in 1995 by Polity Press in association with
Blackwell Publishers Ltd.

Editorial office:
Polity Press
65 Bridge Street
Cambridge CB2 1UR, UK

Marketing and production:
Blackwell Publishers Ltd
108 Cowley Road
Oxford OX4 1JF, UK

ISBN 0 7456 13047
ISBN 0 7456 13055 (pbk)

A CIP catalogue record for this book is available from the British Library.

Typeset in 11 on 13 pt Bembo
by Pure Tech Corporation, Pondicherry, India
Printed in Great Britain by T.J. Press Ltd, Padstow, Cornwall

This book is printed on acid-free paper.

Contents

Acknowledgements

Many friends, students, colleagues, and others will recognize discussions we had and issues we chewed over together. As I see it, my task as author is less to have 'new' and 'original' ideas than to try to draw together, and then connect, arguments and analyses we make in different contexts and about varying issues. The published work of feminists has played a similar role to those live discussions and analyses – it has become integrated, as it were, into an ongoing discussion.

Academic referencing is not an adequate tool for reflecting the influence that such work, let alone live discussions, has had on my own thinking. On the contrary, the more profoundly someone's thinking has contributed to shaping my own, the less easy it becomes to acknowledge it point by point in the notes. Hence, in this book, the notes primarily serve the conventional purpose of academic referencing.

I would like to thank all those who enthusiastically participated in discussion as well as those who have published feminist work, and to acknowledge how much they have contributed to shaping the ideas in this book.

I would also like to thank John Thompson of Polity Press and Hilke Schlaeger of Verlag Frauenoffensive for their crucial interest in and support of this project, Annabelle Mundy and the staff at Polity in Cambridge and Oxford for seeing it through production. Special thanks go to Connie Hallam for her invaluable help with permissions, and to Henry Maas for his constructive copy-editing and patience in dealing with last-minute changes.

The author and publisher are grateful for permission to quote from the following works: Extracts (translated from the German by the author) from Ariane Barth 'Schau mir in die Augen, Kleiner', *Der Spiegel*, 7 January 1991 © Der Spiegel/NYTSS, reprinted by permission of The New York Times Syndication Sales Corporation. Extracts from Luise Eichenbaum and Susie Orbach, *What Do Women Want?* (Fontana, 1984), reprinted by permission of HarperCollins Publishers Limited and the authors. Extracts (translated from the French by the author) from Alain Finkielkraut, *La Sagesse de l'amour* (Gallimard, 1984), due to be published in an English translation by Kevin O'Neill and David Suchoff as *The Wisdom of Love* (University of Nebraska Press), reprinted by permission of The University of Nebraska Press. Extracts from Robin Norwood, *Women Who Love Too Much* (Arrow Books, 1986), reprinted by permission of Random House UK Limited. Extracts from Adrienne Rich, 'Disloyal to Civilization: Feminism, Racism, Gynephobia', are reprinted from *On Lies, Secrets and Silence: Selected Prose 1966–1978*, by Adrienne Rich (W. W. Norton, 1979/Virago Press, 1980), by permission of the author and W. W. Norton & Company, Inc. Copyright © 1979 W. W. Norton & Company, Inc. Extracts on pp. 53–6 from Alice Walker, *In Search of Our Mothers' Gardens*, published in Great Britain by The Women's Press Ltd, 1984, 34 Great Sutton Street, London EC1V 0DX, reprinted by permission of David Higham Associates.

Despite every effort to trace and contact copyright holders before publication, this has not been possible in some cases. If notified, the publisher will be pleased to rectify any errors or omissions at the earliest opportunity.

Violence and the will to violence

Violence is a ubiquitous reality in our society.

Violence is also a topic of public debate, although context and manner of discussion vary – from racist violence, sexual violence, the violence of youth and youth culture, the increase of violence in society, to the violence of war and the question whether it could be stopped by the use of greater violence. Violence is categorized into acts of violence, to be listed and prosecuted by the law. Violence is named after its victims: violence against women, sexual abuse of children, exploitation of animals, attacks on old people, hatred of foreigners, anti-Semitism – except where the violence is attributed to such marginal groups of society that any association with those naming it seems out of the question: the violence of today's youth, right extremism and neo-Nazi violence, hooliganism, or racist attacks where this means attacks by 'racist groups'.

What is striking is that the violence which is talked about is always the violence committed by someone else: women talk about the violence of men, adults about the violence of young people; the left, liberals and the centre about the violence of right extremists; the right, centre and liberals about the violence of leftist extremists; political activists talk about structural violence, police and politicians about violence in the 'street', and all together about the violence *in* our society. Similarly, Westerners talk about violence in the Balkans, Western citizens together with their generals about the violence of the Serbian army.

Violence is recognized and measured by its visible effects, the spectacular blood of wounded bodies, the material destruction of objects, the visible damage left in the world of 'objects'. In its measurable damage we see the proof that violence has taken place, the violence being reduced to this damage. The violation as such, or invisible forms of violence – the non-physical violence of threat and terror, of insult and humiliation, the violation of human dignity – are hardly ever the issue except to some extent in feminist and anti-racist analyses, or under the name of psychological violence. Here violence is recognized by the victims and defined from their perspective – an important step away from the catalogue of violent acts and the exclusive evidence of material traces in the object. Yet even here the focus tends to be on the effects and experience of violence, either the objective and scientific measure of psychological damage, or the increasingly subjective definition of violence as experience.

Violence is perceived as a phenomenon for science to research and for politics to get a grip on. But violence is not a phenomenon: it is the behaviour of people, human action which may be analysed. What is missing is an analysis of violence *as* action – not just as acts of violence, or the cause of its effects, but as the actions of people in relation to other people and beings or things.

Feminist critique, as well as other political critiques, has analysed the preconditions of violence, the unequal power relations which enable it to take place. However, under the pressure of mainstream science and a sociological perspective which increasingly dominates our thinking, it is becoming standard to argue as if it were these power relations which cause the violence. Underlying is a behaviourist model which prefers to see human action as the exclusive product of circumstances, ignoring the personal decision of the agent to act, implying in turn that circumstances virtually dictate certain forms of behaviour. Even though we would probably not underwrite these propositions in their crass form, there is nevertheless a growing tendency, not just in social science, to explain violent behaviour by its circumstances. (Compare the question, 'Does pornography cause violence?') The circumstances identified may differ according to the politics of the explainers, but the method of explanation remains the same.

While consideration of mitigating circumstances has its rightful place in a court of law trying (and defending) an offender, this does not automatically make it an adequate or sufficient practice for political analysis. It begs the question, in particular, 'What is considered to be part of the circumstances (and by whom)?' Thus in the case of sexual offenders, there is a routine search – on the part of the tabloid press or the professionals of violence – for experiences of violence in the offender's own past, an understanding which is rapidly solidifying in the scientific model of a 'cycle of violence'. That is, the relevant factors are sought in the distant past and in other contexts of action, while a crucial factor in the present context is ignored, namely the agent's decision to act as he did.

Even politically oppositional groups are not immune to this main-stream sociologizing. Some left groups have tried to explain men's sexual violence as the result of class oppression, while some Black theoreticians have explained the violence of Black men as the result of racist oppression. The ostensible aim of these arguments may be to draw attention to the pervasive and structural violence of classism and racism, yet they not only fail to combat such inequality, they actively contribute to it. Although such oppression is a very real part of an agent's life context, these 'explanations' ignore the fact that not everyone experiencing the same oppression uses violence, that is, that these circumstances do not 'cause' violent behaviour. They overlook, in other words, that the perpetrator has *decided* to violate, even if this decision was made in circumstances of limited choice.

To overlook this decision, however, is itself a political decision, serving particular interests. In the first instance it serves to exonerate the perpetrators, whose responsibility is thus transferred to circumstan-ces and a history for which other people (who remain beyond reach) are responsible. Moreover, it helps to stigmatize all those living in poverty and oppression; because they are obvious victims of violence and oppression, they are held to be potential perpetrators themselves.[1] This slanders all the women who have experienced sexual violence, yet do not use violence against others, and libels those experiencing racist and class oppression, yet do not necessarily act out violence. Far from supporting those oppressed by classist, racist or sexist oppression, it sells out these entire groups in the interest of exonerating individual mem-bers. It is a version of collective victim-blaming, of stigmatizing entire social strata as potential hotbeds of violence, which rests on and perpetuates the mainstream division of society into so-called marginal groups – the classic clienteles of social work and care politics (and of police repression) – and an implied 'centre' to which all the speakers, explainers, researchers and carers themselves belong, and which we are to assume to be a zone of non-violence.

Explaining people's violent behaviour by their circumstances also has the advantage of implying that the 'solution' lies in a change of circumstances. Thus it has become fashionable among socially minded politicians and intellectuals in Germany to argue that the rising neo-Nazi violence of young people (men), especially in former East Germany, needs to be countered by combating poverty and unemployment in these areas. Likewise anti-racist groups like the Anti-Racist Alliance or the Anti-Nazi League in Britain argue that 'the causes of racism, like poverty and unemployment, should be tackled' and that it is 'problems like unemployment and bad housing which lead to racism'.[2] Besides being no explanation at all of why (white) poverty and unemployment should lead specifically to racist violence (and what would explain middle- and upper-class racism), it is more than questionable to combat poverty only (but precisely) when and where violence is exercised. It not only legitimates the violence (by 'explaining' it), but constitutes an incentive to violence, confirming that social problems will be taken seriously when and where 'they' attract attention by means of violence – just as the most unruly children in schools (mostly boys) tend to get more attention from teachers than well-behaved and quiet children (mostly girls). Thus if German neo-Nazi youths and youth groups, since their murderous assaults on refugees and migrants in Hoyerswerda, Rostock, Dresden etc., are treated to special youth projects and social care measures (to the tune of DM 20 million per year), including 'educative' trips to Morocco and Israel,[3] this is an unmistakable signal to society that racist violence does indeed 'pay off'.

If we nevertheless continue to explain violence by its 'circumstances' and attempt to counter it by changing these circumstances, it is also because in this way we stay in command of the problem. In particular, we do not complicate the problem by any suggestion that it might be people who need to change. Instead, we turn the perpetrators of violence into the victims of circumstances, who as victims by definition cannot act sensibly (but in changed circumstances will behave differently). 'We', on the other hand, are the subjects able to take in hand the task of changing the circumstances. Even if changing the circumstances – combating poverty, unemployment, injustice etc. – may not be easy, it nevertheless remains within 'our' scope, at least theoretically and by means of state power. Changing people, on the other hand, is neither within our power nor, it seems, ultimately in our interest: we prefer to keep certain people under control, putting limits on their violent behaviour, but we apparently have no interest in a politics that presupposes people's ability to change and aims at changing attitudes and behaviour. For changing (as opposed to restricting) other people's behaviour is beyond the range and influence of our own power; only they themselves can change it. It requires their will to change, their will not to abuse power and not to use violence.

A politics aiming at a change in people's behaviour would require political work that is very much more cumbersome and very much less promising of success than is the use of state power and social control. It would require political consciousness-raising – politicizing the way we think – which cannot be imposed on others by force or compulsory educational measures. It would require a view of people which takes seriously and reckons with their will, both their will to violence or their will to change. To take seriously the will of others however would mean recognizing one's own, and putting people's will, including our own, at the centre of political reflection.

A political analysis of violence needs to recognize this will, the personal decision in favour of violence – not just to describe acts of violence, or the conditions which enable them to take place, but also to capture the moment of decision which is the real impetus for violent action. For without this decision there will be no violent act, not even in circumstances which potentially permit it. It is the decision to violate, not just the act itself, which makes a person a perpetrator of violence – just as it is the decision not to do so which makes people not act violently and not abuse their power in a situation which would nevertheless permit it. This moment of decision, therefore, is also the locus of potential resistance to violence. To understand the structures of thinking and the criteria by which such decisions are reached, but above all to regard this decision as an act of choice, seems to me a necessary precondition for any political struggle against violence and for a non-violent society.

My focus, then, is on the decision to violate – not just in circumstances where violence is conspicuous by its damage, but in every situation where the choice to violate presents itself. This means a change from the accustomed perspective on violence to the context where decisions for actions are being made, as it were 'before' their consequences become apparent, and which we may not recognize as contexts of violence. Our political analyses of sexual or racist violence have necessarily concentrated on situations where the power disequilibrium between perpetrator and victim is extreme, where, in particular, it is supported by social power structures such as male and/or white supremacy, so that not only is the violence unlikely to receive sanctions, but on the contrary, the perpetrator will find support rather than the victim. Violence, however, is a possibility wherever there is freedom of action, however limited. Such violence may 'look' different, not least because the possibilities for resistance may also be greater in situations where there is relative freedom of action also on the part of the other agent, that is, the violator's envisaged victim.

The feminist critique of sexism, together with our early recognition of the necessity of raising our own consciousness, constitutes an understanding that ideology itself is a site of power and the abuse of power – that is, that our own thinking and, by extension, our own behaviour are already a primary area for a liberatory politics. More-over, a politics aiming at social equality and relations between equals should make it its central concern to reflect upon the structure of such relations – what it means to relate to others as equals. We have analysed and made a critique of abusive behaviour, where men choose to treat women as unequals, or whites to treat Black people as unequals, being able to do so with sanctioned impunity. This would imply an analysis also of action and behaviour which by contrast is based on choosing equality – in particular, choosing to *grant* equality to others, choosing not to violate others in situations which permit that choice, all the more so as it is our conviction that it is not people who *are* (by virtue of their 'identity') unequal, whom we then necessarily relate to as 'unequals', but that inequality is a matter of treating and being treated unequally. Conversely, we cannot assume that if there are two 'equals', their relations will necessarily be (or remain) equal. Rather, we should investigate how relationships of potential equality may, through the action of one or the other or both agents involved, be restructured into relations of dominance and submission. Action – and especially the will to power and violence – is a vital factor in the continually changing 'structure' of a relationship, combining with those factors we normally consider to constitute the structural context of the relation.

This means engaging also with the discourses which construct violence as a phenomenon but obliterate the agent's decision to violate. Our unwillingness to recognize the will of those who act violently *as* their will to act violently, our readiness to exonerate violent behaviour by means of spurious explanations, not only betrays our primary identification with the subjects of violence and our lack of solidarity with the victims. It is itself an act of violence: the exercise of ideological violence, of the power of a discourse which legitimates violence, stigmatizes the victims, and treats people not as the agents of their own actions but as material for ('our') social policy. Ideology, however, is not just made by others; we are all of us subjects of ideology – as the producers of our own thinking and as the recipients of other people's discourse – unless we resist such ideological structures of thought and discourse in a continual critique of ideology itself.

A decision to violate is not necessarily synonymous with a decision to be 'bad' or to commit an injustice. Rather, we have at our disposal structures of thought and argumentation which make such a decision appear rational, justified or even necessary. These structures of thought are deeply rooted in our everyday thinking: they are part of the dominant ideology. We use them in our daily decisions for action – actions which are not necessarily acts of bodily injury and murder, of arson and larceny, and which do not necessarily unleash a major war, but which none the less are acts of violence: violation of the rights and integrity of other people, violation of their dignity and personhood, suppression of their freedom of choice and their self-determination, acts of objectification and of exploitation at every conceivable level – in other words, war, on a small scale and against our nearest if not our dearest.

What is remarkable is that this everyday behaviour, in so far as it does not fall within the competence of criminal law, is hardly the subject of a serious theoretical discussion.[4] Neither does it attract explicit legitimation; rather, the violence of everyday behaviour draws its legitimacy from the ubiquity of such behaviour in our society and the social consensus about its relative 'harmlessness' compared with other, that is, recognized forms of violence. That is to say, everyday behaviour takes its orientation from the tradition of social practice, reproducing itself through recourse to the status quo. It is so naturalized, in fact, that it is not violent action which attracts attention, but any resistance to it: leaving a violent relationship or situations of violence, resisting bullying, pressure and blackmail, refusing to fight back.

Even a discourse on ethics which we might expect to address this issue increasingly addresses problems of a collective social responsibility – leading indeed to enlightened guidelines for social policy, yet leaving the question of personal responsibility unanswered. For an analysis of collective social responsibility tends not to differentiate between the respective responsibility of the members of that collective according to their diverse situations. Yet the single person has to act, has to decide how to act, even if this does not cause a war or change the world at one stroke. It is these decisions for action within the range of competence of persons which are the topic of this book.

This does not mean that I deem the obvious and systematic forms of violence – from the violence of men against women and children, the racist violence of whites against Black people and people of the Third World, to the violence of the state and its military forces, or violence against animals and nature (which is hardly even discussed in the context of violence) – a less urgent problem than individual behaviour. Rather, the obvious importance and magnitude of 'social' problems of violence cannot be the pretext for considering apparently 'lesser' or more 'harmless' forms of 'personal' violence (our own) a matter for postponement until the major problems have been solved. Violence cannot be measured as larger or smaller, more or less, even if the consequences of violence differ enormously. The consequences differ, however, neither in their measurable size as 'damage' nor in the size or measure of the violence which caused them, but in terms of the means used on the one hand, and in their specificity, uniqueness and incomparability as experience on the other. Violence as the structure of action is neither greater nor lesser: it either is or is not violence.

Moreover, personal behaviour is no alternative to 'political' action; there is no question of either/or. My concern, on the contrary, is the connection between these recognized forms of violence and the forms of everyday behaviour which we consider 'normal' but which betray our own will to violence – the connection, in other words, between our own actions and those acts of violence which are normally the focus of our political critiques. Precisely because there is no choice between dedicating oneself either to 'political issues' or to 'personal behaviour', the question of the politics of personal behaviour has (also) to be moved into the centre of our politics and our critique.

Violence – what we usually recognize as such – is no exception to the rules, no deviation from the normal and nothing out of the ordinary, in a society in which exploitation and oppression are the norm, the ordinary and the rule. It is no misbehaviour of a minority amid good behaviour by the majority, nor the deeds of inhuman monsters amid humane humans, in a society in which there is no equality, in which people divide others according to race, class, sex and many other factors in order to rule, exploit, use, objectify, enslave, sell, torture and kill them, in which millions of animals are tortured, genetically manipulated, enslaved and slaughtered daily for 'harmless' consumption by humans. It is no error of judgement, no moral lapse and no transgression against the customs of a culture which is thoroughly steeped in the values of profit and desire, of self-realization, expansion and progress. Violence as we usually perceive it is 'simply' a specific – and to us still visible – form of violence, the consistent and logical application of the principles of our culture and everyday life.

War does not suddenly break out in a peaceful society; sexual violence is not the disturbance of otherwise equal gender relations. Racist attacks do not shoot like lightning out of a non-racist sky, and the sexual exploitation of children is no solitary problem in a world otherwise just to children. The violence of our most commonsense everyday thinking, and especially our personal will to violence, constitute the conceptual preparation, the ideological armament and the intellectual mobilization which make the 'outbreak' of war, of sexual violence, of racist attacks, of murder and destruction possible at all.

'We are the war', writes Slavenka Drakulić at the end of her existential analysis of the question, 'what is war?':

> I do not know what war is, I want to tell [my friend], but I see it everywhere. It is in the blood-soaked street in Sarajevo, after 20 people have been killed while they queued for bread. But it is also in your non-comprehension, in my unconscious cruelty towards you, in the fact that you have a yellow form [for refugees] and I don't, in the way in which it grows inside ourselves and changes our feelings, relationships, values – in short: us. We are the war . . . And I am afraid that we cannot hold anyone else responsible. We make this war possible, we permit it to happen.[5]

'We are the war' – and we also 'are' the sexual violence, the racist violence, the exploitation and the will to violence in all its manifestations in a society in so-called 'peacetime', for we make them possible and we permit them to happen.

'We are the war' does not mean that the responsibility for a war is shared collectively and diffusely by an entire society – which would be equivalent to exonerating warlords and politicians and profiteers or, as Ulrich Beck says, upholding the notion of 'collective irresponsibility', where people are no longer held responsible for their actions, and where the conception of universal responsibility becomes the equivalent of a universal acquittal.[6] On the contrary, the object is precisely to analyse the specific and differential responsibility of everyone in their diverse situations. Decisions to unleash a war are indeed taken at particular levels of power by those in a position to make them and to command such collective action. We need to hold them clearly responsible for their decisions and actions without lessening theirs by any collective 'assumption' of responsibility. Yet our habit of focusing on the stage where the major dramas of power take place tends to obscure our sight in relation to our own sphere of competence, our own power and our own responsibility – leading to the well-known illusion of our apparent 'powerlessness' and its accompanying phenomenon, our so-called political disillusionment. Single citizens – even more so those of other nations – have come to feel secure in their obvious non-responsibility for such large-scale political events as, say, the wars in Croatia and Bosnia-Hercegovina or Somalia – since the decisions for such events are always made elsewhere.

Yet our insight that indeed we are not responsible for the decisions of a Serbian general or a Croatian president tends to mislead us into thinking that therefore we have no responsibility at all, not even for forming our own judgement, and thus into underrating the responsibility we do have within our own sphere of action. In particular, it seems to absolve us from having to try to see any relation between our own actions and those events, or to recognize the connections between those political decisions and our own personal decisions. It not only shows that we participate in what Beck calls 'organized irresponsibility', upholding the apparent lack of connection between bureaucratically, institutionally, nationally and also individually organized separate competences. It also proves the phenomenal and unquestioned alliance of our personal thinking with the thinking of the major powermongers. For we tend to think that we cannot 'do' anything, say, about a war, because we deem ourselves to be in the wrong situation; because we are not where the major decisions are made. Which is why many of those not yet entirely disillusioned with politics tend to engage in a form of mental deputy politics, in the style of 'What would I do if I were the general, the prime minister, the president, the foreign minister or the minister of defence?' Since we seem to regard their mega spheres of action as the only worthwhile and truly effective ones, and since our political analyses tend to dwell there first of all, any question of what I would do if I were indeed myself tends to peter out in the comparative insignificance of having what is perceived as 'virtually no possibilities': what I *could* do seems petty and futile. For my own action I obviously desire the range of action of a general, a prime minister, or a General Secretary of the UN – finding expression in ever more prevalent formulations like 'I want to stop this war', 'I want military intervention', 'I want to stop this backlash', or 'I want a moral revolution.'[7]

'We are this war', however, even if we do not command the troops or participate in so-called peace talks, namely as Drakulić says, in our 'non-comprehension': our willed refusal to feel responsible for our own thinking and for working out our own understanding, preferring innocently to drift along the ideological current of prefabricated arguments or less than innocently taking advantage of the advantages these offer. And we 'are' the war in our 'unconscious cruelty towards you', our tolerance of the 'fact that you have a yellow form for refugees and I don't' – our readiness, in other words, to build ident-ities, one for ourselves and one for refugees, one of our own and one for the 'others'. We share in the responsibility for this war and its violence in the way we let them grow inside us, that is, in the way we shape 'our feelings, our relationships, our values' according to the structures and the values of war and violence.

So if we move beyond the usual frame of violence, towards the structures of thought employed in decisions to act, this also means making an analysis of action. This seems all the more urgent as action seems barely to be perceived any longer. There is talk of the govern-ment doing 'nothing', of its 'inaction', of the need for action, the time for action, the need for strategies, our inability to act as well as our desire to become 'active' again. We seem to deem ourselves in a kind of action vacuum which, like the cosmic black hole, tends to consume any renewed effort only to increase its size. Hence this is also an attempt to shift the focus again to the fact that we are continually acting and doing, and that there is no such thing as not acting or doing nothing.

Rather, the binary opposition of 'action' and 'no action' seems to serve the simple evaluation of the good and the bad. We speak of being 'active' or wanting to be active again, where being active in its simple vacuity is 'good', 'doing nothing' is rather bad, and where the quality of the action seems secondary to the fact of action as such. Quite the reverse, however, if we analyse the past: there, having 'done' anything bears the danger of it having been bad, since the results are available for analysis. Consequently, analyses of the past tend to feature an abundance of victims, who as victims cannot by definition have done anything, and therefore cannot either be 'guilty'. While descriptions of our future actions are thus distinguished by their vacuity – saying nothing about the kind of activity and explaining nothing about its purpose – the past on the contrary seems to cry out for the writing of histories that explain everything. In these rewritings of history as justification, the mark of distinction for personal identity is no longer to have 'been active', but on the contrary, to have been the passive victim – if not of actual deeds by others, at least of circumstances. In other words, in the past we tend to have been passive, while in the future we may become active. The present, however, is the eternal present in which we inhabit states of being, our identity.

The feminist critique of sexual violence has not only analysed patriarchal power relations as the conditions which make violence possible, it also sees the abuser's will to abuse, his choosing to act violently, as the real 'cause' of violence. This, together with the feminist insight that the personal is political, should mean that for feminists the politics of personal behaviour is a central issue. Yet it is barely considered a serious theoretical issue outside the context of sexual violence: personal behaviour (our own) is criticized at most as a side-effect of political practice, an inadequacy of performance in relation to the competence of political ideals. In particular, the opinion seems to be gaining ground that what really matters is the explicit articulation of intention – what I SAY that I want and mean – less what I actually do and in doing express as my will. The emphasis is on the 'content' of politics and political discourse, less on political practice – so that politics is increasingly becoming a matter of the articulation of good intentions.

The rise of cultural identity politics in particular has contributed to the view that violence is exclusively a matter of social power relations.

What feminist analysis has identified as the dialectic between social power structures and the actions of individuals in specific situations is in danger of becoming conflated in the simple transfer of social power structures to the identity of individuals. Far from supporting members of oppressed groups in the consciousness of their right to equality, identity politics tends to inscribe power and inequality, or victim status, respectively in the identity of persons. The analysis of the behaviour of individuals thus tends to lose in importance in favour of an (exclusive) analysis of social relations and the identification of our place in the social power hierarchy.

An analysis of power relations without an analysis of the politics of personal behaviour, however, leads to the classic 'solutions' to political problems: we reach (at least mentally) for the classic mechanisms of social control – state power and legislation – in order to sketch our visions of a future egalitarian society and to ensure its future stability. In the certain knowledge of the nobility of our ends, we give little thought to the significance of means and our own readiness to deploy social control. Since the chance of realizing our political visions appears so remote, we seem to think that we can afford to prioritize the question of aims over the question of means.

The recent involvement of Western feminists and peace activists in the reality of the war in former Yugoslavia, however, has shown that the readiness to deploy violent means does not dissolve in the face of prospective realization, but on the contrary even increases. Thus the German peace activist and Euro MP Eva Quistorp and the journalist Alexandra Stiglmayer vehemently argued for military intervention by the UN to end the war.[8] Swiss women peace activists returning from a trip to Zagreb declared that they were rethinking their commitment to non-violence or giving up their pacifism, now that women in Bosnia were demanding arms.[9] German feminists and women activists again decided to hold an international 'tribunal' in Zagreb, despite protests from women from all the republics of former Yugoslavia concerning the choice and accessibility of Zagreb as a meeting-place.[10] This confirms that for these women politics, even feminist politics and peace politics, are clearly confined to the 'content' of the immediate political aims but do not include the means. And it shows that where it *is* apparently a matter of a politics of means – pacifism or a commitment to non-violence – such politics have been chosen without any expectation of ever having to prove them in actual situations;

that on the contrary, in the face of a real situation, these political principles immediately collapse, or rather are dropped.

This readiness to engage in violence – which rests on the well-known principle that holy ends justify unholy means – shows at the very least a lack of understanding about the relationship between means and ends, theory and practice, not to say cause and effect. Yet neither the means nor their ends make any sense without considering the point of departure, that is, an analysis of the real situation whose change is our aim, and out of which the means have to be developed. More importantly, however, this readiness to employ violence proves our own will to power: the will to enforce my aims whatever the cost, and in realizing them to use whatever means are expedient.

Although it must certainly be the aim of any liberation politics to dismantle the social power structure and thus to decrease the possibilities for systematic violence and abuse, this does not spare us the question of a politics of behaviour in a world which has not yet been rid of these power structures. Nor does it suffice simply to wish for a future society in which power *may* no longer be exercised. Here lies the crucial difference between a utopia or vision on the one hand, and a politics of change whose aims, however utopian they may seem, are derived from a political analysis and critique of reality on the other. For a utopia or 'vision' is the idealist sketch of a future state of society that remains silent about how this state can be reached (or maintained). Its focus is on the happy future, jumping the analysis of the present and the particular problems which will need to be solved on the way to the future. It means not only to abandon any responsibility for the present, but to build this non-responsibility into the future, since personal responsibility is given up in favour of a superior, even if invisible, institution and authority: the abolished power structure. For in the future utopia there will be no abuse of power because there will be no power to abuse, and no violence because it will be impossible to act violently – because, in other words, not only the traditional offenders but also we ourselves would simply be prevented from behaving violently. Not only is it a vision of perfect unfreedom – of being forced to be 'good', it is also a fallacy to believe that if there were no social power structures there would no longer be any opportunities for being violent.

A vision, moreover, is the sketch of a society to which that society itself has nothing to say. It originates in the fantasy of a subject which is superordinated to society, society becoming the material in the creation of a world after the creative subject's pleasure and will. It is a power fantasy *par excellence*, whether it is the vision of a general or a revolutionary. All the more remarkable that talk of visions and utopias is becoming more prevalent in the women's movement, threatening to replace the political analysis of reality and the discussion of aims and means.

A realist politics – that is, a politics which refers to reality – has to start from the present conditions and their changeability. It is the critical analysis of present conditions, rather than any utopian vision of the future, which will indicate the direction and the possibilities of change. This would mean a politics, however, which goes beyond being 'for' or 'against' something, and a comprehension of reality that is gained from analysis rather than an automatic (ideological) perception of it. If politicians and the media increasingly offer 'analyses' conforming to the scheme of a folk tale or Hollywood western, with their figures of good and bad guys, this is no reason for a critical opposition to use the same scheme with at most an inverted cast. Rather, we should aim to expose the ideological construction of these narratives and mythologies and analyse their influence also on our own thinking.

If anything, however, the trend is going in the opposite direction: not only are critiques of ideology and ideological structures becoming rare and unfashionable, but the thinking of individuals increasingly resembles that of official discourse; institutional 'public' discourse shapes 'private' thinking. If George Bush represents the Gulf War of 1991 as the simple story of a courageous good guy who set out to deliver the world from the evil doings of the villain Saddam, 'private individuals' increasingly have recourse to similar narratives to construct an understanding of their own lives. The aim, of politicians and 'private individuals' alike, is less to analyse a situation or to understand a history than to construct a story and to reconstruct history. Hence political struggle, like the struggle to come to terms with one's life, takes place less on the level of actual events than on the level of their representation – as a battle of representation. Thus politicians today offer not so much solutions to current political problems as, in the most literal sense of these formulations, 'answers' to the burning political 'questions' of the day. These answers usually consist in a reformulation of the question as less of a problem than we originally might have thought.

Scientific discourse, too, which is one of the major instruments of cultural and ideological power, certainly is no longer the prerogative of those who rule and administer society according to their will and interests. A comparable pseudo-scientific standpoint, abstracted from any specificity of the actual situation, increasingly characterizes the discourse of individuals – including that of a critical opposition – who then regard the 'problems of the world' from a similarly lofty and lordly view, arriving at similar solutions. So-called standpointlessness, the objectifying look from 'above' and 'outside', and its concomitant subjectless speech are the trademark of any discursively constructed authority. And since it is a speciality of scientific discourse to abstract action from its agents, representing it as (agentless) acts, it is only logical that this action too, this production of knowledgeable scientific speech, is presented as an act without an agent, a discourse without an author, a monological speech product without a producer.

Just as public discourse is the market-place of industrially published discursive products, so-called private communication increasingly takes the form of an exchange of personal speech products, with individuals fighting each other by means of rivalling representations in preference to reaching a common understanding. Many a political meeting, seminar or conversation among several people bears testimony to the fact that, however small this public arena, it is seen and used as an opportunity for putting one's own products on offer and achieving a victory for one's own representation – over any reality to be analysed and any people involved in analysing it.

Science, of course, is less concerned with the question of people's responsible action in the world than professedly with the principle of cause and effect in the reality which is the object of its study – 'nature' in the case of the original natural sciences, long since joined by 'culture' and 'society' as the objects of the social sciences. Causes are the objectified impetuses of actions ('events' or 'processes'), presented without regard to these as actions, while effects are the objectified consequences of these. The changing continuity of action (or a process or event) is separated into its apparent beginning and end, a point of departure and a final outcome, between which a connection, a causal relationship, is then inferred. A rational morality, if any, derives from the evaluation of effects, which are judged as good or bad, useful or harmful, desirable or undesirable – leaving aside for the moment by whom and in whose interests.

A political morality could also be derived from the consequences of action, in terms of the agents' responsibility for the consequences of their actions. However, the scientific representation of the consequences of action as mere states of affairs – as factual effects – serves to evade such responsibility as effectively as once did mythological representations of destiny as preordained. For if we detach the act from the person acting and regard its consequences as an effect, personal responsibility is no longer an issue. On the contrary, this effect now calls for the scientific investigation of its cause. The cause, as we have already seen and shall see again and again, is never found in the responsibility of consciously acting people, but in an array of correlating factors and contributing circumstances which make identifying any personal responsibility virtually impossible. What is of advantage to the ruling interests of society, however, also has its attraction for individuals, who thus similarly seek to evade their personal responsibility by means of a scientific representation of their own actions as the effect of a most complicated set of causes.

In the possibility of representing reality, in the access to the role of the speaking or thinking subject, lies the power of representation – on the level of big politics as much as on the level of one's own thinking and communication. This power implies a responsibility: the question how we are going to use it. Are we going to abuse it in our own interest, enlarging and consolidating our power, and are we willing to do violence to reality, including the reality of other people? Or are we going to use it in the interests of community and communication, that is, in the common interest of understanding and action? Do we try to analyse and understand reality, or to represent it in such a way that it turns out most advantageous to ourselves, enabling decisions which seem justifiable and normal, yet which we would regard differently if starting from a different representation of reality? It is a position of power which everyone has access to – at least as the subjects of our own thinking and where we have the chance to speak. And it is a position of power for which, in determining our actions, we are answerable, in terms of our responsibility for the consequences of our thinking and our actions. It is a sphere of action, moreover, in relation to which an increasing number of women in the West also inhabit positions of structural power and privilege, participating in the production of knowledge and public opinion.

There cannot therefore in the context of specific women's actions be continued and undifferentiated talk of 'women's powerlessness' – viewed simply in relation to men, the state, the power of leading capitalists or any other more powerful groups which can always be found. The discussion about power relations among women or within the women's movement should have once and for all dispelled the simplistic view of women as powerless, impotent or 'victims'. On the contrary, we are trying to gain an understanding of the position each of us has in a variety of power structures, where we are sometimes on the side of the oppressed, sometimes of the oppressors, in a complex network of relative power relations which have to be specifically analysed in each situation and cannot be determined simply in terms of social 'identities'.

Moreover, feminism has produced an analysis – if not of action generally, at any rate of sexual violence – which not only emphasizes the abuser's will and choice of action, but also uniquely recognizes the survivor's action of resisting, and in this her will to resist. While violence constitutes precisely the violator's attempt to reduce his victim's freedom of action to nought – where the ultimate consequence is indeed her total victimization in death – the survivor's survival means that she has recognized and made use of her remaining, even if minimal, scope for action. Feminist analysis sees in the survivor not a passive victim, but a person and agent who has successfully sought to resist. This means recognizing even in her virtual powerlessness the still existing potential for action. Resistance by definition means acting in situations of violence and oppression where our freedom of action is severely limited and circumscribed. All the more vital that we recognize what scope for action there is. All the more vital, also, that we recognize how much greater is our scope of action and resistance most of the time, compared to the extremity of victimization in experiences of life-threatening violence and enslavement – which we invoke metaphorically and all too lightly by claiming victim status on account of oppression.

The question which poses itself, then, is rather how we act in situations in which we do have (relative) power, not only the space to reach our own understanding of the situation, but also a choice, even if it is a limited choice, of action. To ask this question is not to shift from the political to the personal, from the social to the individual or even psychological. Rather, it concerns the most crucial moment of our political commitment, the point where we ourselves are in a position to initiate and effect change. Moreover, it also largely determines in what manner and by what means we think that our political aim of a non-violent egalitarian society will be reached. It implies a conception of politics which sees the process of social change here and now and everywhere, and thus also in our decisions here and now to act in the interests of our political aims.

Political action, in this view, is not something which will take place only in a more propitious future when circumstances have changed so much, or a revolution is already so far under way that it can take its course, and we as the 'politically active' people can join it. Nor can political action mean something we engage in only on condition that there will be enough others, or better, masses of them, who think as I do, and do what I want to do. Political action does not necessarily imply public mass actions whose massiveness will guarantee their success. For such individual conceptions of political mass action reflect the power thinking of generals commanding the troops of the 'masses' to suit their own strategies. Nor does it help to wish for the masses voluntarily to think as I do and to want what I want – that they be like-minded (like me), thus helping to fulfil my dream of a mass action. Even this has happened in the history of generals. My dream remains the dream of a commander who has like-minded masses of volunteer troops at his disposal.

Instead, we could consider that even our thinking is an opportunity for action, that it can be determined in this way or that, that it is the first opportunity, the first political situation, in which to exercise political choice. 'We make the war possible, we allow it to happen', says Drakulić . 'We only have one weak protection against it, our consciousness. There are no them and us, there are no grand categories, abstract numbers, black-and-white truths, simple facts. There is only us – and, yes, we are responsible for each other.'[11] And if we find this too minimal to satisfy our aspirations for political action and change, why don't we do it anyway, for a start?

So I begin from the assumption that all of us, regardless of our relative positions within the social power structure, do permanently have to decide how we are going to act in a given situation. We have described in some considerable detail the many limitations on our freedom of action – it is the first thing (and often the only one) that occurs to us in justifying our actions. But each situation, save that of the absolute and ultimate violence of our destruction, leaves scope for action, however minimal, which permits the decision to consent to violence or to resist. The question remains how we use the opportunities for action we have, and how we deal with the relative advantages which offer themselves. Here we face the decision to (ab)use our power in our own interests and to our own advantage, or not to; here we face the choice to do violence to others, or not to. It is a most political question, and a most political decision.

A note on 'We'

Much has been said about the use of 'we' and the problem of whom it includes and excludes. On the one hand, feminist authors have deliberately developed a linguistic practice of including 'ourselves' (as opposed to 'themselves') in concepts like 'women', 'feminists' (or 'feminist authors') etc., thus positioning 'ourselves' explicitly within our discourse as well as including ourselves in the subject of our speech, in contrast to the academic practice of avoiding all personal pronouns, especially those positioning the author. In turn, there has been discussion in the women's movement concerning an unreflected use of 'we' or 'us women' which betrays a conceptualization of 'us' or of 'women' that does not include women universally, but only the narrow interest-group of the speaker, for instance white and/or middle-class women. So that, contrary to its apparent universal significance, 'we' often excludes many women and their interests from its designation. It is a critique on which I build in the chapters that follow.

However, there have been many misunderstandings arising from this critique – or rather, its reception. Our response cannot be henceforth to avoid using the pronoun 'we' in the hope of avoiding problems arising from it, and in particular, of escaping any reproach that we are practising exclusion. A conception of 'us' is already implied in how the speaker structures her speech, in particular, in her assumption of whom she envisages to be her addressees, whether or not she names them explicitly. Our critique of the apparent neutrality and impersonality of scientific or academic discourse is not that there is no 'I' and 'you', but that it constructs them implicitly, and as it were surreptitiously, on problematical assumptions. The point is to make structure and assumptions explicit so that we can analyse, reflect on and, where necessary, change them.

Similarly, the critique of the use of 'we', say, in situations where it is meant to designate 'all women' but in fact applies exclusively to a few, is less the use of the word 'we' than a form of thinking, conscious or unconscious, which is exclusionary – racist, classist, nationalist or in other ways discriminatory – constructing an alleged 'universality' of women on the basis of the interests and living conditions of but a few. The meaning of the critique is to make us conscious of this practice and to open it up for scrutiny as to who exactly is 'us' in any given speech context and whether we mean it to be so. The consequence is neither that we should avoid the words 'we' and 'us', nor speak of 'us' only universally and all-inclusively. While the former would return us to the feigned neutrality of scientific discourse, which simply hides the discursive structuring, the latter would allow us to speak only of a future utopia of universal equality, where all are included in an egalitarian community of 'us'. Instead, the critique points us towards a conscious and responsible use of the pronoun 'we'.

It is a responsibility of author and reader alike: 'we' is not the name of a group whose members we recognize by the sheer mention of the label. It is what linguists call a 'shifter' which, like 'this' or 'that', may be used to designate ever-changing referents, in this case groups in which you and I may (or may not) be joined by inclusion. If you are a feminist, you will feel included in my use of 'we' in the context of 'we feminists'; if not, you will recognize that I include myself in that group and am speaking to you from that position. My use of 'we' however does not always designate 'feminists' or the particular position of feminism which I argue for; I also include myself, and many, even if diverse ones of you, in groupings which according to the context may be 'women', 'white women', 'Western women', 'humans', 'speakers', or those who engage in a particular practice I am describing.

However, I am speaking less of particular people like you (of whose specific activities I know nothing). Rather, my 'we' usually refers to the subject position of a dominant discourse which divides us into 'us' and 'them' without our having consciously chosen or assented to it. If we speak of 'foreigners', for example, a 'we' is already implied: though we may never say it, 'we' are the citizens of the state, those 'legitimately at home' 'here', those belonging to the nation.

Discourses, language habits, the way we express ourselves, structure the world, and ourselves in it, in specific ways. It is precisely the subject positions of 'we' constructed by dominant discourses which socialize not only men, but also women into an androcentric, sexist subject position, or people growing up in the West or through Western education systems to assume a Eurocentric view, whatever their personal social identity may be. Much more problematical than any spelt-out 'we' are the many verbal constructions which simultaneously imply and disguise the subject position. My aim is to make these structures as explicit as possible, to make visible that there is a subject – a subject in relation to a verb, an activity – that is, that there are people (us) responsible for our actions. This means that I use 'we' much more often, saying for instance 'when we exclude other women' rather than 'the exclusion of other women' etc. The point is to see ourselves in our responsibility of deciding how we act and to ask ourselves whether we do indeed want to act in this way and to constitute ourselves – in relation to every respective discursive 'us' – in this manner and through this practice as a community of 'us'.

Finally, I use the pronoun 'we' because I consider myself to be participating in a process of collective self-criticism and hence dialogue, a process which may precisely involve a change in how 'I' or 'we' conceptualize ourselves *as* 'we'. In saying 'we', I neither speak *for* a designated group, nor do I always speak about you; I am engaged in a dialogue with 'you', who will know, or will have to decide according to the context, whether you are included, or include yourselves, in my respective 'we' or not. Nor will you always be unhappy if you are excluded: discursive 'exclusion' is not just an act of injustice, but one of analysis. If we talk about structures of power and oppression, there is no all-inclusive 'we' about which we could speak: there are oppressors and oppressed, in either the one or the other of which I and my respective readers will have to include ourselves according to the situation, our own social determinants and, most importantly, our politics. So long as we need to deal with power and inequality, we will have to deal with categories describing the divisions that exist among us; the responsibility, as I see it, lies in deploying these categories in the interests of a political analysis and a politics which aim at the abolition of power and inequality.

Reading what kind of 'we' is constructed in each context, and deciding whether you belong to it, or wish to continue to belong to it, is part of the political work which, I am arguing, it is necessary for us to do, whether as speakers or listeners, authors or readers, or just thinking to ourselves, taking position politically with regard to the structures of power and oppression.

But you are right, of course, to feel that I *do* include you in a specific 'we' of mine, namely the group – whoever we may be – who share these aims.

1

Why the personal is political, and where the private comes from

There is no them and us ... there is only us – and, yes, we are responsible for each other.

Slavenka Drakulić

Basically, there are only two major political attitudes to distinguish: self-interest on the one hand, and a responsibility for the whole on the other. Everything else is but a variation of the two. 'The whole' as an abstract horizon of political thinking would encompass humanity as a whole, but also the world as a whole; more immediately, however, it is the entirety of a situation in which a person acts: not only the other people and circumstances with whom the person interacts, but also the full reach of the consequences and significance of these actions. In other words, it is a question already of perception, namely how much of any action context we choose to include as being part of 'the situation', or what we screen out as irrelevant, and why.

These two fundamental attitudes are mutually exclusive; we cannot hold them both simultaneously. For they are based on structurally incompatible conceptions of people and reality, of the self in relation to the 'whole': on the one hand a conception of self as subject – as 'I' which can also become the plural 'we', and for which the world, everything else, becomes 'it', the object. This conception of the self is the basis for a conception of self-interest, while self-interest is the basis and motive for such a conception of the self.

A different conception, such as Drakulić implies in speaking of the responsibility of 'us for each other', requires a radically different understanding, constituted not through the entities of self and other, but through relation: the radical equality with which all are encompassed in the entirety of 'us', that is, the lack of differentiation with which all relate to each other *as* a whole. A 'we' which knows no 'us and them', and therefore neither a separable 'I', implying a conception also of oneself as *in relation*. Not as a singular entity that first will have to enter into a relationship with others, having the choice whether or not to do so, nor as a subject facing a world of objects, but as self permanently and already in relation.

Self-interest here does not mean a morally reproachable excess of interest in oneself, which could be curbed to a more even measure. Rather, it describes a structure of thought, a conception of the self and the world, which if anything precedes and underlies any moral considerations. Nor are the two principal political attitudes the equivalent of egoism and altruism, of selfishness and love of thy neighbour, a concern for myself or a concern for others – where we could try to achieve a fair and balanced mixture of both. On the contrary, the opposition between egoism and altruism already relies on a primary conception of the self in opposition to the others, of the others in opposition to the self: an opposition which gives me the choice between myself and others, between 'us' and 'them'. Thus even in moral considerations or personal rationalizations which are committed to a concern for the common weal, the structure of self and self-interest is primary, the common weal defined in opposition to it.

Once the self and self-interest have been conceptually installed, any common weal, any 'humanity' or humaneness, any love and responsibility for others can only be conceived on the basis of, and in opposition to, the self and self-interest. This is apparent in the expressions we use: selfishness and selflessness, self-love and self-sacrifice, self-interest and disinterestedness, love of self and love of others, 'humanity' as in 'a person of great humanity', charity, philanthropy etc. The self and its interest are given and the norm, the opposition being expressed as self and other, self and non-self or 'un'-self, or as self on the one hand and humanity on the other. That is, even humanity and love of neighbours are forms of a love and benevolence of the self and towards the others – neighbours and humanity – humanity thus being a concept to describe everyone apart from myself, those who are the issue when I am not.

Even though in everyday speech we use 'politics' mostly in contrast to self-interest, the basic attitude of looking after one's own interest has to be regarded as a fundamentally political attitude, being of considerable consequence to society and social relations. Moreover, much that we traditionally include under the rubric of 'politics' is of this kind. How a person decides to act *is* political, whatever the content of their action and regardless of whether anyone else is 'present' or not, since it necessarily has consequences for society. A person acts *in* society, and even a so-called withdrawal 'from' society and into the 'private' is a social act affecting the rest of society. The very term 'private' still is testimony to an understanding of humans as fundamentally social beings, whose retreat or banishment into an exile of 'privacy' was considered a deprivation – a loss of society and company. What today is being claimed from society as the individual's 'right' was once understood as a punishment and a loss.

It is not difficult to describe the attitude of a structural self-interest in terms of today's discourses: many of them have expressions for and provide legitimations of it. In everyday language we call it 'apolitical' or non-political, that is, the attitude of people who are not interested in 'politics' and who instead pursue their own interests. Here 'politics' designates the concerns of others – society, humanity – to which I, as a private individual, and my concerns, as my private interests, stand in contrast. A 'sensible' political attitude is seen as constituted by a 'healthy' mixture of self-interest and an interest in 'politics'. Christian or moral discourses and personal ethics concerned with the behaviour of individuals make the harmony of personal behaviour with the person's (or God's) moral ideals a first priority. Even though a concern for other people is usually part of these ideals, the responsibility for others is subsumed under the person's self-interest – the fulfilment of personal moral aspirations.[1] Discourses of philosophy and psychology whose premise is the self or the ego, take from grammar the concept of the subject and its object-relations. Hence it appears 'natural' as well as sensible for the subject to be concerned in the first instance with its own existence and subjectivity, or respectively with putting its psychic household in order, so as to become capable in the second instance of sociability.

In the everyday language of the women's movement, this model of a primary concern for oneself derives additional legitimation from the claim that women historically and through caring for others have been practising too much selflessness and self-sacrifice, so that now they need to 'put themselves first'. Little does it seem to matter that the women who historically have been consumed in the care of others rarely are the same as those who now most avidly try to compensate for this historic disadvantage. Nor is it considered in such cases that 'selflessness' is less a historical fact than an attribution of patriarchal mythology: the ideological construction of an ideal of feminity – of the subjectivity of ideal women – which real women should attempt to match. What *is* a historical fact is women's exploitation in the slave labour of 'love' and care, coerced out of them through a patriarchal social order which allowed no alternatives. To describe this labour as self-motivated by women – as the product of a virtuous attitude or even a feminine disposition – is to psychologize a political and social reality, the better to justify the oppression of women by men. Only rarely do we attribute to slaves a comparable selfless devotion to building the colonies or the United States.

As our analyses of women's socialization have shown, so-called selflessness can become rational self-interest, namely the means by which to realize the advantages (however meagre) which patriarchal society offers to women. This is not to say that therefore all is well since women may also have realized their self-interest. Rather, we should understand that the deprivation of women in patriarchy consists not in the loss of self through self-sacrifice, but in the lack of political rights and material opportunities to survive and exist other than through the labour of 'love' and care, that is, other than as dependants and primary carers of men.

As Andrea Dworkin has argued in her book *Right-Wing Women*,[2] women pursuing conservative politics and advocating a traditional role for women neither advocate selflessness nor act against their own interest, but rather in what they consider to be their best interests: the protection of women and their dignity through marriage and the law, social recognition of the role of mother and wife, financial security through marriage, and protection from 'hard' labour, prostitution and pornography etc. The critique is less that these women advocate selflessness or lack self-interest than that they prioritize the self-interest of relatively secure wives and mothers, to the detriment of others and single and poor women in particular.

If contemporary discourses make it easy to describe and legitimate self-interest as a political, moral or psychological attitude, it seems very much more difficult even to conceptualize, let alone express, its opposite, the primary conception of a responsibility for the whole. So naturalized is the conception of the individual who is his own first responsibility that even attempts to postulate the sociability of humans, or their being part of nature as a whole, still usually start from the individual, representing sociability as his self-interest. Thus many a modern holistic and ecological theory presents the belated recognition of our dependency on the whole of humanity and on the entire planet as the last possibility of securing our own survival. The ecological arguments heard most frequently in the West during the second Gulf War of 1991 concerning its eco-catastrophic effects almost unanimously highlighted the fact that these might ultimately affect us too. In other words, the oil slicks in the Gulf are our concern, not because the people and inhabitants of the area are our concern, and not because the lands and the seas are our concern, but because the ecological effects could even touch ourselves. Not only is such an ecological concern based primarily on self-interest, but the argumentation also betrays that for Europeans, a sense of being 'affected' is constructed more effectively through a sense of being part of the ecosystem than through being part of humanity. So defining is our self-interest even in this apparently 'holistic' view (and so basic our opposition to humanity) that an ecological catastrophe anywhere on the globe constitutes a far more immediate and direct threat to us than does the catastrophic assault on the lives and livelihoods of hundreds of thousands of people in another part of the world.

That even a so-called interest in other people, in humanity and the planet as a whole, is postulated almost exclusively in terms of our own self-interest is due to the fact that the dominant discourses are fundamentally committed to individualism and its ideology of self-interest. For these discourses – their form and structure – *are* the dominant ideology, their function to legitimate the status quo. The ideological structure of a discourse makes it possible to express any content, even critical and dissident ideas, without any serious threat to the basic ideology, since any content is shaped through and ultimately brought back to its structural foundation: subjectivity and the self-interest of human individuals. Hence even a moral discourse postulating responsibility for 'others' as a duty does not seriously challenge the legitimacy of one's principal interest in the state of one's own soul;

even an ecological discourse postulating a concern for the wholeness of the ecosystem does not necessarily put in question the fundamental primacy of humans and their self-interest; and even a psychological discourse whose concerns are the subject's balanced object relations does not challenge the subject's primary interest in its subjectivity and well-being. We therefore need to consider not just the political content of a discourse, but above all its ideological structure and function.

Individualism and the principle of self-interest are crucial to maintaining the phenomenal power disequilibrium in society and to legitimizing its constitutive practice of profit and self-enrichment. Once this principle is installed, we may argue about why some are getting rich more successfully than others and whether a certain redistribution might be advisable. What is at issue is no longer the principle of self-enrichment, only the current state of affairs as a result of its application. Thus the liberal theory of the state and its philosophy of the rights of the individual are based on the premise of mutually conflicting self-interests, their concern being to mediate between them. The conception of the 'individual' as the universal model of 'man', however, is not just the hallmark of political liberalism, but the heart of Western ideology altogether, including many oppositional and critical schools of thinking.

The historical conception of the 'individual' underlying the foundation of the European civil state has been based, as is known, not on universal criteria, but on criteria which characterize the male citizen in the nation-state. Through the fundamental division of humankind into the communities of nation-states, the national citizenry, as if 'naturally', becomes the ultimate horizon of human society – what we usually simply call 'society'. Moreover, as Carole Pateman writes, 'the apparently universal criteria governing civil society are actually those associated with the liberal conception of the male individual, a conception which is presented as *the* individual.'[3] These are criteria which rely on the basic division of society into the 'public' and the 'private', two separate spheres in which men and women are differentially positioned and which are governed by distinctive and contrasting forms of social association.[4]

Civil patriarchy is founded on 'fraternity', the rule of the sons rather than the singular father.[5] Basic to the understanding of the (male) individual in the capitalist nation-state is his conception as 'the owner of the property in his person, that is to say, he is seen in abstraction from his ascribed familial relations and those with his fellow men',[6] as an apparently incorporeal entity.[7] 'The idea of the individual as owner' makes the individual 'so like all others as to be interchangeable',[8] or 'equal'. Thus 'owners of the property in their person' may enter contracts with like owners, including contracts whose content is individuals' property in their person, that is, their capacities and attributes (such as for instance their labour power).

Although the individual is thus abstracted from *all* his social relations, his abstractions from these relations differ since his social relations differ. The 'ascribed familial relations' are the relations of the male subject to women and children, relations in the 'private' sphere which, as is well known, are relationships to legal and conceptual objects. 'The family' is 'his family', his possession, until then part of his chattels, his movable household goods. Members of the family are not owners of the property in their persons, they are, on the contrary, the property owned by some other person. Thus the conception of the male citizen as *subject* depends on his relations to women and children, their status as objects constituting his subjectivity. There is nothing new about this.

What is new is that, with the emergence of 'civil society' and the citizen–subject as individual, this subject–object relation is becoming exclusively gender-specific, determining the identity of the national collective of men, subjectivity now constituting itself for *all* men in this manner and on principle in this manner. Men stand to other men of the nation in a different mutual relationship, namely as (abstracted) equals in a community of equals. The social subject–object relationship, now allowed only in the relationship of adult men to women and children (and animals), that is, in the citizen's 'private' sphere, used not to be so restricted, but included men as slaves, serfs or servants who were equally part of a master's chattels. Thus the subject, or the subject–object relationship, was not exclusively determined by (and determining) the gender relationship, but also other relationships of domination and subordination, those of a master over his slaves, servants or serfs. The establishment of 'civil society' means the abolition of such relationships of domination among the men (citizens) of the nation, every one of them now being the legitimate owner of the property in his 'own' person.

Hence the political emancipation of (adult) men – the abolition of slavery and serfdom and the emancipation also of men without property – is constitutive of men's gender (though simultaneously also their national) identity, as well as of the definition of 'universal man'. The status of the political and juridical subject is now equivalent to (adult) 'male/human', defining the concepts of 'masculine/human', 'free', 'citizen' and 'individual'. 'Everything else' belongs to the status of object, that is to say, is potentially part of the private property of men. The alleged greater 'closeness' of women not only to children, but also to animals and nature – which today is again increasingly invoked and intuitively felt, underlying certain currents of ecofeminism and feminist animal rights – is a result of this new drawing of the conceptual boundary between adult men (citizens) on the one hand and everything which is part of their property on the other: women, children, animals and land, all of whom and which are thus subjected to their rule, their violence and exploitation.

Yet even with the emancipation of 'all' men to be citizens of the state, men do not stand to each other in a social relation in the sense of a whole from which only women and children (and animals and nature, and other nationals) are excluded. Rather, the individual is abstracted and extracted also from the collectivity of men, to stand as an individual opposite other individuals, as a single entity opposite other single entities, as a subject opposite other 'subjects', with whom he may then choose to enter into relation. The term 'subjects', originally an expression of their subjugation to the feudal lord, here deserves quotation marks since the coexistence of a subject with other subjects is a contradiction in terms, the subject by definition being unique sovereign ruler in his world of objects. In liberal discourse it is replaced by the term 'individual': the patriarchal sons – subordinates of their fathers – having become 'brothers'. Thus their coexistence as equals or brothers is conceivable only from a meta-level, say from the perspective of a fatherly state as the coexistence of equal citizens, and from the perspective of a philosophy of rights as equality among legal subjects.

This means that the construction of the individual continues to constitute itself principally by means of a hierarchy, namely his relation to the level 'above', to the state, and his relation 'down' to the private sphere. The qualification as citizen is constituted on the one hand through the subject–object relation of the adult man to women and children and other property, while on the other equality among these free subjects requires their subordination to a state which constitutes them as a community by distinguishing them from other men outside the nation, and regulates and guarantees relations between them. That is, the qualification for freedom and equality is constituted through every single democrat's 'private' relationship of domination and his own subordination to the state which holds the monopoly of 'public' power. The superordination of the state in turn constitutes a subject–object relationship, a relation in which the citizens are objects. Yet this seems of less concern to the citizens than that the establishment of a superior level should guarantee the regulation of relations between them, since their major concern as citizens is not to be dominated and made an object by other citizens.[9]

Hence the civil state permits the citizen to constitute his subjectivity by means of his subject–object relation to 'his family', granting every one of them the free zone of his 'private sphere'. Here, in the privacy of his family and home, he remains largely unmolested by the laws of the state,[10] freed in particular from the obligations of citizenship and non-violence with regard to other people. For in the family there are no other citizens, nor indeed any individuals, hence there is no obligation to acknowledge 'freedom, equality and brotherhood'. The 'private' sphere is the sphere of his sovereignty as subject, where he may do as he pleases, where nobody else is watching and no one intervening, where he is the sole ruling lord and master.

What is not the 'private sphere' of individual citizens is the 'public sphere', which belongs to them all equally. However, citizens and individuals whose understanding of themselves is based on the conception of a subject in relation to objects, that is, on 'private' domination, cannot simultaneously be part of a collective, even if only the collective community of male citizens. These two conceptions are mutually exclusive. Hence even the mutual relationships between citizens are structured according to the primary assumption of the self-interest of every single and individual citizen and can be regulated and kept in check only by the hierarchically superordinated state, or those in charge of it. Hence the state in turn necessarily develops its own self-interest, which on principle is opposed to the interests of the citizens, leading to the well-known expansion of state power at the cost of citizens' rights. Above all, however, the principle of self-interest is thus institutionalized as *the* legitimate basic attitude of the citizen among citizens, regulatable and regulated through the control of the state. Its protection and preservation becomes the central concern of liberalism, democratic theory and the philosophy of rights.

As Carole Pateman writes,

[The individual] is a 'private' individual, but he needs a sphere in which he can exercise his rights and opportunities, pursue his (private) interests and protect and increase his property. If all men ('individuals') are so to act in an orderly fashion, then, as Locke is aware, a public 'umpire' (rather than a hidden – private? – hand), or a representative, liberal state, is required to make and enforce publicly known, equitable laws.[11]

The sphere of his possible action as a 'private' individual, as one who exercises his rights, pursues his interests, protects and above all increases his property, must not be restricted to the small sphere of the family which, despite everything, is quite limited in its possibilities for exploitation and accumulation. That would not be freedom. For the exercise of his rights, of his 'freedom' and his claims to the acquisition of property, the individual requires the public sphere of the entire society – which hence is declared the 'private sector'. On the level of the citizens and the state (free zone 'family' excepted) there is a second division into 'private' and 'public':

The separation between private and public is thus re-established as a division *within* civil society itself, within the world of men. The separation is then expressed in a number of different ways, not only private and public but also, for example, 'society' and 'state', or 'economy' and 'politics', or 'freedom' and 'coercion' or 'social' and 'political'.[12]

So-called 'political' responsibility, that is, the self-interested desire and need of citizens for a regulation of the competing self-interests of citizens, is handed over to and invested in the state and is what remains properly 'public'. This results in a considerable shrinkage of what is 'public' and 'political', while 'civil society is seen, above all else, as the sphere of private interest, private enterprise and private individuals.'[13] And as Pateman comments, 'in the late twentieth century the relation between the capitalist economy and the state no longer looks like that between Locke's umpire and civil society.[14] Rather, the economy seems to have become the umpire in relation to the state.

Moreover, in the twentieth century and with the political emancipation of women, the citizenry has doubled. This has not, however, resulted in the abolition of the original division of society into the familial 'private' sphere and the 'public' sphere. Through the continuing existence, for instance, of marriage law, women continue to be implicated within men's original 'private' sphere, though they are now entitled not only to participate in the state, but also to pursue their own private interests in the public 'private' sphere – to launch private enterprises and to consider themselves private individuals. Even so, private enterprise and participation in the private sector of course remain the privilege of few, whether they are women or men, since increasing one's property presupposes the existence of property, while exploitation as a means of accumulation requires that there be masses of people to exploit.

Although the political ideals of civil society – of freedom, equality and brotherhood – are starkly contradicted by the realities of the capitalist world order, individualism still remains a shining ideal, as if the one had nothing to do with the other. In particular, the 'right' to a 'private' sphere – its patriarchal genesis and its contradiction to the concepts of democracy and equality notwithstanding – remains the uncontested claim not only of every male citizen, but increasingly also of many women citizens. If we cannot all be successful in the public 'private' sphere of the economy, at least we may understand ourselves as private individuals, pursuing our interests in the 'private private' sphere.

Women may not have a state-provided disenfranchised 'sex' at their disposal with which to construct their 'private' sphere (leaving aside children, who however remain the joint possession of men and indeed are increasingly claimed by them),[15] and women may still be deprived of the integrity of their own persons. Their bodies may continue to be part not only of the private sphere of men but of the public sphere of the state's reproduction, over whose products the state continues to decide. It may still be impossible, in other words, for women to free themselves from *being* somebody else's 'private' sphere and from being the state's public sphere, let alone to *have* a 'private' sphere of their own. Yet the desire to be a 'subject' after the model of the male citizen subject, this 'private' interest of the 'private individual', may be carried into every encounter and fought out in every relationship in order to establish a different kind of 'private' space, where the power of the subject to make another into an object, where domination over another person, may nevertheless be experienced. It simply requires that we continue with unregenerate tenacity to call this most political sphere of interpersonal relationships a 'private' sphere – a free zone where for the subject, as for the male citizen in his family, 'freedom, equality, brotherhood and sisterhood' have an end, where different rules are operating than in the public sphere, an oasis of domination for the self in the midst of 'equality' and even 'gender equality'.

As Catharine MacKinnon writes, 'privacy' in patriarchal society

> is everything women as women have never been allowed to have; at the same time the private is everything women have been equated with and defined in terms of *men*'s ability to have . . . The very *place* (home, body), *relations* (sexual), *activities* (intercourse and reproduction), and *feelings* (intimacy, selfhood) that feminism finds central to women's subjection form the core of private doctrine.[16] (my emphases, except for 'men')

From the perspective of women, or 'in feminist translation', 'the private is the sphere of battery, marital rape, and women's exploited labour; of the central institutions whereby women are deprived of (as men are granted) identity, autonomy, control, and self-determination; and of the primary activity through which male supremacy is expressed and enforced.'[17] If, then, a 'private' sphere for women citizens necessarily has to be constituted without the free zone of home, marriage and family (and for male citizens in addition to these), that is to say, without the state-sanctioned possession of a wife of one's own, this 'private' sphere none the less fulfils the doctrine of the private in all central points: the 'private' is the place *body* (of another), *sexual relations* (with another), the activity *sex* (with another), and the *feelings of self in the intimacy* (with another). From our experience as women, that is to say, as the historic and ideological prototype of men's 'other', we admittedly know and recognize this 'privacy' as the realm of the bodily-sexual abuse of the 'other', the violation of the integrity of the person of the 'other', the rape by means of the activity of sex of the 'other', and the exploitation of the labour of the 'other', including the so-called emotional and reproductive care for the subject for whom we are the 'other'. That is, we recognize it as the realm in which male domination, the domination of the subject, traditionally realizes and asserts itself. Notwithstanding, this modernized version of the 'private' seems increasingly to represent also for women *the* chance to realize themselves as subjects – that is, to experience, express and enforce dominance over another.

While thus women's political 'equality' in the liberal state has not led to the deconstruction and abolition of men's crass supremacy over women – as a form of domination that is in contradiction to the ideals of democracy and equality – it is now not only male citizens, but increasingly also women citizens who model their aspirations on the 'freedom' and the privileges of the male citizen. That everybody cannot have privileges, that the supremacy of the one means the oppression of the others, that privileges are not so much rights as advantages which are to the disadvantage of others, seems to matter as little as it matters that everyone cannot be a capitalist. 'Freedom and equality' in liberal democracy do not mean freedom equally for all, but free rein for the free competition of the self-interest to dominate (others), and a free market for a free economy to exploit (others). And it means 'freedom for all' to fight out the supremacy and privileges of 'privacy' in their so-called 'private relationships'.

If it is not clear to individual citizens that they cannot all and equally become rich at the cost of others, that they cannot all and equally dominate and rule over others, it certainly is clear to those experienced in rule and domination. It is by reason of state and government, and of the leading powers of the economy and society, that only some may succeed in dominating, while others must be subjected. Only then is the free democratic state guaranteed, only then are power and government secured, only then is the economy really free. And it tends to be clear to individual men that however many aspiring subjects there may be, and however fierce the competition for that role, the pleasure of the subject consists in dominating another as object. If those traditionally condemned to object status, if those continuing to be oppressed and exploited, either by the state and through structural oppression or by individuals – if rather than objecting to power and domination they now themselves aspire to them, it will only strengthen the legitimacy of dominance and cement the power of the already powerful. It would mean that any resistance to power had successfully been checked.

Individualism, the principle of self-interest and acquisition as the proper meaning of life, remains also in modern times the uncontested basis of rationality, to whose pursuit every effort in every area is dedicated. The 'subject' continues to be the model of the individual's understanding of self, even if as a consequence of the emancipation of women it is beginning to lose its gender specificity. 'Becoming a subject' is not only the goal of patriarchal psychology but has become the highest priority also for many women in the Western women's movement, who seem to be of the opinion that till now they have been walking the earth as objects. Women in fact are not objects, nor ever have been, though we may indeed be on the way to perfecting ourselves as subjects – whose claims to power, whose readiness to use violence and whose will to exploitation are hardly lagging behind those of men. Women admittedly continue to lack the collective means to do as men collectively do, to equal men in their collective acquisition, and women admittedly lack a collective sex or gender or class which they could dominate as men continue to dominate women. Yet nothing seems to stop us from wanting to equal them in doing as they do, at least in principle, and wherever the opportunity presents itself – even if equalling individual ones among them has to remain the lonely privilege of individual women.

It is part of this development that capitalist principles have long invaded all spheres of life, transforming every kind of value into value in the capitalist sense. This means that other values may also be accumulated, other 'products' also be circulated, and that private enterprise may flourish also outside the traditional sphere of production. Capitalist thinking is not restricted to capitalists and the super-rich, to entrepreneurs and market profiteers who stockpile their profits of exploitation in the banks. The radical permeation of our everyday thinking by the fundamental principles and values of capitalism means that critics and advocates of capitalism alike have internalized them. Socialization in our Western culture does not just transmit sexism, racism, classism etc., it also transmits the fundamental values of capitalist power and exploitation: individualism, self-interest and acquisition.

2

Love of foreigners and love of the 'other'

Now I understand that it was nothing but this 'otherness' which has killed the Jews, and it began with them being reduced to 'the other'.

Slavenka Drakulić, *Balkan Express*[1]

Outside, the roll call had been interminable . . . Those poor creatures, haggard, fleshless, dirty, dragging the dogged remaining flicker of life within them around, these women . . . more dead than alive – for us they were 'the others'. An awful term . . .

Fania Fénelon, *The Musicians of Auschwitz*[2]

The subject can be posed only in being opposed – he sets himself up as the essential, as opposed to the other, the inessential, the object. He is the Subject, he is the Absolute – she is the Other.

Simone de Beauvoir, *The Second Sex*[3]

At least since Simone de Beauvoir's *The Second Sex*, feminist critique has been based on the insight that the subjection, exploitation and discrimination of women 'begins with' calling and reducing women to 'the others', the other sex, the Other. The conceptual objectification of women is the ideological foundation of men's material assumption of power over women, the basis of their self-empowerment as the collective subject of androcentrism and the patriarchal order. The subject can be posed only in being opposed – he affirms himself *by* posing 'the other' as inessential and as object. Thus men's collective identity is constituted through women's banishment into the category of 'women' – only by explicitly naming women do they implicitly become 'men', the norm of gender and the subject of patriarchal gender-thinking. Hence the subject's self-affirmation lies in the act of naming the other:[4] in the exercise of the power of discourse by which the thinking/speaking subject gathers his addressees unto himself and into the 'we' of discourse, relegating those spoken *about* into the object status of 'them', the objects, the 'others'.

Of course, this insight into conceptual and discursive objectification of the 'others' is not exclusive to feminism, nor is it limited to sexism. Rather, feminists have taken over the analysis of objectification from the analyses of racism, anti-Semitism and classism, extending it to sexism. All the more remarkable, then, that some feminists, academic feminists in particular, increasingly revert to this discourse of 'us and them', of 'we' and the 'others'. Under the banner of a 'politics of difference' – whose provenance or political implications are rarely analysed – differences are being 'recognized' with a vengeance, constructing a plethora of new 'others'. *What* differences are to be recognized by whom and for what purpose are they to be recognized seem to disappear as questions, and with it the insight Fania Fénelon had when, herself a prisoner in the concentration camp of Auschwitz and a member of the girls' orchestra there, she watched the roll call of the women condemned to forced labour: 'For us [the girls in the orchestra] they were "the others". *An awful term*' (my emphasis).

Since the rise of the women's liberation movement and feminist politics, what is called 'French feminism' (standing for academic, theoretically 'sophisticated' feminism) has conquered the academy, translating the feminist critique of sexual power relations back into an analysis of 'sexual difference' and locating women back in the biological destiny of a female body.[5] Similarly, the newly fashionable discourse of 'otherness' seems to celebrate its comeback and academic rehabilitation at a moment when the critique of racism has begun to achieve relative public prominence – that is to say, on the level also of white-dominated public and academic discourse. In the United States, for example, where since the repression of the Black Liberation Movement of the sixties and seventies, public discourse has become a major site of struggle, the critique of racist power relations is now in danger of being neutralized by the staging of a vast cultural festival of 'celebrating diversity'. As A. Sivanandan writes, 'whereas in the '60s, the rebellion on the street swept into the campus and politicised it . . . today the street cultures of resistance have been appropriated by academia and "disciplined" into literary theory and cultural studies, and therein depoliticised.'[6] Similarly, in Germany, where until recently white academia and the media were barely concerned with racism, we may observe in concentrated miniature how the emerging critique of racism, at a time of a drastic increase in open racist violence in society, has led to a frenzied exploration of 'otherness' and the 'other', of the 'stranger' and the 'strange', among white intellectuals and academics.[7]

As far as concerns the critique of racism, Black people and migrants in the 'first world' and people of the 'Third World' of course are the obvious experts: they have analysed the racism of white society in its structural and individual, material and ideological, national and international manifestations, they began to write the manifold history of racism and have developed the theoretical analysis and the political critique. Their critique of Western historiography shows that racism is at the core of European history, a history of the violent conquest of other continents and the subjection or genocide of their indigenous people; that racism is the foundation of the Western economy – an economy of centuries of slavery and the colonial exploitation of the colonized continents, including their people, an economy from which not only the leading slave-trading nations and colonizing empires amassed unlimited profits, but on which Europe and the West as a whole built their political, economic and cultural supremacy as the so-called 'first world'. Their critique of Eurocentrism shows that the racist ideology which legitimates this murderous exploitation permeates the whole of Western culture and 'civilization', the pride and glory of European (and Western) identity. Their political critique shows that racism not only was the basis of colonialism, but remains the basis of postcolonialism through to the latest version of the 'new world order', which secures and cements the fruits of the old world order – the history of the exploitation of the South by the North – for the changed modern conditions of an allegedly democratic 'family of nations' and the 'multicultural' societies of the West. Racism is the basis of European nationalism, which not only reached its abject extremity as nationalism in the National Socialism of German fascism, but as the murderous racism and genocidal anti-Semitism of the Holocaust.

Hardly surprising, then, that white opinion-makers would prefer to avoid the term 'racism'. The struggle for power begins at the level of naming. There is hardly a political meeting or demonstration or candle chain against racism in Germany today which does not include in its title the terms 'hatred of foreigners' or 'hostility towards immigrants' (*Fremdenhaß*, literally 'hatred of strangers', or *Ausländerfeindlichkeit*, literally 'hostility towards aliens'). 'Hostility towards immigrants' and 'hatred of foreigners' are the preferred terms of a public debate which only reluctantly recognizes the compounding racist violence in our societies at the time of their consolidation into fortress Europe. To rename racism – so named by those who are its victims – as hatred of foreigners and hostility towards strangers is radically to redefine the problem and to prepare the ground for a different analysis, serving a different set of interests. It serves the interests, not of those who suffer from racism, but of those who benefit from it, who share in the responsibility for it and who stand to lose considerable privileges if racist oppression is abolished. In other words, it serves the general and the specific interests of the speakers who, in the very act of renaming the problem, decide to exercise their power and (ab)use their privilege as subjects of public discourse, in the interest not of an anti-racist politics but of preserving their own power and authority unaffected by or indifferent to any insight that power 'begins' with the power of naming.

The euphemisms 'hostility towards immigrants', 'hatred of foreigners' and 'xenophobia' not only sound nicer, since they suppress any explicit reference to racism, but in reformulating the problem they also imply its 'solution', namely friendliness towards immigrants and love of foreigners. Thus neither the power of categorizing nor the power relations inherent in the categories are at issue. The categories are simply 'given', in the autocratic inclusion of 'us' into the status of the subject and 'them', the foreigners and immigrants into the status of the objects. We are 'we' and they are 'the others'; we have the choice of how to treat them: with hostility or friendliness, with hatred or love. Thus the problem has successfully been moved out of the political arena and into the realm of individual humanism or Christian love of neighbours, into the arena, that is, of interpersonal relationships.

As women and feminists, we should know about love in the Christian West. Sexism has never been exclusively a problem of hostility and unfriendliness towards women which could be solved by greater women-friendliness. Women have suffered from nothing as much as from love: men are the first to assure us that they subject, imprison, abduct, rape, prostitute, consume, pornographize and kill women because they love them so much. Women are the objects of their desire, both their sexual desire and their economic greed. Every man wants to have at least one of them. Women have not just been hated and degraded, and their representation was never just 'negative' and derogatory: women have been loved to death, put up on pedestals, revered as the guardians of morality by the self-designated representatives of immorality, and they have been celebrated and consumed as the embodiment of beauty.

As women, as the targets of sexism, we know that the problem is less the content of the attitude to our 'sex' than the structure of our definition *as* a 'sex'. Once this structure is given, once we have been designated the objects of the attention and attitude of the male sex, it matters little what form this attitude and treatment takes: it is a matter of gradation and of individual luck. Even if the treatment happens to be kind, it confirms the possibility that it could be malevolent. Above all, any possibility of autonomy or self-determination on the part of the woman 'object' has thereby been precluded, her existence as a person destroyed: they are not part of the options of good or bad treatment; they are not on offer.

Of course, on the level of women's experience it does make a considerable difference how the treatment turns out, whether it tends towards hatred and malice or towards love and kindness. Yet it is a question of principle by definition to be the victim of somebody else's determination. What counts among the 'positive' forms of love – protection, care, help and charity, tenderness and the desire to 'have' the other – shares with the more obviously 'negative' forms of hatred the structure of domination – from patronization to possession, from violence to destruction. The sexual exploitation of a girl is no less a form of exploitation and violence if it is executed with loving tenderness. The patronization of a woman means no less her destruction as a person if she is guarded by her husband like 'the apple of his eye'. And the sexual harassment of a woman is no less a form of sexual violence if it is accompanied by compliments and motivated by desire. Our feminist analysis of violence has focused precisely on the structure of violence: the abuse of power in a power relationship. And it has revealed the patriarchal categorization of violent acts from not-so-bad to bad, and from harmless to harmful, to be part of the naturalization of violence and the mystification of the power relations in society.[8]

The fundamental problem is the conception of the self as subject in relation to an object. Once this structure is given – once the self has empowered itself to a position over and above reality and as the subject of its own 'view', in which everything and anything becomes the 'other', the object of and in my sight – the power relationship is established and the relation becomes a relation of opposition: 'I' and the 'other', I and 'my' opposite. I can choose how I am going to encounter her, in love or in hatred; I as the subject have the choice how I will treat her. Whatever the content of my treatment, it remains a treatment, and there remains the person treated. What a subject chooses to do to an object is a form of aggression: a transitive action determined by the subject, from the subject to its recipient. Even a good deed remains a deed (against the other) and contains within it the latent threat of the misdeed. The fact of the deed – the good deed as much as the misdeed – confirms the power relation between the one who does and the one done to.

So some scepticism might be in order regarding this newly emerging friendliness towards foreigners, this sign of the times following the rise of the critique of racism. Popular advice reassures us that an encounter with foreigners or 'the foreign' not only enlarges our minds but holds other rewards, from the delights of a multicultural cuisine to the benefits of a multicultural workforce, which replenishes our pension funds and guarantees the maintenance of our living standard. It is a plea for the love of foreigners, since like all love it is a blessing to the lover. Love in our sexist, racist, capitalist culture of the West is a matter of exploitation, accumulation and desire; a matter of assessing its usefulness, of calculating costs and benefits, investment and returns; and a questions of needs and their fulfilment. The love of feminists seems to be not so different in this respect.

'To do research as an an academic and journalist is like taking hot and cold baths', writes one feminist researcher about 'living and working in a foreign culture': 'high spirits alternate with frustration, the strange alternates with the familiar, reward alternating with dispossession.'[9] If you think that this journey to the 'other' is motivated by a wish to gain an understanding of and enter into an exchange with the 'others', by a genuine interest in the other and in the interest of the other, you are mistaken. The journey is undertaken in the spirit of love, and hence begins with the immediate calculation of the gains and losses, benefits and costs, investments and returns: every euphoria has its price in the currency of frustration, every enriching experience exacts its payment through the alienation of cash. The enterprise is in the interest of the entrepreneur, in the interest of a subject who is looking around in her object world and there – how could it be otherwise? – only finds the mirror image of herself: 'The expedition to the Other is invariably also a journey to oneself, to the other parts of the self. The researcher here does not really differ from the tourist.'[10]

Despite the astute comparison, no analysis follows of what makes 'foreigner studies' so like a version of intellectual tourism, and what exactly would be our feminist critique of that. Instead, the author contents herself with describing the symptoms – the self-mirroring of the subject in a world of objects she herself has created and depopulated. And she stays with the current categories of 'us' on the one hand and the 'Others', the 'women of the Third World' on the other, and 'the confrontation with the strange and unfamiliar', all confirming the basic outlook of opposition. At most, she sees her task in correcting the image which the women's movement at home has of 'women in the Third World', an image which is said to veer between 'backwardness' and 'bearers of hope'.[11] The problem for her, however, lies in the content of this image, namely that neither the (negative) image of the others' 'backwardness' nor the (positive) one of them as 'bearers of hope' is quite accurate: 'the images brought along from home are not applicable, what we have learnt simply is not true.'[12]

But the problem lies less in the content of the images and that 'their "backwardness" makes us superior' – which implies that an image of them as 'bearers of hope' makes *them* superior, while perhaps one somewhere in the middle would make us equal. Our 'superiority' stems from the fact that it is we who are making the image of the 'others', never mind what is its content. Out of the unassailable safety of our status as subjects, making the picture and organizing the comparison, we may even put 'them' on a pedestal as those who will save the world; as the creators of the picture and the judges of its content we remain unchallengeably superior.

This pictorial discourse about the 'other' is no less an act of violence against them than is a verbal discourse of naming and defining: a coercive objectification of them out of a position of power. I am the subject making an image, the 'Other' becomes the object and content of my image. This violence, moreover, reproduces and propagates itself, since the created image has a function beyond being a nice or an accurate picture: it must be applicable, and it is being applied, namely *to* women in the Third World. Hence these women not only are the victims of a process of objectification which makes them the object of representation; they in turn become the victims of an 'application' of this representation: a confrontation with this image in a renewed encounter, where the women are not perceived in their reality, but where an image is being 'applied' to them, projected on to them, superimposed on them. The real women who first were the 'model' for a picture are now being reduced to the created image. If first they were model in the creation of the picture, now the picture is 'model' for their reality.

To make an image of somebody is an act of ideological violence, a determination and definition to which the other has nothing to say. To have an 'image' of the other means to select particular factors of my perception on the basis of criteria which I choose, reducing the other to these factors. The image is a fiction, a work of my own creation, a 'knowledge' of my own making. It is the expression of my subjectivity, my fantasy and my thinking, which says nothing about the so-called object of my representation. The reality of the other woman, everything I have not perceived and also cannot perceive, but above all her self-determination and her continuing changing, remain out of consideration, are suppressed and excluded.

The arrogance of such imaging consists not only in mistaking my perception for knowledge, but in thinking that what I know is everything there is to know, is my unwillingness to reflect my own subjectivity, according to the principle that 'reality is where I perceive it.' It betrays not only an incapacity for reality, but an unwillingness to realism, a will to power. For it is this same arrogance which moves me anew to reapply my image *to* reality, to travel there with my learnt knowledge in order to approach reality through its screen. Hence it matters little whether the image is 'negative' or 'positive', insulting or flattering. The image is made in the interest of the imager, a means of controlling the 'other' with her 'knowledge', fortifying herself against the risks of an unknowable reality. It shows her decision to affect the other while taking preventive measures against any possibility of herself being affected by the other, let alone changed in the fortress of her self-built Self.

If the researcher thus sets out anew in order to change her first image, it is not out of an insight into what her imaging means to those imaged, what violence it constitutes against them. We set out to change the picture because it is not 'applicable', because what we have learnt as knowledge is not true, that is, because we cannot use this picture and this knowledge. It does not lead us to give up making pictures, it makes us want to make better ones. Any 'critique' of the image remains within the framework of the subject's calculations of its own advantages and benefits – it remains the subject's interest to have the knowledge and to have the image. The interest of the other does not appear in the calculation, it is not a factor. Hence it comes as no surprise that the desired 'encounter with the Others' once again does not materialize, that, as the researcher is obliged to recognize, 'encounters often take place within a prison of images.'[13] Yet the foundations of her own subjectivity which is building this prison – her own subject-object thinking and her own will to power – remain unshaken and unchanged.

And so it remains a matter of hot and cold baths for the researcher – an apt image, since she sits in her bath all alone. There is no 'other' to be seen anywhere, only the water in which the subject takes her bath and which at one time is hot and another time cold, at one time euphoria and another time frustration. The subject sees herself on both sides of her equation, entering herself in both columns of her accounting: on the one side her takings and on the other her expenses. The profit is mine, and the costs are mine. It is not, say, a question of the costs the other has to bear, of what the encounter means to the other. There is no attempt at an equation here, between the concerns on both sides, assessing the responsibility for the situation and considering the other's situation as well as her own.

Hence it is but logical that where the subject apparently does attempt to consider the other, it only happens within the balancing of the subject's own accounts and is registered in the currency of the subject's own exchange rate. For if the image of the other turns out not to be true, that is not an injustice towards the other, but a blow to the researcher's authority and confidence – it makes her 'insecure' and 'disconcerted'. Her admitted 'captivity in images, projects, prejudices'[14] does not constitute a danger to the others, but an impediment to her own enterprise. If her glance never dwells on what her own actions mean to others, the others' actions on the contrary are considered exclusively in terms of what they mean to her: 'At the same time the white woman is also continually imaged by her opposites.'[15]

My 'opposite' has no position and no significance other than being opposite to myself. In the opposition of this 'encounter' she becomes 'equal' – as my opponent in a free arena, who has me as her opponent.

Any existing power relationship falls outside the sphere of vision, in particular the consideration how this encounter has come about, in whose interest it is, and how the other ever came to be my opposite. That the encounter is forced onto the other, that it has been chosen and willed by myself, and that it is undertaken in my interest, becomes immaterial once the match has begun. The name of the game, consequently, is 'getting to know each other'[16] – an apparently symmetrical affair which requires no differentiation between the two players. They are joined as the collective (deleted) subject of a 'joint' action, as if both of them equally wanted to play, as if both were taking part in the same game. 'We get to know each other', we each are a subject in the 'we' and object in the 'each other'. 'It is a process of particularization and social differentiation, in which prejudices are corrected and projections reduced.'[17] 'We' particularize, and we differentiate, from now on 'we' do everything together, we correct prejudices, because we both equally have them and both equally need to correct them. The white woman has an image of the Black woman and the Black woman has an image of the white woman, the researcher constructs a picture of her research object and the research object constructs a picture of the researcher – in wonderful mutuality. In this empty arena of the personal relationship one prejudice apparently is like another, and is, in particular, but a universal human weakness.

The great danger zone – the multiple power relationship between 'myself', a white research tourist from the first world with my project on the one hand, and the 'strangers', the 'others', 'the mostly poor country women' or even 'middle-class women' in the Third World on the other[18] – has successfully been circumnavigated. Above all, what has disappeared from sight is the primary power relation of this encounter, the power relationship between a researcher and her object of study – between the subject of the encounter who seeks and wills it, and the object of the encounter who is required for it and to whom the encounter happens.

This power, however, this violence of the will of the initiator, continually reflects and betrays itself also in her text: 'Togetherness is neither just there nor does it come about automatically – it must be established.'[19] It must, because I want it. I do not only ask questions, I 'declare that I also want to be asked questions'.[20] The questioning may change direction, but the will to ask them, as well as the will to be asked them, remains the will of the selfsame subject.

It is not the unequal relationship that is being analysed. As if such 'togetherness' was a shared interest, a project chosen equally freely by both, an enterprise undertaken jointly by both, for which the costs, too, have to be shared equally by both; the unequal costs borne by the subject also immediately come to the foreground: 'I, as the intruder from outside, have to make the effort to reduce anxieties and distance, to take colonial and cultural barriers down.'[21] I as the one intruding from outside do not have to think about my intruding, but about the resistance to my intrusion. The resistance must go, the anxieties must go: this will of the other manifesting itself in her actions must go. The language as well as the scenario remind one of the notorious lament by men (before the sexual revolution) that *they* always have to make the effort and *they* always have to take the initiative to chat women up – in their arrogant assumption that His goal is Her goal too, that the 'shared goal', the obligatory coupling, is beyond question. What coupling is to heterosexism, 'togetherness' is to the love of strangers. What remains discernible is that it is a matter of love, a love which is neither strange nor unfamiliar: 'I approach the women, make physical contact where a common language does not exist. By means of physical contact I am trying to break through the wall of glass which often stands between myself and these women: I observe them, we can interact and yet I never really get there.'[22]

Haven't we heard this somewhere before? Have we not experienced it hundreds of times? Trying to get there – yet never quite getting there, pressing closer and closer, and yet never getting close enough? Still, the obligatory climax does not fail to come, presenting itself infallibly: 'again and again the euphoric feeling comes . . . in embracings, in the laughing and giggling of which African women never can get enough'[23] – when you push closer and closer, that is, and get where you could not get any closer. If we did not know that this was written by a woman, what would we say? What outcry would there be about this blatant harassment, this violation and transgression? About this unrelenting 'chat up', as it is euphemistically called, whose only possible outcome is its success? Whose arrogant vision stunted by will and desire perceives 'giggling African women who never can get enough of it', as all women apparently 'never can get enough of it'? What remains to be said except that women seem to be learning well?

Laws may tell us that the dignity of a person is inviolable,[24] but a person is touchable, grabbable, aggressable, approachable, in short, eminently violable: it suffices that the violating subject wills it and is ready to assert its will even against the other's will. This is all the easier since the subject does not even perceive the other's will: it does not feature in the subject's representation and is no factor in its considera-tion – it is denied, negated and suppressed already by and in the subject's perception and representation.

This love of strangers – this desire for the 'Other' and for 'together-ness' with the 'Others' – is not, however, the exclusive problem of researchers of foreign cultures and certainly not a specific problem of this particular researcher. Her text merely serves as an example for analysing the structure of this love. The desire for the 'stranger', the 'unknown', the 'Other' is a much more general phenomenon, and in particular has re-emerged as a reflex in response to the critique of racism. Where, as white women, we have been addressed with regard to our power, we respond by proving (to ourselves) our love.

We prove it in the first instance by now talking about the 'others'. If before the 'others' appeared barely or not at all in (much of) our public discourse, we now lovingly put them into it. If before there was a problem of exclusion, there now is a problem of inclusion – the inclusion of the 'others' in the position of the objects of our discourse. So long as we remain masters and mistresses of the discourse, we can deal with the 'others', can even integrate them. This also allows us to reformulate the critique, even if we say 'racism' rather than 'hatred of foreigners'.

We will, for instance, make 'the oppression of the Others through our culture explicitly part of our feminist work'.[25] Thus the 'culture' becomes the proper culprit and the agent of oppression, while we merely demote to the passivity of being 'bearers of the problem', members of 'the culture which *is* the problem and which *creates* the problem'.[26] We have gone half the way, away from our own actions and doings and to the deeds of our culture,[27] so that it is only a short step to full victim status:

> Racism and anti-Semitism are our 'sickness', the evil which pursues us. They are a misery of the white world, its spiritual and moral misery. They confront us with our history and our present . . . with people of our culture towards whom we cannot be indifferent; with our own identity which has been shaped by this culture and which often we do not even want.[28]

The great danger zone – our own position within the power structure and our own behaviour and (ab)use of power – has thus apparently been circumvented. While Black people, migrants, refugees, Jews, Cinti, Roma or travellers and others singled out by European racism are pursued by racist mobs and murderers, 'we' are pursued by the evil of racism and anti-Semitism. You might almost think that in racism we have a common problem, one which the culture has presented us with, but you are wrong, because it ceases to be a problem altogether of those who are actually oppressed by racism. Rather, we ourselves are the ones really 'oppressed' by it: *we* are being pursued by it, for *us* it is an evil and a misery. As before it was 'culture' assuming the role of the culprit, now it is racism and anti-Semitism rising to the status of agent: *they confront* us with our history and our present (which otherwise we would not have), *they* confront us with people of our culture towards whom we cannot be indifferent (because they belong to 'our own' culture), and *they* confront us with our own identity, which perhaps we don't even want but which we cannot do anything about – while we happily impose an identity on 'the Others', whether they want it or not, which we could indeed do something about. Not only is there a continuing struggle for power between 'us' and 'them', 'we' even fight about the problem. And since we are in a position to determine the matter, the problem will from now on be all ours: it becomes *our* problem, and 'working on these questions is our business. It is work in our own interest.'[29] If we did not know it before, we know it now: the enterprise is in the interest of the entrepreneur.

If only, however, it left the 'others' alone, if only they were untouched by our problem and our undertaking. But ours is a project of love, it stands under the auspices of desire, the desire for the 'other'. We are on our way to the Others: 'The way to the Others requires experience with the Others, the confrontation with reality, a real encounter with the Others.'[30] And even if it is the way which requires the experience, it is our way and our need to take it. The desired confrontation and encounter, like the coupling, is our own wish and will, the 'Others' are not being asked. We assume that they will be pleased and grateful, that they have just been waiting for us. *We* now are in need of the experience: we need the encounter, and we need the 'Others' for it. Suddenly it is the case that 'we are missing them, that we do not only need them, but miss them.'[31] The Others are what we still want for our happiness, we need them for our cause – and we are willing to (ab)use them in our interest.

The whole argument is a defence of the love of the 'Other', for the love will be a blessing to those doing the loving. It is an advertisement for a worthwhile investment, for it promises good returns: 'We will experience that we no longer disappear in an undifferentiated mass of women' – on the contrary, we will 'locate' ourselves in the identity of dominance and supremacy, 'as for example, a white Christian hetero-sexual middle-class woman without disability, who is continually developing and growing'.[32] Thus relocated in the standard categories of power – of racism, anti-Semitism, nationalism, heterosexism, clas-sism and ableism – we not only find our new identity which distin-guishes us from the 'mass' of women, we will properly be able to flourish. And the ultimate dividend is nigh: 'We will' – at last – 'be able to encounter Jewish women and Black women.'[33]

'Togetherness', the grail of the love of the Other, thus seems to have come within reach, the way there to have been found. At least from our perspective, which discursively constructs and imposes 'to-getherness', suppressing the other's interest by subsuming it under our own. The subject's desire for the other, the subject's will to have her, finds its fulfilment in an 'encounter' which the subject takes firmly in hand – pushing closer and closer, even if one never really gets there.

It is with good reason that feminists have begun to question the term 'sexual abuse', seeing that there is no 'use' of people which is not an abuse, and that using them means exploiting them. Exploitation, as we know, rests on power and the ideological objectification of the other as 'other', the prerequisite of domination. Behind the categorization, behind the objectification, behind domination and exploitation, how-ever, is the will of the subject to objectify, to dominate, and to exploit.

3

Personal communication behaviour is political

How is it, then, that we are suddenly on our way to the 'others', what have Black women said that we suddenly miss them, want them, need them? What has prompted this sudden new love, this desire for the 'other', for the 'different' and the strange, and set us on our way in quest of an encounter with the 'other'?

As I have already said, this phenomenon seems to coincide with the critique of racism gaining ground within 'public', that is to say, white-dominated discourse and consciousness. Within the women's movement in particular it has been Black feminists' critique of racism and the analysis of the interlocking oppressions of sexism and racism, which also included a critique of the behaviour of white women and feminists. It has been a critique concerning both the theory, the interpretation of feminism as it has been defined by white women, and their actual behaviour and (ab)use of power. Yet as bell hooks, for instance, explicitly states in her essay, 'black women and feminism', published in 1989, her aim in writing her earlier book, *Ain't I A Woman* (1981), 'was not to focus on the racism of white women. Its primary focus was to establish that sexism greatly determines the social status and experience of black women.'[1]

White women's response to, and interest in, the work of Black feminists, however, has focused primarily on its implicit or explicit critique of the racism of (white) feminist work, understanding it principally as a 'critique of feminism'. Hence, discussion between Black women and white women indeed shifted increasingly to the issue of white women's racism. While white women should indeed take seriously this critique and its implications for feminists' theory and practice, the terms of the debate suggest that (many) white women's motive has been less a shared concern for an anti-racist feminism than a concern to shift the issue to where white women are concerned. Consequently, an increasing amount of Black feminists' critique – oral and written – endeavoured to clarify and explicate what white women's racism consists in – where their theorizing is racist, and where their behaviour is so.

The behaviour, moreover, which has been criticized is the kind of behaviour we as feminists have most vehemently criticized and continue to criticize in men, but which is increasingly being deployed also by privileged women: (ab)use of power and power structures for one's own benefit and advantage, which is to say, at the cost and to the detriment of others. It includes abusing the power of discourse to represent reality from a Eurocentric, white-centric point of view. This serves not only to maintain the already existing social supremacy of white women in relation to Black women, but also creates a 'white-women-centrism' focused around the interests and the perspective of privileged white women. Thus if Black theorists have (among other things) made a critique and analysis of Eurocentrism, Black feminists, besides developing a feminist analysis of racism, have also produced a specific critique of the Eurocentrism of white feminist theory and practice, of 'white-women-centrism'.

Thus Alice Walker created her famous term 'womanist' as a critical alternative to the term 'feminist':

> *Womanist* 1. From *womanish*. (Opp. of 'girlish,' i.e., frivolous, irresponsible, not serious.) A black feminist or feminist of color. From the black folk expression of mothers to female children, 'You acting womanish,' i.e., like a woman. Usually referring to outrageous, audacious, courageous or *willful* behavior. Wanting to know more and in greater depth than is considered 'good' for one. Interested in grown-up doings. Acting grown up. Being grown up. Interchangeable with another black folk expression: 'You trying to be grown.' Responsible. In charge. *Serious.*[2]

This crystallizes much of what Black feminists criticize in white feminist practice – a practice which in the few years of the new women's movement has coloured the term 'feminist' white to such an extent that for Walker a new term for Black feminists or feminists of colour has become a necessity: a term which reflects the experience of Black women. Points of the critique include the lacking maturity of white feminists, their lacking sense of personal and political respons-ibility, a critique which has been articulated again and again by Black feminists (and is being overheard again and again by white women). 'Being grown-up', 'responsible', 'in charge' of oneself – not a 'victim' with diminished responsibility. As Toni Morrison writes on the same topic,

> Black women have been able to envy white women (their looks, their easy life, the attention they seem to get from their men); they could fear them (for the economic control they have had over black women's lives); and even love them (as mammies and domestic workers can); but black women have found it impossible to respect white women . . . Black women have no abiding admiration of white women as compe-tent, complete people . . . they regarded them as willful children, pretty children, mean children, but never as real adults capable of handling the real problems of the world.[3]

It is a criticism which women have also made of men, and other domestics of their masters – from the vantage point of an experience of service which reveals the infantilism and incompetence of masters and mistresses.

Walker further criticizes the separatist tendencies of some white women in the women's movement who demand that Black women enter an *a priori* coalition with them and against Black and white men, even though many Black women have repeatedly made their position clear, as for instance the Combahee River Collective in 'A Black Feminist Statement' of 1977:

> We believe that sexual politics under patriarchy is as pervasive in Black women's lives as are the politics of class and race. We also often find it difficult to separate race from class from sex oppression because in our lives they are most often experienced simultaneously. We know that there is such a thing as racial-sexual oppression which is neither solely racial nor solely sexual, e.g., the history of rape of Black women by white men as a weapon of political repression.
>
> Although we are feminists and lesbians, we feel solidarity with progressive Black men and do not advocate the fractionalization that white women who are separatist demand. Our situation as Black

people necessitates that we have solidarity around the fact of race, which white women of course do not need to have with white men, unless it is their negative solidarity as racial oppressors. We struggle together with Black men against racism, while we also struggle with Black men about sexism.[4]

Walker's second part of the definition of 'womanist':

2. *Also*: A woman who loves other women, sexually and/or nonsexually. Appreciates and prefers women's culture, women's emotional flexibility (values tears as natural counterbalance of laughter), and women's strength. Sometimes loves individual men, sexually and/or nonsexually. Committed to survival and wholeness of entire people, male *and* female. Not a separatist, except periodically, for health. Traditionally universalist, as in: 'Mama, why are we brown, pink, and yellow, and our cousins are white, beige, and black?' Ans.: 'Well, you know the colored race is just like a flower garden, with every color flower represented.' Traditionally capable, as in: 'Mama, I'm walking to Canada and I'm taking you and a bunch of other slaves with me.' Reply: 'It wouldn't be the first time.'[5]

'Committed to survival of entire people, male *and* female', recalling the premise from which feminism originally started, namely that women as much as men are part of humanity, that the political distinction between men and women is a social construction which we reject and oppose. It is a premise which is incompatible with a separatist practice which sees separatism not as a means but an end, thus postulating the superiority or at least the priority of the female sex. At the same time Walker recalls the political meaning of separatism as a temporary form of political organizing, to which Black women are increasingly obliged to have recourse – 'periodically, for health', that is, as a strategy also of self-protection in a racist women's movement.

Above all, however, Walker rejects the appeal to female incompetence and weakness, the self-perception as 'victim' so widespread among white women: the womanist is 'traditionally capable', be it even as a child or as a slave or both. That is, even in conditions of extreme oppression and disempowerment, or rather, precisely in such conditions, the womanist is concerned with resistance, mustering all her capabilities and her competence. Far from invoking her 'inability', her 'powerlessness' or 'helplessness' on account of being oppressed, she wants 'to know more and in greater depth than is "good" for [her]'. Being disadvantaged to her is no reason for justifying and contenting herself with ignorance – even where such ignorance might be 'good' for her, even where, as part of the feminine (or black) role, it would have its advantages. The womanist is wilful, resistant and resisting, sensual and full of the will to love: '3. Loves music. Loves dance. Loves the moon. *Loves* the Spirit. Loves love and food and roundness. Loves struggle. *Loves* the Folk. Loves herself. *Regardless.*'[6] She loves her body, life, the community, and also herself – she does not think she first has to learn it. And she rejects and resists the dualisms of white male culture which divides body from mind and spirit, self from society, political 'work' from 'pleasure': she loves music, dance, and struggle.

Walker's coinage is a means (also) of making white women conscious of their practice, of revealing the historical tradition of 'feminism', that is, the history of the new women's movement and its selective inscription in theory, as 'white' and racist, in order to argue for an inclusive feminism: '4. Womanist is to feminist as purple to lavender'[7] – more feminist than 'feminist'. Having found the term 'feminist' to be white and watery, Walker leaves it to white women (even if she still requires it for the definition of a Black feminist or feminist of colour) in favour of the strong and inclusive sense of 'womanist'.

bell hooks on the other hand, who has also contributed much to the critique of racism in the women's movement, argues not only for a definition of feminist theory and practice which is more 'feminist' than that of white feminists hitherto, she also pleads for retaining the term 'feminism' for it. For it is in the name of feminism that 'white feminism' is being criticized: 'white feminism' is a contradiction in terms, a racist women's liberation movement a mockery. Should this 'feminism' remain white, that is, racist, then it is no feminism worth the name. hooks writes:

> Black women must separate feminism as a political agenda from white women or we will never be able to focus on the issue of sexism as it affects black communities . . . there are a few black women (I am one) who assert that we empower ourselves by using the term feminism, by addressing our concerns as black women as well as our concern with the welfare of the human community globally . . .[8]

And although at present it is above all Black women who develop an anti-racist feminism deserving the name, bell hooks none the less argues against calling it, as does for instance the Combahee River Collective, 'Black feminism':

> I believe that women should think less in terms of feminism as an identity and more in terms of 'advocating feminism'; to move from emphasis on personal lifestyle issues toward creating political paradigms and radical models of social change that emphasize collective as well as individual change. For this reason I do not call myself a black feminist. Black women must insist on our right to participate in shaping feminist theory and practice that addresses our racial concerns as well as our feminist issues.[9]

In the last analysis the question is less who advocates a theory than what theory and politics they are advocating, less a matter of the identity of the advocate than of the content of her politics. Not the 'feminism' of white women is 'white' and racist, but the politics – theory and practice – of white women calling themselves feminists. The fallacy lies in thinking that the label women give themselves is necessarily an adequate description of their politics.[10] Identity is no guarantee of politics, rather, we should analyse the actual politics: the radical models of social change as well as the personal changes in behaviour which go along with such aims. Feminism is not an identity, but a politics: it is not so much that we *are* feminists, as that at best we can advocate a feminist theory and live a practice of feminist behaviour.

This includes the behaviour of advocating feminist theory, that is, the communicative behaviour in a shared and collective feminist discourse. While the critique made by Black women is a communicative step in a collective process – an analysis of and argument with the statements of white feminists – the discursive behaviour of many white feminists increasingly tends towards scientific discourse, that is, solitary monologue. Scientific discourse is the prototypical discourse of (white, male, educated, etc.) power in our society – a discourse in which no one speaks, which makes 'standpointlessness', or as Catharine MacKinnon has called it, 'aperspectivity', its standard, all the better to disguise and maintain the standpoint of power and the perspective of ruling interests.[11] Although it is an instrument of power which feminists have criticized as a mainstay of patriarchal dominance, women with educational privilege increasingly seem themselves to wish to take advantage of it.

As in mainstream public discourse 'racism' is in the process of becoming a white-dominated expert discourse and a new academic discipline, so feminist public discourse shows a development towards a discourse of expertise which precludes dialogic structures and collective discussion. Once racism has become a 'topic' of public interest there begins a power struggle: a struggle by the legitimate producers of knowledge for the monopoly on the production of knowledge, and by the producers of public opinion for the monopoly on opinion-making. Thus in Germany, white philosophers and professors are toying with the thought of instituting 'racism studies' at the university, while a glance at the new literature reveals a daily growing plethora of emerging experts, mostly white male academics. Racism as a 'topic' is in demand in publishing and at public events generally and in the German women's movement, but Black women authors and speakers remain a dwindling minority.

It is a phenomenon which we may witness again and again, whether the 'topic' is sexual violence, the sexual exploitation of children, pornography as raised by feminists, or racism as raised by Black people. It is a power struggle, however, not just about maintaining the position of power of white or male opinion-makers – their supremacy is already firm and established even without the 'topic' of racism or sexual violence. It is a matter, also, of how the 'new material' is being constructed as knowledge: (re)shaped in the interest and from the perspective of the powerful, that is, processed 'scientifically'.

In published feminist discourse as well as in live exchanges between women we can see a parallel tendency to counter critique by means of the classic strategies of the power of discourse: a struggle to keep control of the discourse and to re-present the alleged state of affairs from the point of view of apparent standpointlessness. This means that the response to critique takes the form, not of a direct engagement with the speech of the critics, but of a correction and adaptation of one's own speech. On the speech of Black women there follows a counter-speech by white women, a speech of their own which is less concerned with discussing what has been said than with reprocessing what has vaguely been heard. It is a speech which above all re-presents the 'state of affairs' from a new point of view, that is to say, reformulates it 'scientifically'.

While in Germany the response to the critique of racism is currently literally and crassly taking this form, we have also known it in the Anglo-American women's movements. And if we think that in Britain and the United States we have progressed beyond this stage, we should look at what shape this progress is taking. After a period of direct and interpersonal struggle on the level of live encounters, the struggle for discursive dominance has largely shifted to the level of published discourse, the structure of speech and counter-speech of live encounters giving way to a situation of parallel speech at the level of published discourse, a 'pluralism' of voices of separate competencies, of scientific monologues which reprocess (select) feminist speech. The power relations governing published discourse automatically take care of regulating this 'pluralism' of voices, replacing the live fight for dominance. With the institutionalization of women's studies and the emergence of academic feminism, moreover, scientific discourse not only has ceased to be an object of critique, but is increasingly being rehabilitated as being a proper medium for 'feminism'.

Scientific standpointlessness, however, is no longer the exclusive province of recognized scientists and academics. So-called 'scientificness', a standpoint from 'above and beyond', is establishing itself increasingly also in everyday language and thought. As the scientific subject speaks from nowhere, making an 'objective' representation of reality from a standpoint above and beyond that reality, so the speaking subject increasingly does not speak from a position within a speech situation, as a person in communication with another person: the subject speaks from the position of 'truth', the 'objective' view of reality, the objectification of reality. As a speaking subject it refers not to the other's speech, but to the alleged content of that speech, of which it now makes its own representation. The structure of the interaction is not a process of establishing mutual understanding, of searching for common points of understanding between two communicants: it is a competition between representations of the 'state of affairs'. The emphasis is on the 'content' of discussion, at the expense of the process of communication, the professed aim to understand the 'matter' under discussion rather than one's interlocutor. The communicative situation is seen no longer as the coming together of people wishing to understand each other, nor is the process of communication seen as another 'matter' to be understood: communication is seen as an encounter, an arena for a competition between opinions and a struggle between rivalling representations – the stage for a battle between speaking subjects.

A semblance of critical discussion is maintained in that some points of the critique, having indeed been heard, turn up reworked in the subject's own discourse. The necessity for dialogue has thus been evaded and the subject stays in control of the discourse. Thus it became common place to re-render Black women's critique by reformulations such as that 'Black women have been excluded from the women's movement and from feminist discourse', that they have been 'invisible' and have been unable to contribute to feminism, or that they are 'criticizing feminism'. As Black feminists have pointed out again and again, this renders the women's movement identical with white women, feminism identical with the feminism of white women, reproducing the very white-women-centredness, the arrogant perspective of white women who consider themselves to be 'the movement' and declaring it to be reality. It gathers 'us' together as the movement and 'them' as those outside criticizing 'it'. Hence the issue no longer is white women's oppressive behaviour, but Black women's absence from the movement – to which the quick response has been to issue an invitation addressed to Black women to 'join' the movement (ours), to participate in our conferences and to fill the ranks of our rallies so that these will no longer suffer from the stigma of exclusive whiteness. The enterprise remains in the interest of the entrepreneurs, but Black women are now in demand and needed to stave off any future critique that white women are excluding Black women.

If this seems to be going over old ground, it is because however old it is and however often it has been explicitly analysed and criticized, it has not been overcome. If specific things are no longer being said, it is less because the critique has been understood than because it has been understood that they should no longer be said. Specific expressions may disappear, but the principle of their construction lives on, becoming if anything more 'sophisticated'. Hence it not only continues to be necessary to analyse them, but to analyse in particular their transformation into more sophisticated forms of discourse.

How far feminist discourse excludes Black women would require an analysis of and differentiation between different discursive strategies.

We need not only to distinguish between oppression and exclusion of people on the one hand, and forms of suppression and exclusion on the level of discourse on the other. The problem of a dominant discourse, as we know from sexist discourse, is less the discursive exclusion of women from this discourse, than on the one hand their subsumption under pseudo-universal categories like 'men' and 'humans' (which do not in fact apply to women), and on the other their inclusion in the discourse as objects of discourse – as 'women' or the 'other'. That is, the fundamental problem is a discourse which is shaped from the perspective of power, and which itself is an exercise of power: of controlling and instrumentalizing the 'other'. Similarly, the original problem of a white feminist discourse was less that white women set out to exclude Black women than that they claimed to include them in concepts like 'women', 'all women' and 'us women', where these concepts were framed specifically from the perspective and interests of white women. As we have seen, the problem of a new white discourse is increasingly not just this (implicit) subsumption of Black women under 'universalizing' concepts which do not apply universally, but also their explicit inclusion as 'the other' – in the Anglo-American tradition including a reference to the 'others' being the competence of the 'others'. In other words, the problem of this discourse is not just 'the discourse', but that it constitutes the continued exercise of discursive power by the white women who are speaking, who continue to control and to arrogate the speaking voice to themselves, excluding Black women from communication by reprocessing their voice.

Neither were Black women ever invisible: if white women consider them to have been 'invisible' it can only mean that we who are speaking and looking have not seen them, or indeed have made them 'invisible' in our own discourse. If we do not hear the voices of Black feminists audible in our midst or in their vast published literature, it is a sign of our unwillingness to hear rather than of the inaudibility of Black women's voices.

If, however, we attribute this process of exclusion as a quality to Black women, making it one of their 'properties' – they *are* 'excluded', 'not included', 'invisible' etc. – we thereby achieve that the acting (and here speaking) subjects disappear from view and from the linguistic construction, while the allegedly invisible, inaudible and excluded Black women become the problem (and as such very much

visible). Black women's contribution becomes a non-contribution –
they have been unable to contribute to the feminist movement[12] –
even if this contribution is there for all to see but has not received any
attention from the specific women who are also now speaking. In
particular, this contribution continues to get no attention, since it is
made to 'disappear' once again in the very profession of our regret.
That is to say, the discursive perspective takes over the view – or
rather the highly selective view and non-view – of white women,
confirming it as the real and objective state of affairs. The objectifying,
'descriptive' discourse reinstates the perspective of power, using the
power of discourse to do so.

Such formulations – reformulations of the problem by means of
linguistic constructions like passives which remove the active agents,
or adjectival constructions which render an action as the 'property' of
the objects of action etc. – are all constructions we are familiar with
from our critique of androcentric and in particular scientific discourse.
They have the function and the effect of rendering the subjects of
action invisible, of removing from view and possible scrutiny the
responsibility of those who had the power to act, as well as of those
who identify with them and at this moment are exercising their power
to speak. Thus the consequences of action appear as independent
'facts', states of affairs to be described, no longer as consequences of
actions which could be analysed with respect to their agents.

The women's movement is neither a place from which women
could be excluded, nor an organization with the power to grant or
withhold membership. The exclusion of specific groups of women
does not take place at the level of 'the women's movement', but in
concrete situations, contexts and projects on the one hand, and on the
level of discourse on the other. Yet if we abandon our position as
white women whose own behaviour in specific and real situations is
at issue, assuming instead a scientific standpoint which views the
matter from above and beyond, we not only escape from critique and
analysis, we at the same time reformulate the state of affairs. The
problem no longer is the specific behaviour of specific women (ourselves): the problem is 'the women's movement'.

Thus it is for instance a sociological discourse (whose usefulness as
a means of social control should be beyond doubt), which makes the
women's movement nevertheless into a 'place' with spatial and geographical dimensions. Based on the analysis of the sociologist

Jo Freeman, Dagmar Schultz writes 'a few words concerning the structure of certain social movements and their relevance for the development of feminist research':

> Freeman argues that a social movement, in contrast to spontaneous, collective behaviour on the one hand and the formation of interest groups or parties on the other, usually has a structural and cultural centre, with those more or less concerned at the periphery. Like other researchers of social movements, she regards an already existing communication network which can be used for the new ideas as a necessary condition (Freeman, 1975, pp. 48–9) . . . The white women's movement . . . had as its cultural and structural centre white intellectual middle-class women, who either belonged to professional circles or were younger women who had been active in the civil rights movement or the students' movement. Poor women and working-class women, whether coloured or white, as well as middle-class 'women of color' were not included in the movement, or else were at the periphery . . . In the following years and with the growing professionalization of the women's movement the narrow focus on themselves in particular of white women who were not engaged in grass roots projects increased.[13]

Uncritically a sociological model is here taken over which makes social movements into an object of study which apparently is fully accessible to the researching eye. Whether the social movement is really being seen, or whether in fact it is being constructed as an object, seems not even to arise as a question – presumably because the feminist researcher is in the good company of 'other researchers of social movements'. Despite the apparent empiricism, what constitutes a condition for the social movement is derived not from the movement under observation but supplied by the sociologist and her classification, which orders phenomena into 'movements', 'spontaneous collective behaviour' and 'interest groups or parties'. In order to qualify as a movement the object requires a centre, as well as an already existing network of communication. Since the women's movement calls itself a movement, it is studied through this screen, and lo and behold, the object throws back exactly this picture into the researching eye. The centre is more or less where the researcher is standing and looking, namely with the white educated middle-class women. A few other concerned women can be faintly made out in the distant periphery. The second scientific requirement for qualifying as a movement apparently is also present – in the national and international (that is, Western) network of the educated white middle-class women's private and professional relationships – and QED, it is a social movement!

From the perspective of women who do not describe the movement as observing social scientists, who regard themselves as part of the movement yet suspect its existence also beyond their own field of vision, there emerges a different understanding. The aim never has been to build a movement after the model of other social movements in order to qualify as one. The aim has been, and in many places remains, the liberation of all women from oppression, as well as the development of a politics and practice which support and facilitate all women's struggle for autonomy and self-determination. This means, amongst other things, no centralizing organization, no fixed place, no membership – hence no power for any woman to exclude other women, and hence no power to include them either: no inside and outside, but only the choice of every single woman to identify with this 'movement' and its political aims or not. Above all, no hierarchical sociological geometry as we know it already from Eurocentrism, of a 'centre' and its 'periphery'.

Regardless of this self-definition by an autonomous movement, however, a centre is scientifically assigned to it, both in the original diagnosis of its white bias, and now in the proposal of a remedy, the acquisition of proper *leaders*:

> The particular social position of 'women of color' [as the group bearing the brunt of sexist, racist and classist oppression] should really make them the *centre* of the movement, since they are the least co-optable by a conservative ideology . . . A *leadership role* of these women, however, would require that white women recognize their privileges and be prepared to give them up . . .[14] (my emphasis)

The refusal of large sections of the women's liberation movement to designate leaders, directors and presidents has precisely been one of its most characteristic features – and one of its most effective forms of resisting the existing power relations and hierarchies of society. If at the alleged 'centre' self-styled leaders have none the less emerged, this is a problem of the practice and understanding of these particular women, as well as of those who have helped to 'elect' them. It does not mean a leadership, however, which has been recognized or accepted in the women's movement at large, just as the 'centre' is not generally deemed to be the centre except by those who consider themselves in it. What has been recognized, however, is that this constitutes an attempt to take power and control the movement.

Rather, it is a problem of a feminist social science if it scientifically declares as centre what deems itself to be the centre – if, in other words, it assumes the dominant white point of view. The sociological method constructs its object of study, the 'movement', as if it were an object and not a historical (even if collective) subject. As object it becomes a thing, which the subject may view from all sides and apparently is in a position to encompass as a whole. The scientific subject describes and measures its object according to standards and criteria which are not defined by the movement itself, but which are imposed on it from outside. This is a process of objectification and hence an exercise of power which is identical to that which constitutes scientific discourse as a whole, and which does not either differ from the androcentric construction of women as objects.

Nor does it improve matters to call the chosen object of study the 'white women's movement' in an attempt to recognize the white bias of the women described, if the scientific perspective remains equally white-biased and continues to regard these white women as 'the women's movement'. If it seriously was a matter of restricting the object of study to a 'white women's movement', then it would hardly make sense to criticize its exclusion of Black women or to recommend it to choose Black leaders. The problem of white supremacy in large parts of the Western women's movement is not that white women decided to found a white women's movement, which would at least be a clear situation like, say, with the Ku Klux Klan, where we would hardly speak of the exclusion of Black people from this social movement. Rather, many 'women's contexts' have been and continue to remain exclusively white, but think of themselves as 'open' to 'all women'.

Yet this empirical fact – that there are indeed power relations operating between women and in the women's movement – is no reason for sacrificing the theoretical political aims of autonomy and non-hierarchical structures and making this fact the basis of a new theory about the 'nature' of the women's movement. Rather, this discrepancy between theory and practice should be seen precisely as the problem to be solved, an occasion at the very least for a feminist self-critique: a reflection of our practice in the light of our political principles – including the practice of taking over uncritically such concepts as 'leaders', 'centre', 'social movement' and the attendant methodologies. Such self-criticism, however, is at present undertaken above all by non-dominant groups of women, and includes the critique of precisely this kind of behaviour by privileged white professional and academic women.[15] Making instead a scientific diagnosis of the inadequate state of the movement means to have successfully reformulated and replaced the critique of the behaviour of specific white women, and to have projected the problem into the object of study, the women's movement. Instead of serving as a means for recognizing reality, this scientific method has on the contrary constructed a new reality: a scientific picture, a fictional object.

If by contrast we stay with the critique and take it seriously, we find that the critique is less that white leaders should be replaced by Black leaders than that there are any leaders at all in a movement which is committed to equality and the deconstruction of power hierarchies.[16] Once again it is a sociological perspective which obstructs our view of the connections between actions and their consequences – if we expect the social position of women of colour to 'make' them leaders (whether they want to or not), as if it ever was the qualities and aptitudes of people which 'make' them leaders, presidents, professors, or indeed housewives or prostitutes. Such roles are created by means of power and power structures, and people are appointed to them by means of decisions on the part of those in a position to decide. That those occupying such roles are also those most apt for those roles is part of the carefully cultivated myth of meritocracy which serves the legitimation of this distribution of power.

So we would do well to recall bell hooks's advice to desist from identity politics and to pay attention instead to women's political actions. Not the identity and the (imposed) living conditions of a group of women guarantees these women's politics – else all women would at least be anti-sexist. Not the factor of their being 'most' oppressed qualifies them or 'makes' them the least co-optable, but their deliberate choice (where they make it) to resist co-optation and corruption. Such a politics may indeed be derived from one's own experience, if that experience is being politicized, but it does not necessarily 'develop' from that experience. That the probability of a politics of integrity may be higher where women's experience of oppression is greater, or conversely, that the likelihood of being co-optable and corruptible increases correspondingly with one's privileges, seems to confirm itself in as much as it is above all Black women, working-class women, women of 'minorities' who continue to recall feminism to its own principles – although this by no means proves that all Black women, all working-class women, all women of minorities share this politics.

Such a view, however, and its calculation of probability, seems to correspond above all to our desire to attribute the responsibility for women's politics not to the women themselves, but to their circumstances. To privileged women it may indeed seem a mitigating argument to blame their privileges for their own co-optability; but it means in any case not taking women and their political will seriously. In particular, it is an insult and a failure to take women seriously if we explain their political integrity as coming to them more easily – on account of their extended experience of oppression. For no woman is it easier because things are more difficult for her, and for no woman is it more difficult because things are easier for her. Nor is a woman's sacrifice any the greater because, in choosing resistance, she has more privileges to lose. Rather, such accounting of advantages and disadvantages reveals how deeply we are steeped in the social values of profit and bargaining – that we regard political choice as a personal sacrifice, and measure our own oppression as well as our own alleged sacrifice against the oppression and the sacrifices of others. Choosing resistance constitutes a risk on every level of the social hierarchy; and every woman has to develop her political understanding in the situation she finds herself in. In every situation she faces the choice either to consent to the social status quo, taking what meagre (or not so meagre) advantages it has to offer her and trying to maximize them in her own individual interest, or to resist a political order which attempts to co-opt her through her individual interest, and to act in the interests of all those oppressed.

bell hooks is right, of course, to emphasize the unusual position of Black women as a group in the social hierarchy, which Dagmar Schultz also refers to when she recommends them as leaders: that Black women as a group are at the bottom of the occupational ladder, and that their overall social status is lower than that of any other group, that in contrast to both Black men and white women they bear the brunt of sexist, racist and classist oppression.[17] It begs the question, however, whether Black women therefore have 'not been socialized to assume the role of exploiter/oppressor in that [they] are allowed no institutionalized "other" which [they] can exploit or oppress' (bell hooks specifically denies that children are such an institutionalized 'other' even though they are exploited by their parents);[18] whether socialization means that we just learn our particular attributed roles, or whether it does not precisely apprentice us to the values and perspective of the powerful and, particularly, to the aspiration to power.

More important, however, is the question whether we regard this as the reason why (many) Black women fight against oppression – because they are 'allowed' no one to oppress. hooks does not quite draw this conclusion; her emphasis lies more on the 'special vantage point' marginalization gives Black women to develop a counter-hegemonial view.[19] Her argumentation, however, suggests this: 'Black women with no institutionalized "other" that we *may* discriminate against, exploit or oppress',[20] 'with no institutionalized "other" that we *can* exploit or oppress.'[21] (my emphases). In this sociological snapshot of the collective position of Black women the differences between Black women are eliminated, and in particular, their political will has disappeared from view: their decision (where they make it) for a politics of liberation and their resistance to an ideology of personal self-interest.

If bell hooks is seduced here to present the 'most oppressed-ness' of Black women as 'advantageous', as constituting a particular vantage point and experience from which Black women have 'a contribution to offer which is unique and valuable',[22] it reflects the pressure of white domination, including the pressure to produce 'scientific arguments', *against* which she means to assert herself: 'Though I criticize aspects of feminist movement as we have known it so far, a critique which is sometimes harsh and unrelenting, I do so not in an attempt to diminish feminist struggle but to enrich, to share in the work of making a liberatory ideology and a liberatory movement.'[23]

Not just the collective social position socializes, but also the specific experience of oppression, exclusion and disdain – here the experience that Black women have to legitimate their usefulness *vis-à-vis* white women, and legitimate it in terms based on the interests of white women: use and enrichment.

4

Is the political psychological?

The choice of formulation is political; it is an expression of one's political attitude. Not only does it reveal how the subject constitutes itself – whom it chooses to address and to constitute as the 'we' of its discourse, and whom and what it chooses to make an object of speech. It also shows what the subject considers to be the 'whole' of the speech or action context and what it chooses to exclude from it. That is, it reveals the subject's communicative intention.

If we lock others into the status of 'the others', for example, it is a sign that we do not wish to enter into communication and dialogue with them. Allocating 'them' the status of the 'other', 'we' are speaking to 'ourselves'. As androcentric discourse is speech from men to men and about women, and Eurocentric discourse is speech among Europeans at the 'centre' of the world and about those at the 'periphery', so a white-women-centric discourse is a white women's soliloquy, power speaking to itself. Its addressees are 'white women' – not other white women addressed as communicants in a dialogue, but 'white women' as the plural of the white woman subject – 'we' as the plural of myself, talking about 'them'. It also means that, while we acutely object to being objectified through men's sexist discourse, considering it to be a form of violence, we do not apparently consider it an act of violence if we ourselves objectify other women – all the less so if those women are absent from the specific speech context. That is to say, we do not consider those we objectify and speak about to be a relevant part of the speech and action context, nor do we consider our act of objectifying them to have any consequences for them worth thinking about.

A 'kind' interpretation of this discursive behaviour would see it as a result of patriarchal socialization – acquired from dominant discourse as we acquired our 'mother tongue' from the speech of our mothers, so that we have unconsciously internalized racism, sexism, classism and scientificness, which now trap and implicate us in our own speech. It is an explanation which, just as Alice Walker criticizes, starts from the assumption of women's weakness and damagedness, appealing for indulgence on account of diminished responsibility. It is an explanation which also has its respectable model in the 'high' theory of semiology, which as Deborah Cameron points out 'sees experience and indeed the individual herself, as a product and function of an institutionalised system of signs', where language 'defines our possibilities and limitations, [and] constitutes our subjectivities'.[1] As an explanation of limitations and their causes, it is closer to excusing incapability and inadequacy than to positing them as a problem to be overcome. As feminists or Walker's womanists, however, we will start from the assumption of women's traditional competence and ability and attribute responsibility to ourselves. For our aim is less to describe these symptoms in the interest of a precise diagnosis and aetiology of our speech impediments, than to analyse the power of discourse and the abuse of this power, in the interest of overcoming them.

Nothing prevents us from questioning language use, least of all our own, from asking who we are speaking to when we say 'we', who is meant and who is not, and whether what we say applies to this group; when we say 'women', from asking 'all women, or which women?', and when we describe facts, whether they are as we say, and if we are in a position to judge them. Nothing stops us asking about the acting subjects which have disappeared from passive and adjectival constructions representing actions, or from statements concerning perceptions, by whom 'excluded', by whom 'oppressed', to whom 'invisible', and so forth. That is, nothing stops us from attempting to render concrete again what has linguistically been abstracted. For here we can take a first step towards changing political reality, analysing the contexts of action and naming the agents. Only when we recognize the connections and know those responsible for action can we begin to intervene in political reality and to know where to put up resistance. All the more so if the actions concerned are our own which we have thus tried to withdraw from (our) view.

If we nevertheless fail to do so, if we continue to treat communicative and discursive behaviour as if they were a natural and individual
attribute of ourselves like, say, the colour of our hair, it must be
political intention. If we are unwilling to question our use of language
and to analyse the power relations in our linguistic behaviour, it
betrays our willingness to use the relative power of educational and
academic privilege and to abuse it in our own interest. To the extent
that our language conforms to the structures of dominant discourse –
in particular, its abstraction which conceals the substantial connections
and relations of reality – it betrays an intention conforming to the
meaning and function of that discourse: to legitimate and maintain
power and the distribution of power in society.

Communication is not just a question of speaking and formulating,
but also of listening, that is, understanding what has already been said.
If in the context of the critique of racism white women confuse
'feminists' and 'feminism', it is not just a choice of the wrong word, it
is a sign of not having understood or having misunderstood what has
been said, and on two distinct levels: first, at the level of the critique
which is directed at the behaviour of specific feminists, which is
'misunderstood' as a critique of feminism; secondly, at the level of our
own understanding – of feminism as well as of how what has been
said may fit into it – for which we ourselves are responsible and which
we cannot blame on what a specific other woman may have said
(even if she said 'feminism' rather than 'feminists').

To reformulate what a woman has said is an act of violence.
Adopting and reformulating her speech from our own point of view
not only shows that we do not wish to speak with her, but that we are
unwilling to hear what she said. Not only do we not hear what she
says, but in not letting her speak for herself in our speech we show that
we do not want our own addressees to hear what she has said. Instead,
we replace her speech by our (mis)representation of it, which we put
up for discussion as 'her speech'. Objectifying the speaker together
with 'her speech', we are inviting our audience to join us in the
position of discursive subjects, that is, to join in objectifying 'them'.

Such reformulations, however, are constantly being produced, in
discussions as well as in texts – so-called paraphrases in our own
words.[2] Whether there is a conscious intention to misrepresent, or just
an assumption that our paraphrase will do as well as the original
speech, it is problematical communicative behaviour towards the

person whose speech is being paraphrased. If I take a woman seriously, I take seriously what she has said, that is, precisely what she has said and how she has said it. I assume that she means what she says, and that she says what she means. And I can reply only to what she has actually said, not to what I think she has said. If a woman criticizes the behaviour or statement of another woman or even a group of women who identify themselves as feminists, this does not mean that 'feminism' has been criticized, and should not be reformulated as such. If Black women criticize the fact that many white feminists prioritize sexism over racism, they do not thereby question feminism or even sexism, but the insistence of some white women that sexism can be separated from racism and that sexism has to come first.

But the point of such reformulations is evidently not to engage with the critique or to enter into a dialogic exchange with the critics – to try to understand, to ask for clarification, to contribute to the analysis and to continue to think further. The point is to establish discursive power, to reformulate the problem, replacing it by one's own definition, and to win the audience as allies in this venture. This explains why critique is rarely quoted verbatim, why the critics are not given the chance to speak for themselves. It is an exercise of power and control, eliminating 'the other' together with her speech and controlling what is heard. In this way, not only her critique is suppressed, but also the communicative significance of her critique as a speech act, that is, her intention of speaking *with* us to reach a common understanding. What was an act of social communion becomes an act of opposition, through the discursive restructuring of the communicative parties of 'I' and 'you' as the oppositional parties of 'us' and 'them'.

While discursive strategies, such as paraphrasing the speech of others for an audience of an 'us' which excludes those speakers, are thus signs that 'we' prefer to remain mistresses of the discourse and to converse among 'ourselves', it yet is not the case that 'the others' could simply stay where they are. Rather, many white women, as we have seen, are on their way to 'the others', seeking an encounter with 'the others'. They may not wish to let Black women speak to them and to hear what they are saying, but they want to encounter, counter and confront them. As we have seen already, this, too, may manifest itself in white women's speech.

Where Black women have made a critique of racism and racist behaviour, white women feel reproached with racism. This is not just the wrong choice of word. While a critique – the discussion and analysis of formulations, meanings, interpretations and practice – is a form of social behaviour, the collective self-criticism of a movement referring to common principles, standards and political aims, the term 'reproach' shifts the frame of reference to a radically different domain, namely the arena of personal relationships.

What is of interest is not what has been said and whether it is true, but rather who has said it and what it means for 'us', its recipients. What is being heard is less the issue of racism that has been raised – the analysis of reality, here of specific racist practices – than the mere fact that someone has spoken and expressed a viewpoint which is different from mine and which may concern my own behaviour. If usually we focus on the 'content' of communication, at the expense of the meaning of communicative behaviour, here we shift our attention from the content of the critique and turn to the fact of critique. Since for the subject, however, a relationship by definition is an opposition between the subject and the other, which thus excludes the possibility of a joint process of understanding, the subject does not recognize communication for its communicative intention, the interest in dialogue. Rather, it sees the speech of another as a challenge to a duel of words, which can be resolved only through victory and unity, victory of one (my) representation over the other, and eventual unification under one point of view (mine). The mere speech of another is a threat, critique a sign of dissent and disunity, where 'I' am not only being 'opposed', but 'reproached' for what I've said, which I regard as hostile behaviour towards myself.

Audre Lorde, for one, has constantly underlined the significance of critique as a joint communication, as for instance in her famous 'An Open Letter to Mary Daly':

> . . . I write this letter to you now, hoping to *share with you* the benefits of my insights as you have shared the benefits of yours with me . . . what I want *us to chew upon here* is neither easy nor simple. The history of white women who are unable to hear black women's words, or to maintain dialogue with us, is long and discouraging . . . *I invite you to a joint clarification* of some of the differences which lie between us as a black and a white woman.[3] (my emphases)

As the addressees of this passage (which we have become together with Mary Daly since its publication), we may see ourselves addressed in Audre Lorde's 'you' – that is, as feminists talking together – joining her in thinking about what she invites us to think about together: the history of the relationship between white and Black women and the differences which lie between us as Black and as white women, and the specific criticisms she makes of Daly's text (and by implication of similar discursive behaviour). Or, as white women we may ignore her communicative speech act, choosing instead to identify *as* white women, that is, as members of a racially constituted group, a party whose interests are in conflict with those of Black women. Thus we will see Lorde's text as an attack, and leap to white women's defence, either by trying to prove the 'attacker' wrong (say, arguing that 'not all white women' are doing what Lorde here criticizes), or explaining where white women's fallibilities come from, in the hope of negotiating mercy in Black women's judgement of white women. Speech – here Audre Lorde's 'letter' – then becomes less a communication from a speaker to her addressees than a move in an ongoing war between opposing parties.

This view of critique, which regards the critical discussion especially of our own texts, statements and interpretations, and also our behaviour, on principle as an attack, is also manifest in the increasing use of the term 'debate', which indeed designates a contest of opinion, an adversarial battle of arguments. And it is reflected in the desire, much vaunted among German feminists, for a 'culture of quarrelling' (*Streitkultur*) and 'strategies of conflict resolution' among feminists. The choice of terminology is revealing, since it betrays its origins in the domains of personal relationships and military conflict, where the central activity is indeed quarrel and battle rather than discussion, and where the reason for the quarrel usually recedes behind the fact of the quarrel. Conflicts and quarrels, moreover, are a matter less of the disputed content of the quarrel than of the relationship of the quarrelling parties.

What the feminist movement needs is less a culture of quarrelling than, on the contrary, a recollection of the fact that critique is a matter of discussion which requires the separation of arguments from persons, thus allowing us to engage with each other's arguments without personal conflict. If on the one hand, however, we refrain from engaging with the arguments of others and on the other respond to critique as if it were a personal attack, a collective discussion cannot take place. Yet we should ask ourselves what is the point of public feminist discourse if critical discussion of each other's arguments is considered undesirable, if everyone wants to make her statement but is unwilling to refer to anybody else's, let alone have her own discussed – because we think that analysing and responding are forms of personal aggression while listening is a form of submission. If it really is our goal that everyone should be able to express her opinion without anyone responding, it is not obvious why we have to express our opinions publicly – unless the issue of course is a power struggle, a struggle for supremacy on the level of public speech, whose aim can only be victory, where victory means speech in front of a silent mass audience.

If the issue, however, is feminism or indeed any cause, then the question is the common cause rather than who represents it or a particular view. And we represent a particular view not because it is ours, but because, according to our present understanding, it seems to us right. We would perhaps all agree with this in theory; our practice, however, consumes itself in the opposite. It shows itself, amongst other things, in the choice of expressions such as 'reproach', 'debate', 'quarrel' and 'conflict'.

This shift from the level of political discussion to the level of personal relationships is particularly marked in the history of white women's discourse in response to Black women and women from the Third World. Walker alludes to it in her critique of white women's perception of themselves as victims, their habit of taking recourse to having been damaged by patriarchal oppression – that is, their self-pathologizing. Such alleged damage apparently not only dispenses a woman from her responsibility in general, but specifically from her responsibility for seeing her own oppression in relation to the oppression of other women. We know this practice to excess from experience in projects and contexts of the Western women's movement, where one's oppression credentials or even one's personal situation – from overwork to illness – are ritually offered as a reason for diminished responsibility, and in particular as a reason why one's responsibility should be taken over by the other women present. But it is manifest also in white women's theoretical argumentation in relation to Black women's critique of racism. Self-pathologizing and its attendant claim to incapability are thus the last resort of the relatively powerful in trying to outbid those with less power in terms of victim status. It is a strategy which has all the more chance of succeeding where the women competed with are in turn struggling for competence and capability, and refrain from pathologizing themselves.

One of the most typical symptoms of this shift from the political to the level of personal relationships is the practice of psychologizing political reality. While the point of a political critique is to analyse political realities in terms of their power relations in the interest of changing them, an ever-growing part of the work of white and Western academic feminists is dedicated to *explaining* political reality, and explaining it in terms of psychology. No sooner is the extent of men's sexual violence discussed and documented, no sooner is their consumption of pornography raised as an issue, no sooner is the racist violence of whites a topic of public discussion, than theories emerge to explain this behaviour, and explain it by pathologizing those who engage in it: men are said to have a deep-seated fear of women or female sexuality, 'people' are said to have a deep-rooted fear of the 'strange' and the 'different'. That is to say, the active agents themselves are the 'victims', if only of their own psychology. There is no question whether such explanations in fact explain anything, for their function is less to clarify a problematical reality than to exonerate those responsible for it. They become all the more popular if the behaviour in question is that of the explainers themselves, here when white women and feminists are questioned about our own use of power. Having explained problematical behaviour psychologically, it follows that, if we look for solutions at all, we look for psychological solutions – say, where behaviour is seen as 'motivated by fear, hate or ignorance', suggest replacing it by love and desire.

Adrienne Rich's article 'Disloyal to Civilization: Feminism, Racism, Gynephobia' is a case in point, all the more important as Rich is one of those feminists who have taken the critique of racism extremely seriously. The article dates from the late 1970s and thus cannot be taken to represent Adrienne Rich's current understanding as a person, while my critique of course is made with the benefit of hindsight, that is, after years of feminist critique of racism. Yet the article traces a movement of thought and feeling which has characterized that of many white women and feminists since, namely responding to the insight into the realities of racism by explaining our response to the reproach of racism – followed by the desire for a personal relationship with Black women.

In the very course of recognizing white women's historical and present-day racism in the United States, Rich continually feels obliged, or feels the need, to find an explanation for this horrendous fact, namely that white women who suffer so much from sexist oppression nevertheless themselves oppress Black people. White women's implication in racism, however, appears above all in terms of their relative lack of power and responsibility, rather than in terms of their relative power. That is, Rich highlights white women as 'women' in relation to 'men' (white men), where they appear as victims of sexism, rather than as white women in a comparison of power in relation to Black women and men. Concerning the role of white women in slavery Rich writes:

> Women did not create the power relationship between master and slave, nor the mythologies used to justify the domination of men over women . . . but in the history of American slavery and racism white women have been impressed into its service, not only as the marriage-property and creature-objects of white men, but as their active and passive instruments.[4]

Every formulation immediately takes back any responsibility and relative power that white women might have ('did not create', 'have been impressed into its service'), constructing them instead as victims, as white men's 'property' and 'objects'. Even in the approximation to their active participation in racist oppression, this participation is rendered not as active action but as 'being instrumentalized to be active': they *have been made* into active *instruments*. When the formerly enslaved Frederick Douglass speaks of the 'irresponsible power' of his former white mistress, Rich corrects and improves, writing:

> She was not, I suggest, corrupted by 'irresponsible power' in the sense that a male tyrant or patriarchal despot could be so described; but rather, torn and maddened by false power and false loyalty to a system against which she had at first instinctively revolted, and which was destroying her integrity. Powerless in the institution of marriage, the institution of slavery *did* give her near-absolute power over another human being, her only outlet for rage and frustration being the control she had over that person.[5]

Feminists have been fighting against structurally similar arguments meant to exonerate rapists and sexual abusers: that they have less than absolute power compared to the most powerful of the powerful white despots or millionaires, while appealing to the necessity of a safety valve, an 'outlet' for rage and frustration. Yet here, in the context of white women, they suddenly seem reasonable. Thus the white woman is not responsible for herself, she is the victim of a system, 'torn and maddened'. It is not she who gives up her original integrity, the system is 'destroying her integrity'. It is not she who decides irresponsibly to abuse her 'near-absolute power over another human being'; the system of slavery gave it to her — from which we apparently are to infer that she could not but exercise it.

In other words, in her legitimate concern with the position of white women as oppressed by white men, Rich foregrounds their oppression *at the cost* of the oppression of Black people — in this case at the cost of the oppression directly caused by the white woman herself. Our understanding of structural, systemic oppression is used to show understanding for the specific actions of the white woman at the very point where that woman's behaviour towards her slave, Frederick Douglass, is in question. To put it bluntly: where the woman's behaviour towards others is the issue, we speak of others' behaviour towards the woman. In the context of the present, that is, the early women's movement, Rich argues:

> If a shallow 'life-style' brand of feminism can shrug off the issue of racism altogether, it is also true that more 'political' white feminists still often feel vulnerable to the charge that 'white middle-class women' or 'bourgeois feminists' are despicable creatures of privilege whose oppression is meaningless beside the oppression of black, Third World, or working-class women and men. That charge, of course, resolutely avoids the central fact of male gynephobia and violence against all women. It also diverts energy into the ludicrous and fruitless game of 'hierarchies of oppression' . . .[6]

A sensitive understanding is here being extended towards the psychological vulnerability of political white women — and the analysis moved to the level of personal relationships, where critique becomes a 'charge', and white women are being judged and sentenced as 'despicable creatures', that is, on the grounds of their identity (which they cannot help) as being white and middle-class. As a result they in turn feel vulnerable and presumably hurt indeed, all the more so as being seen as despicable means personal rejection. The words of the critique are not quoted but paraphrased by Rich, and paraphrased from the perspective of white women's reception, their subjective and emotional response.

Rich's concern is to show how men in patriarchy are prepared to use any pressure, manipulation or violence to prevent women from organizing as women – historically and in the present operating the 'divide and conquer' strategy which effects deep divisions between women, of which racism is one of the deepest, and the one which is the theme of her article. Yet what in the passage above begins as a discussion of the 'issue of racism' turns into a discussion of male abuse of white women: 'the charge of "racism" flung at white women in the earliest groupings of the independent feminist movement was a charge made in the most obscene bad faith by white "radical" males (and by some leftist women) against the daring leap of self-definition needed to create an autonomous feminist analysis.'[7]

While such male behaviour, and in particular the cynical abuse of 'reproaches' of racism, classism or anti-Semitism (by anyone), is indeed reprehensible behaviour, it substitutes at this point of the discussion for a discussion of our own behaviour: that of political white women (in contrast to the shrugging-off of the issue of racism by 'life-style' feminists). Any legitimate issue of racism disappears from the discussion while we are concerned with the cynical charge made in the most obscene faith. Whether critics of 'the issue of racism' really consider white women 'despicable' and regard sexist oppression of white women as 'meaningless', or whether in fact their critique concerns behaviour rather than identity, does not get raised. It is less important than considering white women's feelings.

Hence white women's response of feeling outbid in their oppression, and of entering into competition with Black women and men, also seems a product of such abusive charges, although we know it also as an autonomous response by white feminists to the (legitimate) criticism of racism, in particular as the attempt to prioritize sexism over racism. Yet by discussing men's behaviour of flinging abuse, women appear indeed in a relation where they are the victims – as the white slave mistress is a victim in relation to her white husband. But they are victims more crucially of the violence of abusive charging, be

it by men or by anyone, less of their general structural position as
(white) women which, if it were the issue, would need to appear in
relation to that of Black men and women. Thus even in the context
of 'racism' (as a charge or reproach), white women are victims rather
than those with power – although it is white women who at this very
moment are taking advantage of the power of discourse, deciding
what to foreground and what to exclude.

The issue of racism thus appears above all as a counter in the strained
relations between white women and men on the left, rather than a
political issue which white women might consider as a question they
(also) pose themselves – which in particular Black people, and especially Black women, might have raised apart from white men. And it
seems that the cynical bad faith of white leftist men (and some Black
men) and the 'intense negative pressures by the male-dominated Left
in the 1960s'[8] are being used to *explain* if not to excuse white women's
'retreat from anything resembling rhetorical demands that white
women "deal with our racism" as a first priority'.[9]

Finally, the author herself insists that really this is no argument at all:

> But surely such demands have a different meaning and imperative when
> they come in bad faith from the lips of white – or black – males, whose
> intention is to discredit feminist politics; and when they are articulated
> by black feminists, who are showing themselves, over time, unflagging
> and persistent in their outreach toward white women, while refusing to
> deny – or to have denied – an atom of their black reality.[10]

If Black women have, over time, unflaggingly and persistently been
speaking to white women, reaching out to them, why not discuss
what they have been saying? But Black women, it appears, have not
yet formulated their critique in a way that we as white women can
accept:

> I can easily comprehend that when black women have looked at the
> present-day feminist movement, particularly as caricatured in the male-
> dominated press (both black and white), and have seen blindness to, and
> ignorance of, the experience and needs of black women, they have labeled
> this 'racism', undifferentiated from the racism endemic in patriarchy. But
> I hope that we can now begin to differentiate and to define further,
> drawing both on a deeper understanding of black and white women's
> history, and on an unflinching view of patriarchy itself.[11]

Black women's critique (if indeed they have any) has not apparently been based on their experience, but just on their 'looking at the feminist movement'. Moreover, they have probably been looking less at the women's movement than at caricatures of it in the male press. Their visual impression that there is racism in the women's movement is therefore (1) more of an appearance (a male representation) than an experienced reality, and (2) wrongly labelled as racism. Black women, we gather, first need to differentiate more carefully between the racism of white women and the racism 'in patriarchy', just as Rich differentiated the 'false power' of Douglass's white mistress from real power (as men have it in patriarchy).

In other words, if anything is standing between white women and Black women, it is above all white men's violence towards white women, and it is Black women's undifferentiated labelling of white women — standing in the way, at least, of white women's ability to consider the issue of racism. Which suggests that it is Black women who have the power of naming and defining, that is, power over white women. If there is any impediment to a joint women's movement on the side of white women at all, it is not anything that white women are doing, but their psychological vulnerability to the charge of racism, a vulnerability due to their being oppressed by men. And it is two further weaknesses and disabilities: 'ignorance' and 'blindness'. All the more reason, it seems, for Black women to tread carefully when they label — for they have become (in this account) the (wrong)doers, with white women being the victims.

Where Black women are exposed to the real violence of racism — by white men and white women — white women escape to the level of feelings (even if exclusively their own), which are ultimately beyond disputation. For what a woman *feels* cannot be disputed; what she thinks she has heard can be judged only by herself. What could on the other hand very well be discussed is what has in fact been said and whether it is true, for it is a reality to which we all have equal access. It could also be clarified by analysis how appropriate a feeling may be — whether it relates to any real action or statement, or in fact to my subjective impression of what I think has happened or I have heard, or I have heard somewhere else. Feelings, however, enjoy such a privileged status among Western women that their appropriateness is rarely analysed, let alone questioned.

Shortly afterwards Rich explicitly shifts to the level of personal relationships, addressing 'Black woman' first in a poetic monologue, then in a dialogue:

> The images we have of each other. How black woman and white move as myths through each other's fantasies, myths created by the white male psyche including its perverse ideas of beauty. How have I handed my own sexuality, my sense of myself as deviant, over to black women, not to speak of my own magic, my own rage? What illusions do we harbor still, of our own and each other's Amazon power or incompetence, glamor or disability, 'smart-ugliness' or cerebral cool-ness, how do we play the mother or the daughter, how do we use each other to keep from touching our own power? . . . What caricatures of bloodless fragility and broiling sensuality still imprint our psyches, and where did we receive these imprintings? . . . How has the white man, how has the black man, stood to gain from pitting *white bitch* against *nigger cunt*, 'yellow gal' against black?[12]

In the 'personal' relationship of 'I and you', of 'us' with 'each other', Rich and the Black woman have apparently escaped the historical and social power relationships which Rich just before had so painfully analysed. They meet in a mutual encounter where each is 'I' and the other her 'you', where power and risk are apparently even in the denuded opposition of two subjects. The images each has of the other, the prejudices about the other, the illusions each has about herself and the strength or weakness of the other, are here common and evenly distributed – and also linguistically joined in the common subject 'we': 'the images we have', and 'what illusions do we harbor'. Even so, as is usual with the conception of personal relationships, the subject's own subjectivity occasionally obtrudes and casts the other in the stereotyped role of the object: 'How have I handed my own sexuality, my sense of myself as deviant, over to black women, not to speak of my own magic, my own rage?' Both however are damaged, victims of the same master, the white man and his defining power – the myths and images 'not created by them' apparently remaining outside their own responsibility even in their own imagination and fantasy. The commonality of their victimization as women, each being pitted against the other, lets us forget the asymmetry and hierarchy even in abuse.

It hardly comes as a surprise that this encounter – the speaker's attempt to overcome the political power disequilibrium through a personalized relationship – eventually turns into an erotic fantasy of love:

> Taught to deny my longings for another female body, taught that dark skin was stigma, shame, I look at you and see your flesh is beautiful; different from my own, but taboo to me no longer. Whether we choose to act on this or not (and whatever pain we may explore in touching one another) if we both have this knowledge, if my flesh is beautiful to you and yours to me, because it belongs to us, in affirmation of our similar and different powers, in affirmation of scars, stretch-marks, life-lines, the mind that burns in each body, we lay claim to ourselves and each other beyond the most extreme patriarchal taboo. We take each other up in our strong arms. We do not infantilize each other; we refuse to be infantilized. We drink at each other's difference. We begin to fuse our powers.[13]

After the manner of desire, the subject infers from her desire for the other a common and mutual desire of both for each other, goes over from 'I' to the joint subject 'we': 'I look at you and see your flesh is beautiful . . . taboo to me no longer . . . Whether we choose to act on this or not . . .' On the basis of a mutuality which has been linguistically constructed, her 'knowledge', her own reaching out to the other's flesh, is assumed to be the same on the part of the other, is projected on to the other with only a rhetorical proviso of 'if' – in a speech act which renders the other silent, which extinguishes the other's will and wish by subsuming it under my own, since, despite the 'if', it is henceforth conceived of and treated only as identical. The shared identity of being women and lovers shall suffice to guarantee equality and mutuality, indeed to extinguish the inequality of a history of racism – desire sufficing to annul the difference between two persons in this 'personal relationship' where we 'fuse our powers'.

Rich here poetically makes explicit what usually remains implicit but generally underlies the practice of psychologizing the political and resolving it through personal relationship, namely that the issue is love and recognition – the other's love and recognition of myself. It is the bounty love yields to the one who loves, hence she is willing to get it by force. Having chosen the encounter, her own love 'lays claim' to the other and her love, regards it as a right. 'For you are my rejected part, my antiself.'[14]

To this personal desire, any collective cause is sacrificed time and again – in the present context Black women's communicative concern for a joint understanding of feminism and a joint political struggle against racism. Through the reformulation of their critique as a 'reproach', their analysis as a 'charge', Black women are discursively coerced into a personal relationship, with their political intention recast as their own desire for relationship. No matter that Black women keep repeating how they cannot respect white women who continue to behave like wilful 'children'. But respect is not the issue, our desire is for 'love' and a personal relationship. For a relationship, even a quarrel, even a 'confrontation' is proof that the other has entered the game, that she is playing a match with me – that she has recognized me, even if only as an opponent.

It hardly seems to matter that thus not only the common cause, but also the other has been sacrificed: that this recasting of politics as relationship constitutes an act of violence against the other in which her intention, her self-expression and her self-determination are annihilated. The enforced 'togetherness' – togetherness even in quarrel and confrontation – apparently justifies the means. Nor does it seem to matter that in this shift to a 'personal relationship' my own subjectivity remains dominant, egocentrism replacing white-women-centrism. Rather, the fact that the question of the other's wish and will does not even arise, any more than the question of my own love and recognition of the other arises, shows that this so-called personal relationship, this erotic relationship, is the desired private sphere in which there is only one point of view, mine, and only one interest, my self-interest, and the other has become part of my self.

5

Psychotherapy, or the legitimation of irresponsibility

The fact that the parameters of subjectivity, feelings and opinions have become such a solid part of commonsense 'rationality' is not unrelated to the uncritical status which psychology enjoys among discourses. While even on a theoretical level its status is rarely determined in relation to other disciplines, that is, other levels of analysis of social ('human') phenomena, in practice its ubiquitous relevance seems beyond any doubt or question. Psychological truths – say the much quoted adage that 'the strange' and 'the unfamiliar are always threatening' – become the axiomatic starting-point of political analyses or philosophical treatises. Through the phenomenal expansion of psycho-therapeutic practice in our society, moreover, a discourse of popular psychology has become so firmly established as to inform our most commonsense notions of people in society.

In our enthusiasm for all things psychological we tend to forget that the original impetus of psychoanalysis as well as other kinds of therapy was the investigation of psychic (and social) disorders – leaving aside for the moment what was considered as such – and that even the study of the psychology of so-called healthy people is based to a large extent on clinical data of 'pathologies'.[1] The aim was to study and explore disturbances in people's thinking, feeling and behaviour, or crises in their ability to cope with their lives, in order to help them overcome them. If Freud in the course of developing his science eventually came to the diagnosis that (Western) adults in general are basically neurotic, this means less that neurosis is the normal state of the human psyche than that there is something seriously wrong with the conditions of life in modern Western society.

Yet in the course of the development of psychological theory and above all with the explosion of psychotherapy as a booming business, it has become a central tenet of Eurocentric thinking to regard the neurotic inhabitants of Western urban societies not only as 'normal', but as at the highest stage of development of human sensibility. That is to say, the empirical evidence of a high degree of neurosis in our societies has become a reason less for trying to heal it than for people to try and 'accept' it and to learn to 'live with it'. Although therapy is being offered as a universal panacea, it simultaneously teaches us that we are basically incurable. But since it is a scientifically attested incurability which moreover is quite 'normal' in the most 'advanced' societies of the world, it loses the stigma of an incurable disease, becoming instead the proud certification of our highly strung, highly sophisticated postmodernist sensibility. In confirming our suffering and discontent and assisting us in accepting it, if not indeed in taking pride in it, psychotherapy has a key function in stabilizing and maintaining the social and political status quo.

Hence there is a tendency also among feminist psychotherapists to recommend to women a cure on the couch as a progressive step in their struggle to come to terms with patriarchal oppression. The political aim of changing social structures and behaviour gives way to the scientific aim of explaining 'women's psychology'. Although what is found empirically to be the psychology of (many) women is also understood to be socially determined, it is nevertheless scientifically attested *as* 'the psychology' of women. Hence the client's political aim of changing society correspondingly gives way to the aim of asserting her socially determined psychology more effectively. That is to say, women's project of affecting society is replaced by the project scientifically to describe and therapeutically to cement the way society affects women.

Luise Eichenbaum and Susie Orbach, who explicitly identify themselves as part of the women's liberation movement, describe how and why 'through the process of trying to change our society'[2] they discovered psychoanalysis and other therapeutic methods: despite feminism and consciousness-raising they 'continued to feel unentitled, unexperienced, or unequal . . . This discovery on a feeling level led us to try to discover the vital connections between the social world that women inhabit and the inner private world that governs us in the deepest reaches of our personalities.'[3] While this largely corresponds to the aims of feminist consciousness-raising, the crucial difference is that here the non-hierarchical structures of collective self-help are being replaced by a hierarchical and commercial relationship between therapist and client – that while the 'content' apparently remains the same, the political 'form' has been abolished. We shall see moreover that the political aim of changing society also disappears without trace, while the women undergoing therapy in search of political liberation equally emerge from the therapy 'incurable'.

The three advantages which the therapeutic techniques selected by Eichenbaum and Orbach in their own view have to offer are, first, that they hold 'the possibility that people could get in touch with their feelings more speedily than through psychoanalytic methods'; secondly, that they '[encourage] individuals to act on their own behalf', and thirdly, that they '[demystify] the process of psychological change'.[4] That is, the clients, like their therapists before them, will discover 'the feeling level', and apparently get there more speedily than through any other methods. In particular, they will learn to give up their political aspirations and have the 'courage' instead to act on their own behalf, that is, in their self-interest. And if the process of psychological change is thus being demystified, there is no mention even any longer of any process of political change. The psychological change open to the client is the change from a feeling of social discontent and critique of political conditions – 'unentitled, unexperienced, unequal' – to an acceptance of her feelings as part of her innermost self. For as we shall also see, the client is mistaken if she thinks that her feelings of discontent and displeasure are due to the social and political conditions of her life as a woman in patriarchy, that is, due to real experience of social and political inequality.

Thus this feminist therapy reproduces the very turn-about which Freudian psychoanalysis performed at the beginning of the century, when from being a potential means of recognizing reality it turned into a scientific theory in support of the status quo, scientifically certifying feelings as psychic products and explaining away any causes in social reality. The same theory 'demystified' the sexual exploitation of girls by men in their family, explaining that the experience of women and girls is not a social and political reality, but a product of their imaginations, a wishful fantasy.[5] Numerous women objected to this 'discovery' on the 'feeling level', amongst them Bertha Pappenheim and Charlotte Perkins-Gilman, who after escaping from their respective therapies with Breuer, Freud or Weir Mitchell as well as from their respective families, spent their lives fighting for women's rights and against the sexual and economic exploitation of women and girls,[6] not without incurring further slander, both from the great master Freud and from their own families.

Thus a descendant of Pappenheim asked her interviewer Ann Jackowitz: 'Why are you interested in Pappenheim? She was nothing but a nut and a lesbian.'[7] Freud, on the other hand, wrote to Marie Bonaparte about Pappenheim: 'She never married. And she has found great joy in life. Can you guess how? What she does . . . She is active in societies for the protection of white women. Against prostitution! She speaks out against anything sexual.'[8] To Freud, speaking out against the sexual exploitation and enslavement of women and girls is equivalent to speaking out 'against anything sexual'. And that Bertha Pappenheim never married but campaigned against what was then called the 'white slave trade' or 'founded the German Jewish feminist movement under the name the League of Jewish Women'[9] proves to the great master that she continues to have a sexual hang-up. Had she stayed in therapy instead, she would surely have been cured of it. Above all she would have refrained from political activity.

What was clear to Freud, in other words, also became clear to many women patients, namely that therapy contributes to the social control of women. For Pappenheim, as for so many women of the first women's movement who had been therapized, the 'healing' step consisted in leaving the power relationship of the therapy, casting off its patriarchal ideology and seeking the causes of her suffering no longer in personal 'illness' but in political (including familial) social conditions. While their recovery began precisely when they exchanged their dependent existence as suffering daughters or wives of the bourgeoisie for an active political life in their own right, feminist therapists today advise women to give up political struggle in favour of starting a career as a patient. The therapy's 'content' may have been adjusted 'feministically', yet the ideological foundations of psychological theory and the political structure of therapy remain unchallenged and unchanged.

Psychology and therapy today not only orient themselves by the highly neurotic standards of human sensibility in the metropolitan societies of the West, but they are also primarily based on the development of the psyche at the stage of babyhood. Since Freud – until his radical U-turn back to an 'instinctual determinist' as a consequence of his denial of the sexual exploitation of children[10] – was convinced that problems in adult life often stemmed from unresolved problems in childhood, childhood increasingly became the focus of analysis. But while psychoanalysis originally saw itself as an instrument for resolving these difficulties – raising such childhood experiences into the consciousness of adults to enable them retrospectively to come to terms with them and to recover their ability to cope with their lives – psychological theory increasingly sees early childhood *per se* as determining the adult's future, that is to say, as the 'cause' of adult mental life.[11]

Hence it is less the extreme, traumatic experiences of a child (not to mention an adult) which the person at this stage is unable to cope with that are seen to cause disturbances in later life. Increasingly it is the experience of early childhood in general, the conditions of life as a being who has not yet matured, who is not yet capable of surviving alone, who is dependent on care and nurture, which are declared the paradigmatic determinants of the psychic structure of the adult personality. Birth, if not indeed prenatal experiences in the womb, consequently become traumas from whose after-effects people may continue to suffer until death – or until their encounter with the relevant psychological theory or therapeutic treatment which, if it cannot remove the after-effects, at least can alleviate them.

Thus the mother's breast offered for nurture but periodically withdrawn – not to mention the affront of being brought up on the bottle – become the understandable 'cause' of adult men's phenomenal sexual violence against women, in particular their obsession with stuffing women's mouths literally in sadistic torture and symbolically through political silencing, as a revenge for the fact that the breast was ever withdrawn.[12] In other words, the mere condition of childhood as such, of having had a person, let alone a woman as a mother, suffices to predict the relative inability of future adults to cope with their lives. And indeed 'I refuse to have been born by a woman', one valiant adult protests against this particular childhood deprivation.[13]

On the other hand, progressive medical science and high-tech gynaecology prophylactically support this understanding of human psychology, recommending birth by Caesarian operation to grant the child, but above all the future adult, a gentler entry into the world than his or her mother would provide.[14] But whether by birth or by

Caesarian operation, to have had a human being as a mother at all, someone with personal dimensions, with interests and aspirations of her own instead of a continuous caring and nurturing service or a permanently available slave, will, as we shall see, become one of the chief causes of the problems of adult humans in modern Western society.[15]

Far from using such observations about adult mentality to point out the infantilism of grown-up men (and women), thus to enable them by means of therapeutic consciousness-raising belatedly to overcome it, psychology on the contrary makes the infantile needs of babies the standard of the emotional life of adults. While Freud, for instance, still regarded the need to gaze at genitals as a characteristic of the pre-oedipal infant, contemporary Western society is celebrating genital scopophilia as the latest progress of a liberatory adult culture attempting on the contrary to protect children from it, to whose developmental stage in fact it corresponds). Similarly, feminist psychologists and therapists today derive their understanding of the mental life of adult women from the structure of feelings and needs of post-natal infants, that is to say, from what a psychological theory imputes to children as their structure of feelings and needs.

Thus the Women's Therapy Centre in London, for example, explicitly bases its approach on the object relations school, a loose grouping of theories about infantile development (Fairbairn, Winnicott, Guntrip and others), as well as on the work of Melanie Klein, who sees in infantile fantasy the paradigm of the future personality structure of the adult, and for whom the crucial period of childhood is limited to the first two years of life or so.[16] While Klein is an instinctual determinist, object relations theory emphasizes the infant's social experience, in particular her or his relationship to the primary carer, the 'mother'. What object relations has in common with Melanie Klein, however, is that both consider the first couple of years after birth to be the crucial period for the 'construction of personality', that is, the personality of the future adult: 'Ego development begins at birth and in relation to the primary caregiver, the mother. This early period, which Fairbairn calls "infantile dependency", is the pivotal period in ego development.'[17]

Consequently the adult individual becomes interchangeable with the infant, the infant with the adult individual. Thus Eichenbaum and Orbach explain why they have chosen object relations theory:

It posited a materialist view of psychological development on the basis that *the individual* has a need for relationship and a drive for contact with another human being, and that the first two years of life are the most important time for the development of the inner core of the *person*, the psyche and the personality together, which Fairbairn and Guntrip mean when they refer to the ego . . . The *infant* has a *primary* need for human contact.[18] (my emphases except 'primary')

Or:

'Whereas Freud saw libido as primarily seeking satisfaction, Fairbairn believed that the *individual* has a drive for relationship, a drive for contact with another human being. Thus the *infant* has a primary need for human contact.[19] (my emphases)

So we are hardly surprised to find that adult sexuality, too, is seen principally as the problem of an infant. According to Joanna Ryan, 'the idea that adult sexual activity can stir up infantile feelings in adults is basic to any psychoanalytic approach.'[20] Thus E. S. Person argues that 'sexuality expresses many aspects of personality and motivation, originating in both infantile and later experiences.'[21] Generally it is assumed that the adult individual whose infantile personality developed during the first two years of life continues to yearn for the *state* of infancy, especially in matters sexual, as Ryan further explains quoting Person: 'because of the real dependence of a helpless child on a relatively powerful adult, "it is unlikely that sexuality will ever be completely free of submission–dominance connotations".' For 'sexuality expresses an enormous variety of motives, predominantly dependent or hostile, and the force of sexuality exists precisely because sexuality is linked to other motives.'[22]

Nancy Chodorow, followed or paralleled by large numbers of feminist psychologists and psychotherapists,[23] again takes it as read that the aim of sexuality is a 'return' to 'oneness' with the imaginary mother.[24] It has long been a central cliché in our culture that men's sex, that is, their genitally penetrating women, constitutes their attempt to return to the womb and the state of an embryo – even though, to the best of my knowledge, there exists no evidence of infants and children manifesting a like desire to return and regress. Notwithstanding, this myth has since been adapted also for the adult woman, who in yearning for a 'merger' with the 'other' is said to

express a like desire. Only rarely does one come across a hint in the
expert literature like the following by Joanna Ryan, namely that 'in
adult–adult relationships we are also trying to be adults.'[25] Which is
why this aspect of adult mental life continues to remain largely
unexplored.

But since it is the 'core of the person' which allegedly is formed
during the first years of life, it is not just in sexuality that this infantile
personality manifests itself: the infantile personality *is* the personality
of the adult. Hence, an adult's view of the world and attitude to reality
equally originate in the perception and cognition of a newborn baby.
Eichenbaum and Orbach describe this baby stage of human cognition,
which is characterized by the fact that it is *fantasy*:

> For Klein, the instincts sought objects as their aim, rather than pleasure
> as Freud posited. The objects – the people – were, however, objects of
> an internal nature rather than the images of the actual people in the
> child's life. The internal objects were part of the heritage that an infant
> brought into the world along with instincts. Where an instinct arose so
> did an image of an object to satisfy it. Real people were screens upon
> which the infant could project its internal fantasies. Experience of
> people in the world confirmed the experience of the child's internal
> object relations.[26]

Although, due to their greater emphasis on social influences, the
biological determinism of object relations approaches such as Nancy
Chodorow's in *The Reproduction of Mothering* seems minimized in
comparison with the theoreticians of inborn instincts, there still remains the fundamental structure of childhood experience *causing* the
adult personality structure: 'Women come to mother because they
have been mothered by women.'[27] Though in this case men would also
have to come to mother, since they too had been mothered by women
– unless it is for a different reason that women come to mother.

It is a corollary of such theories and their corresponding therapies
that motherly care or 'nurturance' – an amalgam of warmth and
nourishment – must form a central part of the therapeutic relationship:
'What comes across clearly in Guntrip's descriptions of his work and
clients is the importance of nurturance within the therapy relationship. This concept is a cornerstone of our feminist psychotherapy.'[28]
This means infantilizing not only the client but also the therapist, and

with them the therapy relationship as a whole – since the conception of this so-called mother–infant relationship is based not on any real relationship between a mother and her child, but on the infant's fantasy of its relationship to its 'internal object' of a 'mother', a fantasy grown out of the insatiability of an infant's needs.

This infantile fantasy of a 'mother–child' relationship, however, becomes the model not only of the therapeutic relationship, but of (adult) relationships in general. That is, it becomes the model for 'love' – emotional needs and fulfilment – in the relationships between adults when we do not mean sex. As Lynne Segal explains in her article called 'Sensual Uncertainty, or Why the Clitoris is not Enough', there are 'all sorts of other emotional needs – to obtain approval and love, express hostility, dependence and domination, relieve anxiety, and repair deep-lying psychic wounds of rejection, humiliation and despair', with which 'sexual desire is knotted through'.[29]

Without distinguishing between theory and practice or pointing to their dialectical interaction, without differentiating between an analysis and an explanation, between a description of symptoms and a diagnosis of their cause, or between a problem and what might constitute its possible solution, therapists take the empirical evidence of the average emotional state of their clients – and amateur psychologists that of their friends – and make it the basis of a 'theory' which clearly reflects the childlike regression effected or found in the patient. Since this 'little-girl' syndrome plays a considerable role not only in feminist psychotherapy itself but in the understanding of relationships in general, it is worth studying its genesis in somewhat more detail. As Janice Raymond has argued, therapy has been central in the development of 'therapism' and the accompanying syndrome of 'relationism' – making a therapeutic context out of one's relationships[30] – which increasingly also informs our politics and our conception of what would constitute a 'caring way of dealing with each other'.

In a series of 'case studies' in their book, *What do Women Want?*, the authors Luise Eichenbaum and Susie Orbach tend themselves to speak in the language of the little girl they postulate as being hidden in every woman. Thus they tell us in childlike earnest how a 39-year-old educated middle-class woman with a job at the BBC – which she is about to give up to go freelance – is thrown into an existential crisis when her husband of two years proposes to go on a business trip precisely during her last week at the BBC: 'Katie felt totally abandoned and wondered how she was going to make it through an entire week without him . . . In fact, she only had one free night in the whole week. And yet she felt dejected, rejected, vulnerable and scared at the thought of being on her own.'[31]

In fact, she survived the difficult week, yet the trauma extends well beyond it:

> Pete returned from the week wrung out and tired. He behaved in a withdrawn and distant way and it emerged later that he was actually feeling lousy about having left Katie for the week. Shortly after his return he got a cold, then he had an accident playing football . . . Katie looked after him and was a tower of strength. He gradually got better but something significant in their relationship changed from that point on. For the next few years, Katie felt suspicious towards Pete and somewhat disdainful. She felt he couldn't really give to her in the way he had in the past and she wondered whether she was right about what had originally flowed between them. But at the same time as she became somewhat contemptuous of him and even undermined his attempts to reach out to her, she became increasingly dependent on the relationship and felt more insecure than she had for ages. She kept looking to Pete for some sign that he still loved her and wanted her.[32]

What seemed a crisis in the relationship in fact turns into a crisis of self:

> Katie discovered with an unpleasant jolt that she could not rely on maintaining an independent stance while she was in a close relationship. As soon as she had opened herself up in this relationship all her hidden and forbidden dependency desires came up and overwhelmed her. She was caught out by the intensity of her feelings of abandonment and rage at Pete. And she resented being so affected by these emotions.[33]

So much for the description of the case in the paraphrasing words of the therapists. Their analytical explanation follows with hardly a change of style:

> The unfortunate sequence of events had destabilized Katie. Nerves had been touched and her self-confidence shattered. The explanation for this went back years before Katie was involved with Pete. From beneath the layers of rationality and life experience, Katie's unconscious asserted itself. With different players and different goals, Katie was reliving with Pete her very earliest childhood steps towards independence.[34]

These were, so the therapists tell us, her first steps of 'separation-individuation' out of a total symbiosis with the mother when she was a toddler. Katie's mother, it appears, had not been able to cope with her baby's needs:

> Katie's needs frightened her, *for they reminded her of her own forbidden feelings*. Sometimes she was unable to be responsive to Katie, to tune in absolutely to what she wanted and, in giving to her, provide a reassurance that all was well. At other times, Katie's mother ignored her needs, just as she was forced to ignore her own.[35]

Because of this inadequacy of the mother to respond to the needs of her baby, to 'tune into' her neediness at all times and 'absolutely', the three- or four-year-old Katie 'came to understand that she shouldn't rely on her mother too much' and should 'hide away her little-girl part':

> She was a little girl who had inadmissible needs now hidden inside her. She made an unconscious resolution to approach the bigger world without the cumbersome neediness of her first years. She couldn't bear to feel the rejection again . . . she was hoping either to have her needs met elsewhere or escape them altogether . . . Every new situation built her confidence that she could cope, that she could take care of herself, that she didn't really need anyone. But every victory had its reverse psychic effect, for Katie became more and more distant from the little-girl part of her inside who had stopped growing, whose needs had been prematurely nipped in the bud, who still hungered for constant attention.[36]

Although she tries to disengage from her little-girl part, the latter in fact remains inside her, unnoticed and repressed:

> The little-girl part did not present itself directly . . . But when Katie fell in love with Pete, a part of her psyche unfroze . . . In her closeness with Pete, her earlier feelings of closeness with her mother were re-evoked . . . When Pete 'left her' for the week at a point when she was moving out of her secure job at the BBC, she felt as though she was being abandoned to face the world once again on her own. More than that even, she unconsciously felt as though his departure was some kind of punishment for her new work decision.[37]

We might wonder why neither the therapist nor her client ever raises the question as to the appropriateness of these feelings with respect to the actual events – why Katie's childlike representation of the 'events', uninfluenced by realism or knowledge, never becomes the subject of discussion. For it is here, in her account, that she expresses her thinking and understanding – how she perceives her problems and how she sees or cannot see her options for dealing with them – and to change which, one presumes, she is seeking help and support. Yet the therapist simply confirms what her client reports. Moreover, she derives from it a theory, or the confirmation of a theory, concerning the nature and function of feelings in 'relationships': the excessive neediness of the adult woman must correspond to a neediness in her infancy, a neediness which moreover was never satisfied. The therapist's theory – her generalized account of universalized 'events' ('every mother', 'when we first come into the world' etc.)[38] – is absolutely congruous with the individual client's account, the two mutually influencing and confirming each other. The theory reproduces the client's childlike subjective understanding without 'if' or 'but', and the client reproduces a therapizing account of her own childhood. The reported content of the one as of the other account remains solid fact: the child suffered from emotional deprivation, from unfulfilled neediness, not because such neediness by definition of its postulated unboundedness cannot be satisfied, but because her mother was inadequate.

Why the mother was inadequate is also quickly explained: there is a 'tug of war', a 'push–pull dynamic' in the mother–daughter relationship. 'Mothers relate to their daughters in this fashion because they were similarly related to by their mothers. Inside each mother lives a repressed little girl who is still yearning for acceptance and love.'[39] That is to say, mother herself is a potential client for therapy, who at the time Katie was little must have suffered as the adult patient Katie is suffering today, and must have suffered as much when she was little as did Katie when she was a little girl. Hence the theory comes full circle back to the problem: the theory is the same as the problem. And the therapy in store is also the same, for it does not consist, say, of working through the fantastic and unrealistic (alleged) conception of feelings and needs of the toddler from the perspective of the realistic and developed cognition of an adult, it consists in confirming and affirming these insatiable and people-consuming needs. The repeated mention of 'forbidden feelings' and 'inadmissible needs' already hints at what direction the therapy will take, besides betraying its own childlike conception of reality as a fatherly authority which 'forbids' feelings and needs.

What Robin Norwood considers to be a central feature of the 'dysfunctional family', namely 'their inability to discuss *root* problems',[40] turns out to be a central feature also of the therapy relationship. What Norwood says about the family can be applied without change to the therapy context:

> What all unhealthy families [and therapies] have in common is their inability to discuss *root* problems. There may be other problems that *are* discussed, often ad nauseam, but these often cover up the underlying secrets that make the family [the therapy] dysfunctional. It is the degree of secrecy – the inability to talk about the problems – rather than their severity, that defines both how dysfunctional a family [a therapy relationship] becomes and how severely its members are damaged. A dysfunctional family [therapy] is one in which members play rigid roles and in which communication is severely restricted to statements that fit these roles.[41]

In other words, this suppression of 'root problems' serves to keep such 'dysfunctional families' precisely functional, that is to say, 'together', real problems not being allowed to surface so as not to threaten the apparent harmony of family 'togetherness' – say, in the form of an insight that, for some members of the family, separating might be appropriate. Just as the 'dysfunctional family', undifferentiated here in terms of the power relations amongst its members, 'has' an interest in maintaining its togetherness at the cost of individual members and their personal liberation, so the 'therapy relationship' has an interest in maintaining itself and not endangering its 'mother–child' harmony. If the therapist in recognizing and discussing real problems risks her client's becoming capable and thus 'liberating' herself, and so stands to lose a paying client, her client, in recognizing and coping with her problems, stands to lose her claim to a warm and comforting, family-like therapy relationship.

Hence the therapy indeed consists in 'workshops on dependency', where the client 'became aware of how disappointed and upset she was about the course of events', became aware, that is, of much the same thing she had originally felt, and just as she had originally felt it – unadulterated by any reflection or insight:

> She realized that she didn't want Pete to do very much at all; she didn't really want to collapse, and felt she could conquer any challenge if she only knew that he was really behind her. Until that fateful week and the ensuing illness she had felt Pete was really there for her, concerned about her. She experienced his week's absence as a withdrawal and a rejection.[42]

The only additional 'insight' in this report is the theoretical postulate of the therapy, namely that the problem lies not in the present, but in the past: 'It flung her back almost thirty-five years to feelings of utter loneliness and anxiety that she had suppressed. She felt that she had been dropped, she had been pushed out . . . She was forced to deny her dependency needs once again. These needs were so forbidden.'[43]

What the therapy has to offer is encouragement by all means to 'admit' those 'forbidden' needs, to become conscious of them and to 'accept' them. Whether this will in fact help the client is doubtful. She may indeed know now that she has insatiable dependency needs, unfulfillable claims to unconditional care and support, but they are not thereby any more likely to get satisfied. Rather, the probability increases that she will be thrown into despair not only by her husband's leaving her for a whole week, but by the slightest sign that once again he is not 'really behind her' – when to be 'really behind her' means not to pursue his own job, to make the timetable of her career the schedule of his own life, and when to be 'concerned about her' means having no concern in the world but her, no concern, that is, but to satisfy the equivalent of an infant's expectation of continual 'motherly' care. While these dependency needs, accepted or otherwise, may thus never be satisfied by Pete, or indeed by any real person, the therapy relationship in turn offers a unique opportunity for the client to experience that her therapist – for the duration of a session – is 'really behind her', having no concern but her concern for her, and to live out this dependency need for as long as the money for a continuing therapy lasts.

There may be problems that are talked about in this therapy – perhaps even continually. But there is no problem to be solved, since neither the client nor her partner does anything that might be a problem in need of changing. In fact, neither of them does anything at all, for there are no persons acting in this account, even though it is about a relationship. The *dramatis personae*, rather, are Fate on the one hand, and her victim, the client, on the other – what happens and to whom it happens. What Pete may be doing is less an action on his part than a move on the part of Fate, using a pawn in her attack on the client: Pete happens to have to go away just when Katie most needs him. Then he falls ill and incurs an injury – a further blow of Fate against the client, who would have preferred being looked after to looking after. That she cannot reproach him for this is obvious even to the client; she does not reproach him for it, she reproaches the course of events for taking such a turn. The therapist too sees the real problem in the course of events: 'the unfortunate sequence of events had destabilized Katie.' They have declared war on her: 'nerves had been touched and her self-confidence shattered.'

So what was this sequence of events, what was their unfortunate course? The course of events is, above all, a sequence of different feelings presenting themselves. It is not a sequence of real events or actions – of abandoning and being abandoned, of rejecting, of inflicting injuries, or of withholding instead of giving: no one abandons Katie, no one rejects her, no one hurts her, no one throws her down, nor does she perish after a week on her own. She *felt* totally abandoned, rejected, dejected and vulnerable, and she *felt* that Pete could not really give to her as he had given to her in the past. And although she survives the week on her own, she wonders whether she was right about what had originally flowed between them – she asks herself but she does not ask him. She keeps looking to Pete for some sign that he still loves her and wants her. The fact that he lives with her, that he is trying to reach out to her (which she undermines) apparently is no sign from him, is not the sign (from Heaven?) she is waiting for. What such a sign would look like is difficult to say, since his acts of love and concern, his apparently model behaviour, clearly are not sign enough.

Whether she in turn makes any signs is not the question, for she is not an actor in this drama, she is the patient and recipient of action. Hence she does not show suspicion towards her partner, she just feels suspicious towards him for the next few years; she does not hold him in contempt, she just becomes contemptuous towards him. Far from being actions on her part and against him, it is, rather, yet another blow of Fate against her that she has to feel this way, since she would prefer to feel happy, knowing that he loves her, knowing that he wants her. Whether she in turn wants him is just as little the question: she does not want him, she wants him to want her.

It is a battle in which she is the victim. But it is not a fight in the relationship, a fight with a partner who does not love or give her enough: it is a fight with the relationship. It is towards the relationship that she becomes suspicious – was it really what she thought it was, or had she perhaps been mistaken? 'Something significant in their relationship changed from that point on', not in her partner's behaviour towards her, but 'in the relationship'. Hence we should not be surprised that it is not Pete she increasingly gets dependent on: 'she became increasingly dependent on the relationship.'

The relationship, it seems, does not consist of the continuing behaviour of the partners in relation to each other; the relationship is the sum and sequence of Katie's feelings. That these are not reactions in response to her partner's actual behaviour we have already seen: it is not his departure for one week that is the problem, but his going at a time when she wishes he would be 'really behind her', when she 'felt utterly unsupported'.[44] Nor was his falling ill the actual problem, but his doing so at a moment 'when she was feeling she would like that bit of reassurance herself'.[45]

Most importantly, however, her feelings are not her own affair for which she herself might be responsible; like the events, they are blows which Fate deals out to her; they appear as Pete's cold appears. Hence she feels suspicious towards him for the next few years, just as he feels ill for the next few days. Like villains, desires for dependency 'came up' and 'overwhelmed' her;[46] and they 'flung' her back almost thirty-five years to feelings of utter loneliness and anxiety. She was 'caught out' by the intensity of her feelings of abandonment and rage at Pete. And she felt resentful about being 'so affected' by them. Her rage, none the less, is directed at Pete – though it remains her that is 'affected' by the intensity of this feeling.

From beneath the layers of rationality and life experience, Katie's unconscious 'asserted itself' – it too, like the feelings and needs, being part of the arsenal in Fate's conspiracy against our heroine. It obliges Katie once again to relive, 'with different players and different goals', another relationship, the relationship with her mother nearly thirty-five years before. In this drama too, our heroine is the principal victim, suffering and enduring the machinations of Fate. In this case, the latter's chief agents are an incompetent mother as well as a 'little-girl part' of the daughter's that had ceased to grow but was still hungering for constant attention. The little-girl part 'did not present itself directly, indeed, [Katie] might never have become reacquainted with her if she had found enough challenges to negate her existence'.[47] But when Katie fell in love with Pete, 'a part of her psyche unfroze' and the little-girl part came back to life again – just as Americans have themselves frozen after death in the hope of being unfrozen back to life again in a few hundred years.

But while the infant heroine of this *relived* drama of a childhood relationship – relived by the grown-up Katie during that fateful week – is cast as the passively suffering Victim, it turns out that the real two-year-old Katie – as presented in the account of her actual childhood – was indeed an active agent in her own life: one who wanted to understand, and apparently did understand that she should not rely on her mother as if the latter were the imaginary mother-object of her own fantasy, one who 'made an unconscious resolution to approach the bigger world without the cumbersome neediness of her first years' and who 'quashed' this part in her; who set about 'to look outside the mother–daughter orbit', hoping to have her needs met elsewhere or escape them altogether, who 'thrust forward, taking up challenges with gusto, proving to herself that she could handle different situations'.[48] While this little girl, in other words, was still acting, taking her life into her own hands according to her best understanding and abilities, it is the 39-year-old Katie who has become exclusively a Victim, passively experiencing and enduring not only the circumstances of her life, but equally the foreign bodies inside her emotional household: ancient feelings of yesteryear, a frozen and unfreezing 'little-girl part', and a myriad of unwanted and uncalled for 'feelings' and 'needs' with which she has nothing to do except for the fact that *they* do to her.

This suggests that it is not so much the experiences of early child-hood which exert their uncanny influence on the adult, but on the contrary, problems of adult life – unrealistic desires and illegitimate claims on other people – which are being projected back into baby-hood and childhood. While toddlers according to their abilities and possibilities actively put up resistance against experiences of violence, attempting to overcome their problems as best they can, adults by contrast project a chosen 'helplessness' and incapability retrospectively on to childhood. While as adults we discover the pleasure of power, the desire to control and use other people in our own interests, and, in general, motives which are 'predominantly dependent or hostile', we project them on to an alleged experience of such pleasures as infants, the better to excuse and legitimate them.

Thus Lynne Segal exploring her sexual needs as an adult discovers that she does not just want to be loved, but equally to 'express hostility, dependence and domination'. Rather than worrying about her violence, her desire for power over another person and for hostility towards them, she tries to legitimate these by projecting them on to babies: 'As babies we have been the passive and powerless, but also powerfully demanding, recipients of enormous parental attention and, hopefully, physical gratification and love.'[49]

The fantasies which are thus projected on to babies are the fantasies of adults, their adultocentric projection of what 'being a baby' might mean. Far from being the fantasies of the powerless, they are fantasies from the perspective of those having power, power for example over babies, and they are fantasies of 'being a baby' which precisely appear attractive to adults for themselves. In particular, they betray the response of powerful adults to the extreme powerlessness of babies, their hostility towards the weak and their competition with them in a 'tug of war' between their own demands and the baby's demands: their conception of the self and the baby based on opposition and struggle. Thus the very existence of another with such obvious claims as a baby becomes a challenge to the self, an impediment to the subject's exclusive pursuit of its own demands.

This confirms itself explicitly in feminist theories of object relations which include the 'mother's' perspective. Yet they no more attempt to address adults' violence against children than do non-feminist theories. Rather, it becomes apparent that the 'mother–child' relationship is conceived as a fundamental antagonism, an adversarial relationship of two opponents engaged in a tug of war between their respective demands, a 'push–pull dynamic' between two competing 'little-girl parts'. And since all women are potential patients, to whom therapy extends its total 'understanding', no one must be found to be responsible for this war, no one held responsible for any violence they commit.

Instead, therapeutic explanation sets in motion a spiral of infinitely regressing responsibility. For no sooner do we turn to the alleged wrongdoer, the mother who caused all the suffering of a patient like Katie, than this wrongdoer equally gains indulgent therapeutic understanding, becoming a patient herself in turn, since she too was the victim of the actions of another and earlier wrongdoer, namely *her* mother. And so *ad infinitum*. None of them experienced happiness and contentment; they all received insufficient care and attention. And as Adrienne Rich explains the white woman's violence against Black people by pointing out that she too is oppressed by patriarchy – 'Powerless in the institution of marriage, the institution of slavery *did* give her near-absolute power over another human being, her only outlet for rage and frustration being the control she had over that person' – so the violence of 'the mother', her abuse of power in relation to her children, is 'explained' as the product of a superior power: powerless in the institution of patriarchal daughterhood (and marriage), motherhood *did* give her near-absolute power over another human being (her baby), her only outlet for rage and frustration. It is not the mother deciding to enter an unfair tug of war, a battle with her small daughter, a push–pull dynamic with a baby; it is not her deciding irresponsibly to abuse her near-absolute power over a child. The system of motherhood gave it to her – from which apparently we are to infer that she could not but (ab)use it.

If the Women's Therapy Centre in London put their emphasis on mothers' incapability to enter into absolute symbiosis with their baby daughters, discharging these in turn dissatisfied on their path through life (and into motherhood), Nancy Chodorow on the contrary sees the problem precisely in mothers' overpowering and unending symbiosis with their daughters.[50] That is to say, if the issue is to legitimate the wish of adults to demand and receive absolute care and nurturance from others, this wish is projected on to the infinitely needy baby who was never sufficiently satisfied (symbiosed) by her mother. If, on the other hand, the issue is explaining why adult women do not take responsibility for themselves, clinging to unrealistic demands and needs, attention shifts to the small child's attempt to separate and individuate from the mother, who however thwarts this bid for independence through her overprotective and smothering nurturing care. In any case, the wish of the child is unfulfilled but legitimate, the behaviour of the mother illegitimate, the wish of the now adult child still legitimate (because previously unfulfilled), and the behaviour of the erstwhile mother 'responsible' for it.

In either case it is not the real behaviour of the mother or the child which is at issue, but the need or incapacity of the 'child' and a corresponding inadequate and unsatisfying behaviour of the 'mother' as constructed from the perspective of the now adult 'child', said to be responsible for her need and incapacity as an adult. The spiral of regressing responsibility has been set in motion, which legitimates the needs in question of any current patient of therapy and exonerates her from any responsibility for them. For there is no longer any responsibility in the present; there are only 'causes' in the past. This adultocentric perspective, however, this legitimation of non-responsibility, is inherent in object relations theory and ego-psychology in general, as they all project the problems of adults on to infants and their 'mothers': adults' fundamental hostility towards the other, their claims to power and their pleasure in dominance and control over others.

To represent the factual powerlessness of infants as their apparent 'powerful demanding' is to play sleight-of-hand with the concept of power (and with the power of representation). The 'power' of a 'powerfully demanding' baby is a projection by adults to whom the legitimacy of the baby's claim on their care appears as a restriction upon their own search for satisfaction. No child demands powerfully, she demands out of a position of powerlessness. As Eichenbaum and Orbach argue rather casually: 'babies taken into care but given no love and personal attention cannot sustain life – they give up and die.'[51] Apart from the fallacious implication that biological mother equals love and care (however insufficient), while fostering means no love and care, we may assume the point to be the absence of love and care, no matter from what source. In such a case a child may demand and cry as 'powerfully' as she wishes, it does not help in a situation of utter dependence on grown-ups, who alone will decide whether they will look after her or not.

If I question this mechanism of spiralling mother-blaming, I do not thereby deny that children do indeed suffer violence at the hands of adults, including mothers. Nor in addressing the issue of violence against children do I argue that all mothers abuse their children. My point is, rather, that neither psychology nor psychotherapy in any way seriously address the question of adult power over children, that on the contrary, they want to have their cake and eat it – want to claim parental violence on behalf of the (adult) children clients, yet absolve any adult (clients) from responsibility for their own violence. If every client by definition is a victim of her past, there are no acting persons left in the present. Hence therapy is not so much taking side with children as taking side with adult children, that is, clients.

Neither can there be any serious attempt to confront violence if therapy proposes to solve the problem on the patient's part, that is, on the part of the victim of violence. For the victim-patient is either to 'accept' the consequences of violence suffered in childhood by accepting an insatiable neediness as an adult, or else to '[develop] a narrative of self understood as a "biographical accounting" with which she or he feels emotionally comfortable'.[52] The issue, in other words, is neither the patient's behaviour in the present, nor her (or his) actual history, the history of any violence experienced and resistance offered to it: the issue is rewriting that history, and rewriting it not according to any criteria of truth and reality, but of what history the patient may feel most comfortable with. No matter that this precisely does not constitute a way of 'cognitively and emotionally' working through and coming to terms with one's history. Nor does the question arise what 'narrative' or 'account' it is in the first place which is either to be 'accepted' or to be rewritten from a more comfortable point of view – that is, nor is the narrative account of adult patients (in the present) ever problematized *as* the construction of a narrative.

Power, of course, is the real underlying issue, which the therapeutic definition of the 'problem' however does everything to disguise. This means in the first instance not to identify, let alone analyse, power relations, reformulating any power – be it the client's power in her own relationships and her power as the subject of her account, or the therapist's power in the therapy relationship – as powerlessness, all the better to legitimate it. And where power cannot altogether be made invisible, it is naturalized.

As patriarchal sociobiology and its amateur camp-followers attempt to naturalize men's sexual violence through (selective) recourse to an allegedly natural male aggression in the animal world, thus to exonerate men from any responsibility for their violent behaviour, so psychological theories naturalize and legitimate the illegitimate desires of adults – their desire for power and control over other people – through recourse to the alleged 'nature' of children. Such 'naturalization' not only serves to legitimate power, it is itself an exercise of power in relation to this so-called nature, here the animal world and children respectively: control over a discourse about 'others' which these others can neither influence nor determine. They are the power-less objects of the discourse, defenceless victims of theories and allegations, screens for projections by powerful subjects who objectify them.

What object relations theory posits as the infant's heritage (innate or otherwise) in reality is the freely chosen method of a scientific dis-course. Take the description of the infantile fantasy process as defined by Melanie Klein and paraphrased by Eichenbaum and Orbach above, substitute 'scientists', 'theoreticians', 'psychologists' for the original 'infant', transpose into the present tense – and already you have the scientific method: 'For Klein, the instincts sought objects as their aim, rather than pleasure as Freud posited.' It appears that science also seeks objects as its aim (even if some posit the pleasure of research). If the pleasure posited by Freud is what makes a 'drive' a drive, the drive is necessary to disguise the power of the subject of the drive. Science may not be a drive, but like the drive it serves to disguise the power of the subjects of science, that is, of the scientists and theoreticians, the masters and mistresses of the discourse. According to our adaptation of object relations theory, then, theory and science have objects as their aim, that is to say, the objectification of reality – the reality of people, animals and nature whom they make into objects.

'The objects – the people – [are], however, objects of an internal nature rather than the images of the actual people in the [scien-tists'] life. The internal objects [are] part of the heritage that a [scientist] brings into the world along with [science]. Where a [science] [arises] so [does] an image of an object to satisfy it.' Where a desire for the power of theory arises, an object of theory is sure to arise to satisfy it.

Real people [and children, animals and realities] are screens upon which [scientists and theoreticians] [can] project [their] internal fan-tasies. Experiences of people [and other realities] in the world of [the scientist] [only confirm] the experience of the [scientist's] internal object relations. Klein explained the inner fantasy world [science] in terms of the struggle between the two great instincts: libido . . . and aggression. These two instinctual forces [meet] in the individual [science] and [form] the battleground on which the [scientific ego, that is, science] develops.

Moreover, we would argue with both object relations theory and with Freud that neither objects only, nor pleasure alone, but objects *and* pleasure are the aim – that the corollary of the object is the pleasure of objectification, and the corollary of pleasure is the power over the 'objects'. For the object only exists under the power of the subject, the pleasure of the subject only in its power over the object. The real aim is the subject's pleasure of power: its power as subject over the object.

So powerful is this method, so successful in empowering the self as subject and opposing the whole world as object, that almost no one today any longer seems to take offence at it. We seem to find it quite normal that not only scientists, but all of us walk the earth like the Kleinian infant with a screen in front of our eyes, on to which we project our own fantasies. We are most likely still to take offence only if it happens to be we who are being used as a screen, when of course we mean to be the projectors. Object relations theory is the apex of a development of psychological theory which also in its other manifestations ceaselessly posits this fundamental power relationship – the conception of self as subject in relation to an object world – as 'normal' and 'human', as 'natural' and given and hence unchangeable. Object relations theory is the apex only in as much as it explicitly names what could not be named more clearly, namely that everybody and everything and all may legitimately be made into an object. And it is of significance in so far as feminists in particular have begun to select it as their preferred psychological theory.

Where once there existed a feminist critique of psychology and a feminist critique of objectification, a critique precisely in terms of power and power relations, there now exists a 'feminist' legitimation of power effected through objectification, propagated by psychology. With women gaining access to positions of power in patriarchal society, with women's growing experience of power and the pleasure of power, there apparently is a growing interest also in legitimating women's claims to power and in undermining the critique of power. Apparently we no longer have a critique of power as such, only of the fact that power used to be the prerogative of men. Apparently we no longer have a critique of objectification and the concomitant subject-ification, but only of the fact that the roles of subject and object used to be distributed according to gender. Hence the term 'empower-ment' and the project of self-empowerment increasingly feature in feminist discourse, replacing the goal of deconstructing the power structure.[53] Equality apparently no longer holds the promise of an end to oppression, but of equal access to the roles of domination and oppression.

Thus we may witness a veritable explosion of 'object worlds', no longer the exclusive prerogative of science (or men): 'A person lives in a multiple object world – in the internal, largely unconscious object world of their psyche which has laid its foundation in the past, in childhood, and in the external largely conscious world of daily life.'[54] That grown-up people view the world like newborn infants, (mis)taking the projection of their fantasies for reality, their 'imaging of the world'[55] for the world, is no longer the problem to be analysed: it is the assumption from which we start and with which we want to stay. Not only the imagination (or the psyche) produces an 'object world', with the inherent problem of the subjectivity of the 'arrogant perceiver'[56] that created it; the world itself, the consciously experienced world of daily life, 'is' an object world. Thus the real world has successfully been made to disappear. There is no reality any longer to consider, there are only the 'internal' and the 'external' object worlds – internal to me, and external of me.

Ego-psychology, or My relationship and I

This demise of the world as reality not only leaves us with a multitude of personal object worlds; like the big bang, it also sets a myriad new 'objects' into the world(s). While on the one hand people (everyone except for the subject) now count among the objects, it is also the case that many non-human and inanimate 'objects' assume the role of subject and take action.

Thus we have seen a veritable cast of actors populating Katie's relationship, taking over directing the play: the events, the needs and feelings, old unsatisfied feelings as well as a little-girl part (in the order of their appearance). The reality of the present becomes the stage for a drama from the past. Katie on the one hand is the centre of the stage, the pivot around which the action turns, yet she is not a protagonist, since she is not herself a *dramatis persona*. Like the princess of fairy tales or the heroine of the bourgeois novel she does not participate in the action, but is passively enduring, suffering and waiting – victim and object of the actions of the *dramatis personae*. Yet she has another role beyond the stage, which tends to conflate with that of her therapist: they both are in the audience watching the drama, which in turn they describe, narrating its plot. In this function of re-presenting the alleged drama as narrative lies the enormous power of the subject – creating a reality as the Lord in the beginning created a world, from scratch and according to his wish and will.

This act of narration, of objectifying and representing the drama on stage, also fulfils the famous postulate of the splitting of the ego into subject and object. In order to become a subject able to make other people into objects, so the theory, the self must learn to conceive of itself as a potential 'object'. Since the growing infant must learn to consider the mother as 'not-I', as not in fact part of the infant's own self, she must learn, not that mother is mother and self is 'I', but to perceive herself as a separate and coherent body entity.[1] According to Lacan this happens during the 'mirror stage', when the child, directing her gaze at herself in the mirror, comprehends herself as an object of sight. Thus the child simultaneously is the subject of her gazing and comprehending, and the object of her own gaze and consciousness.

While this splitting of the ego is considered an important step in the infant's development to a conscious person, we may wonder what is the significance of the development in the modern therapeutic subject towards perceiving itself exclusively as an object. For the patient describes her history as victim of the events without apparently any consciousness of her role as subject. Her focus, like that of her therapist, remains fixed on the stage of the narrated drama, where she figures as the principal object, while her role as narrating subject, as interpreter of the events and as author of her own understanding, never becomes a topic of the therapeutic discussion. While this may indeed be a product of the therapy relationship and the collusive roles of therapist and patient, such an understanding of the self and such a method of representing one's history are by no means exclusive to the therapy context. Representing oneself as the object of circumstances and the victim of events – that is, describing oneself as if from the perspective of one's own therapist – is, as we have seen, a technique of wider application. It generally serves to hide the subject's power and to suppress its role as agent. Yet psychological theory and psychotherapeutic practice have had their share both in propagating and legitimating it as a commonsense method of self-perception.

In her brief overview over the different psychological and psychoanalytic theories, Nancy Chodorow writes: 'The interpretation of psychic structure that stresses the mental personality as object rather than subject is fundamental to the development of psychoanalytic ego psychology, the school that has come to dominate the American psychoanalytic tradition.'[2] She criticizes the determinism inherent in psychoanalysis which, in postulating drives and psychic 'apparatuses', reduces the 'acting agent' to a 'behaving organism'.[3] While the 'cultural school' of psychoanalysis has also criticized this determinism, it only replaces, Chodorow argues, a biological determinism by a cultural determinism: although it is culture and social life that are seen to determine the development of the child, 'the person in this view', too, 'is no longer an agent, has no way to work on or create that which is internalized.'[4] In Chodorow's view, object relations theory remedies all these shortcomings, postulating that while the child is indeed being influenced by culture, she in turn works on the 'culture' she internalizes by means of her fantasy. Not entering the psychic system unmediated, culture thus loses its determining role: 'Cultural school psychoanalysts are right that the outside world affects the inside. But this influence is mediated through fantasy, introjection and projection, ambivalence, conflict, substitution, reversal, distortion, splitting, association, compromise, denial, and repression.'[5]

Note the array of means by which this input from the world outside is 'worked' on, and which constitute the self's most impressive proof of subjecthood. Although in this theory, too, people have innate drives, these too are not as absolutely determining as they are for Freudians, nor does the pleasure principle rule supreme: 'People have innate erotic and aggressive energies. Infants, as psychoanalysis shows, are sexual. But people do not naturally seek release of tension from physiological drives or use their object-relations in the search for this release. Rather, they manipulate and transform drives in the course of attaining and retaining relationships.'[6]

That is to say, people (or infants) are not exclusively being manipulated by drives; they in turn manipulate their drives, making *them* the objects of *their* action. Whether this also solves the problem of regarding people as objects and as (products of) psychic systems remains to be seen. What matters to Chodorow is that the emphasis on object relations necessarily postulates the subject, the 'agentic subject'[7] – a subject constituting itself through objectification. The fact that it is this subject which in the course of its objectifications also makes itself into an object – regarding in particular its own subjectivity, its actions and feelings, as products independent of itself – to her remains outshone by its role as an 'active self'.

One of the most important 'objects' which, in creating its object world, the active subject calls into being is the discursive object 'the relationship'. As we have seen already in the case of Katie's relationship, it takes three to make a couple: myself, the other, and the relationship. As object relations theory moreover makes abundantly clear, the relationship is of considerably greater importance than is the partner. This corresponds to the commonsense understanding of relationships, that is, the 'personal' or 'private' relationship of two: Katie does not so much become dependent on Pete, as on the relationship. Another person, by contrast, constitutes a fundamental problem for the subject and for its relationship: you cannot do anything with a real man or woman, cannot change them, cannot determine their behaviour – unless it be by force; that is to say, you are simply at the mercy of their self-determination, possibly even their own aspiration to the status of subject. Hence it is best to accept the other as a given object in the object world, and set to work instead on the relationship.

As many commentators on social life have observed, we are in love usually with love. Thus our desire for a relationship is usually a desire for relation, while our passionate involvement is an involvement with the relationship: it is the relationship we want. It is the relationship that we make demands on and have expectations of, which 'it' does not always meet; it is the relationship that we fight for, that we are trying to keep, that we do not wish to give up. It is for the relationship, too, that we seek a partner. Although another person is a necessary prerequisite for a relationship, that person is often its principal impediment, the obstacle in our way of making it a happy relationship and realizing its true potential. If only the other were as we imagine them in our dreams, if only the other conformed to our happiest fantasies, if only the other were truly an object which does not periodically fall out of its role, then our happiness would be complete, and the relationship would no longer be a problem: it would fulfil all my needs, taking its gentle yet passionate course, its safe and yet spontaneous development, its continuous yet alternating path full of unforeseen (only positive) surprises. The waves of my needs continually reforming themselves would ensure that the relationship is never boring, lacking, or full of emptiness,[8] for we – my relationship and I – would be having a perfect partnership, a harmonious complementarity: between my needs and it fulfilling them. It is the same partnership, by the way, which I always wanted to have with my mother, but which never succeeded because of her.

The problem is that we make our fantasies and object worlds with the material of reality – that we use people for them and shape events with them. If our power and violence are not sufficient to do so, it may lead to a great deal of unhappiness, discontent and frustration with life which never properly submits to fantasy. Hence there exists a large therapy industry today which deals with this misery of relationships. The therapy, however, has the same theory which originally created the problem, its empirical survey of the facts not only reflecting the problem, but decisively helping to construct and maintain it.

This may be aggravated in the case of some feminist therapy, which on account of the gender identity of therapist and client rests on a veritable symbiosis of problem and therapy. While Margrit Brückner, for instance, identifies as a major problem of women's attitude to relationships their '*powerful fantasy to change others* without a concept of self-change'[9] (my emphasis), that is, exactly what feminists have criticized in men's desire to control women,[10] this insight, even if quoted by therapists or psychologists tends to disappear again as soon we get to the female patient and her relationship. What tends to stay, rather, is the axiomatic rule that the client's relation to her relationship is primary, while any consequences it may have for other people (that is, the partners in question) are hardly worth mentioning, all the less so if the therapy's feminism rests on the assumption that these 'others' in any case are men who for centuries have been oppressing women in relationships.

Hence the trademark of a great deal of feminist therapy is that it psychologizes a political analysis. Thus it tends to attribute to women a centuries-old tradition of self-restriction, selflessness and self-sacrifice, as well as a special ability to take on relationship work – without a worry, it seems, that this exactly reproduces the patriarchal definition of the feminine sex-role. Far from seeing it as the construction of ideal 'femininity', the theory pronounces it historical fact. While patriarchal ideologues at least did and do have a notion of women's actual inadequacy in fulfilling this ideal – whence the countless measures from social control to medical intervention to coerce them to approximate to it more closely – many women and feminist therapists today seem to believe in the total congruity of attribution and reality.

They do so despite the fact that women freely report their own acts of coercion, speaking openly of their own claims to power – how they want to ' "win" the old struggle to be loved',[11] 'to change another person through the power of her will',[12] or make other people do things: 'I made him tell me that he loved me, and I made him give me a hug . . . It never would have happened if I hadn't forced him.'[13] Yet despite this remarkable manifestation of the female self, pursuing its

interests with determination and tenacity, with will-power and per-
sistence – powerfully working on its fantasy of its 'relationship' while
instrumentalizing others in the process – therapists and their clients
unwaveringly stick to their theory of the non-existent female self.
'Women . . . sacrifice themselves for others in their jobs, they are
eager to give up their own interests in the service of their man and
children', they are 'coerced to be selfless', all leading to 'self-sacrifice,
self-devaluation and martyrdom'.[14]

The general misery of relationships is seen as the 'result of a
pathological [social] gender arrangement', in which 'activity and passivity, devotion to others and self-assertion, dependence and independence, satisfaction of instincts and caring for others have been torn
asunder and attributed respectively to the two sexes.'[15] That is to say,
it is taken for a fact that women devote themselves to others while
men indulge in being and asserting themselves, that women are
dependent while men are independent, that women care for others
while men indulge their instincts and drives. Women are attributed
even a 'need to submit',[16] and an inability to act 'self-protectively'.[17]
And if the female self has not been totally destroyed, what is left of it
is exceedingly fragile: 'Your self-esteem is critically low',[18] every little
event in the relationship may suffice to '[deal] a serious blow to her
fragile self-image',[19] or even to '[shatter] her self-confidence'.[20] As
'members of the oppressed group' women have 'internalized and
accepted the prejudices of the dominant group against themselves', as
a consequence suffering from actual 'self-contempt' and 'self-denial',[21]
if not indeed from a total 'loss of self'.[22]

The feminist analysis of social power relations and women's collective oppression by men is applied on the basis of gender identity to
individual women and men, so that women by definition are victims,
men by definition culprits – members of the group of the oppressed
and members of the group of the oppressors. An analysis of the specific
situation in terms of its agents and their actions thus becomes superfluous, gender identity giving us the necessary information. The
political reality of structural oppression is turned into a sociobiological
disease, while the real and varying consequences of oppression for
women in their different situations are dissolved into the shared
damage of a gender 'character'. Hence there is no longer any need to
change or even just to recognize power relations, since these seem to
exist above all in people's psychic structure rather than in reality.

Starting from the unquestioned truth that women are selfless and loving, therapists and their clients set about to heal them of this illness, teaching them and learning 'how we can change and get well'.[23]

The symbiosis between therapist and client considered to be particularly feminist shows itself in the readiness of the former not to exempt herself from the problems of the latter: on account of her own experience as a woman she has a particular understanding of her client. This means less that the feminist method of collective consciousness-raising is applied to the therapeutic context. Rather, the therapeutic method is in the process of informing also the personal politics of the women's liberation movement, what Janice Raymond calls 'therapism',[24] replacing the political understanding of collective consciousness-raising.

Referring to one's own experience as a woman thus tends to signal a special authority to 'understand' and legitimate another woman's experience – 'understanding' usually meaning the unreflected recognition that the other has the experience, rather than a particular analysis of that experience. That is to say, it seems to suffice to have 'had' the experience; its interpretation no longer matters. On the contrary, the sheer congruity of having had the 'same' experience tends to confirm the other woman in her understanding of her experience – confirm, in other words, that there is nothing else to understand or comprehend. Which is why the experience of the one tends not particularly to help the other come to terms with her experience. Yet it is increasingly this unconditional 'understanding' that women are looking for in turning to other women, as opposed to any support in gaining a better understanding, or changing their initial understanding, of their experiences.

The question remains how the relatively accessible insight into women's desire for power and their corresponding behaviour – their desire to change other people, to manipulate and instrumentalize them in the interest of their own conceptions – can be squared with the unwavering belief in women's selflessness. It can be squared, it turns out, by means of discursive reconstruction, by radically reformulating the situation and its actual relations. This means in the first instance to reformulate what in reality is a relation as instead a thing, a matter, an object. Hence a relationship no longer is two people relating to each other, a constantly changing process depending on the actions of the people involved. It becomes a *thing* of which I can have certain expectations that I know it would be illegitimate to have of another *person*. Thus I can want to have a relationship, whereas wanting to have a person would be suspiciously close to wanting to own and rule that person. I can make the relationship my need, whereas needing another person might make it clear that this means using that person for my need.

As 'our common cause', the relationship becomes the screen that hides my self-interest: it is not in my name I am making demands, but in the name of 'our relationship'. Not only does this look unselfish, but in being 'willing to take more responsibility than [the partner] for initiating the relationship and keeping it going',[25] we think moreover that we are taking the sacrificial part, carrying the greater share of the 'work'. Above all, it allows me to shift the identification of any problems away from the politics of personal behaviour – my own as well as my partner's – and towards the common undertaking, as problems 'in our relationship' if talking to the partner, or problems 'in my relationship' if talking to the therapist.

Some therapists too recognize in this shift an attempt, however inappropriate, to gain control or indeed 'mastery over the problems':[26]

> It is true for all of us that when an emotionally painful event occurs, and we tell ourselves that it is our fault, we are actually saying that we have control of it: if we change, the pain will stop . . . By blaming ourselves, we hold on to the hope that we will be able to figure out what we are doing wrong and correct it, thereby controlling the situation and stopping the pain.[27]

Since from the beginning neither my own behaviour nor that of my partner is up for discussion, but on the contrary, an 'event occurs' in the relationship which emotionally hurts me, this will lead not to an analysis of behaviour but to a diagnosis of the relationship. And since we also start from the axiomatic assumption of women's selflessness especially in relationships, this does not lead to a clarification of the woman's own illegitimate claims to power or her own problematical behaviour, but simply to a method of giving up fruitless or ineffective 'patterns' of behaviour as 'unhealthy'. Robin Norwood explains the goal of her therapeutic book as follows: 'Its purpose is specific: to help women with destructive patterns of relating to men recognize that fact, understand the origin of those patterns [in childhood, where else?], and gain the tools for changing their lives.'[28] Her own experience convinced Norwood how unhealthy these patterns are:

I know this only too well, having been a woman who loved too much
most of my life until the toll to my physical and emotional health was
so severe that I was forced to take a hard look at my pattern of relating
to men. I have spent the last several years working hard to change that
pattern. They have been the most rewarding years of my life.[29]

On no account must we question our own wish for power or
recognize our own interest in controlling others, say, so as to give
them up for political reasons. Rather, a 'pattern's' use is being compared to its price (toll) and found not to be at all cost-effective; or the
use of a new pattern compared to the use of an old pattern and found
to be considerably more 'rewarding'. Whereas changing your pattern
of relating means 'redirecting your loving attention away from your
obsession with a man and toward your own recovery and your own
life'.[30] No more wasting of loving attention, in other words, which is
not spent on your own account.

  The practical thing about a pattern of relating is that it, too, is a
thing, and in fact something which we have once surreptitiously been
given like smuggled goods slipped into your bag. In no way is it a
personal behaviour which, if I want to change it, I can change by
behaving differently. For my behaviour is not really my behaviour,
but the product of a pattern of behaviour. It turns out according to the
pattern as knitting does according to the knitting pattern. Exchanging
one pattern for another does not require a change in my behaviour,
but a therapy that enlightens me about the origins of the pattern and
how it came to be in my baggage. We already know, mother has
packed it in there: 'Typically, you come from a dysfunctional home in
which your emotional needs were not met. Having received little real
nurturing yourself, you try to fill this unmet need vicariously . . .'[31]
'To grow up as female in this society and in such a family can generate
some predictable patterns.'[32]

The fact alone of being a person in this society, having been born
and grown up in a family (for where is the non-dysfunctional one?) is
reason enough to develop a pathology. Being a woman and the
daughter of a mother, however, makes everything twice as bad. While
the conditions of life and socialization of girls and women and the
power relations in the patriarchal family would indeed be issues for a
political critique, this is neither about politics nor political change: it
is about pathologizing yourself in the first instance, so as to 'make your
recovery your first priority'[33] in the second instance.

One reason for this is that our critique of men's behaviour and generally of the relationship between men and women in patriarchy must not go too far, so as not fundamentally to threaten that relationship. As an individual woman may not want to separate from a violent man because she does not want to give up 'the relationship', so many women and therapists do not wish to part with a conception of 'the relationship' which is based on the pleasure and power of the subject, because they want that relationship too much. This means that neither our partners' coercive or violent behaviour – even where they are men and thus certified 'oppressors' – nor our own behaviour must be seriously put into question, neither their understanding of relationships be analysed, nor our own.

Hence, rather than questioning the relationship in its conception, we diagnose its state: it is good or no longer so good, it is or 'is not meeting our needs',[34] it is lacking in love, 'unstable',[35] or 'isn't working', and sometimes it breaks apart or 'dissolves'[36] or 'fails'.[37] Thus we may even become afraid of relationships, 'afraid to get involved – I mean, it's nothing but pain every time'.[38] This saves us from asking whether we would not indeed be right to be afraid of a particular partner, one who causes us pain and behaves violently, or conversely, whether my pain and my hurt are the result of the partner's violent action or whether they are in fact, as in Katie's case, feelings of my own, originating in my claims to power. By explaining instead that it is 'the relationship' which causes us pain and the 'event' which is hurting us, we exonerate all possible suspects, thus keeping them available for the role of partner in the relationship. Therapy may help us exchange either a behaviour pattern or possibly the odd partner, to keep the relationship healthy.

Thus therapists as well as their clients stick with the assumption that on account of patriarchy women's selves have been mutilated and damaged – that women really have denied, given up or lost their selves. This means not only claiming the collective and cumulative historical suffering of the gender of women on behalf of individual women – so to speak as an advance credit in suffering or an accumulated capital of personal innocence. It also means overlooking the fact that even an internalized self-contempt meets with the emphatic resistance of the self, and that it is this contradiction, rather than the 'loss' of self, which creates the psychological problem. Yet it seems more important to deny women's resistance than to regard it as a sign of their still existing selves – so that we may continue to consider them reduced to half-people, who first have to find their other halves or heal and restore their damaged selves.

This may appear advantageous to women, since not having a self they automatically are beyond any suspicion of having any self-interest, let alone any claims to power. Yet it necessarily means denying women's political will, collectively as well as individually not taking women seriously. Like Alice Walker and other feminists, we shall instead start from the radical proposition that women are and always have been full human beings, that our behaviour shows our competence in surviving: our ability to make the best of limited possibilities and to act responsibly even within restricted conditions. That this is not all we wish for women, or how things should stay for women, should not need emphasizing, and is reason for feminist critique and political work. The point here is that we should take women seriously, and despite oppression attribute ourselves a self as well as a will, competence as well as ability.

This would mean, as Jessica Benjamin emphasizes, not to 'idealize the oppressed',[39] or in other words, to give up mistaking patriarchal attribution for reality, and to recognize women's selves as well as their self-interest. It means acknowledging women's responsibility for their own decisions and actions, even if they choose to realize their selves according to the principle of self-interest, even if they decide not to refuse and fight power but to claim it. And it would mean taking a political perspective not only on women's behaviour, but also on a psychological theory which propagates the irresponsibility of the 'mental personality', by seeing it as the product of a psychological apparatus rather than as the responsibility of the person. And it would mean questioning a feminist therapy that takes gender identity as its basis and mistakes 'great understanding' of clients for motherly love.

If women and feminist therapists, despite everything, continue to disguise the self as well as the self-interest of the female subject, we must consider it political intention. To speak of 'self-negation' might indeed be appropriate – not because women actually dismiss their own needs, but in as much as the therapeutic discourse negates not just the subject's claims to power, but the self as such. The 'great understanding' which Birgit Rommelspacher sees women 'extend towards men and their psychological situation',[40] thus exonerating them from responsibility, is even exceeded by the great understanding which women extend towards themselves and their own psychological situation, and which 'motherly' therapists show towards their clients. Thus we may replace 'he' by 'she' to describe the latter: 'The internal view extinguishes the responsibility of the perpetrator. Yet the perpetrator must be called to account, in so far as what [she] did was "in [her] power", in so far as [she] had alternative ways of behaving at [her] disposal.'[41]

Since women's behaviour is rarely analysed, much less the alternatives of behaving differently, women are rarely called to account. Rather, their behaviour is viewed with such 'generous empathy' as Rommelspacher sees women showing to men's behaviour: 'The view of the individual from a 'motherly' perspective tends to minimize personal responsibility . . . the 'motherly' view leads to the psychic disempowerment, emasculation [*Depotenzierung*] and infantilization of the [woman]. She understands [her] completely and forgives [her]. [She] couldn't help it. All [her] misdeeds are only expressions of [her] problems.'[42] This 'motherly' view is produced also in the therapizing account of oneself in which the self figures as the victim of circumstances and the object of other people's agency – where the disempowerment and infantilization of the woman (in the object status) goes along with the empowerment of discursive objects to the status of agents, and where both together constitute the subject's supreme self-empowerment. The purpose of this 'motherly' view of oneself, as with the 'motherly' view of men, is to exonerate from responsibility for their actions those who therefore must clearly have been perceived to have responsibility and to have been acting.

Even in the case of Jessica Benjamin, who in her book *The Bonds of Love* has so clearly analysed the relation of dominance between subject and object, we may see how 'power', 'domination' or 'gender polarity' ultimately become autonomous things – not just a 'system involving the participation of those who submit to power as well as those who exercise it',[43] but also the ultimate agents or *dramatis personae*: 'Domination ultimately deprives both subjugator and subjugated of recognition. Gender polarity deprives women of their subjectivity and men of another to recognize them.'[44]

Turning a process and a relation into a thing – a relation whose asymmetry had been the major theme of the book – makes domination and power (like 'the relationship') into a 'system' with two 'participants'. As the superordination of the state over the citizens establishes 'equality' among them, so the construction of a discursive object such as the 'relationship' or 'domination' establishes an abstract meta-level superordinated to the process or relation in question, representing the 'participants' as 'equals' in their subordination to it. Thus it is no longer the subjugator who subjugates, or men who subjugate women, there is 'subjugation' and 'submission'. This may then as easily be represented linguistically as the action of the one or the other 'participant': he subjugates her, or she submits. Although the sudden multiplying of possibilities may make one lose one's orientation in the whole ladder of levels, so that the woman submits (assuming she does) no longer even to the man or her subjugator, but to 'power' or 'dominance'.

While an analysis which includes women's agency would indeed be desirable – as it would for instance allow us to distinguish between their resistance to power and domination on the one hand and their entering into a power struggle, however unequal it may be, on the other – this is not what Benjamin achieves simply by linguistically making women into agents. Rather, it seems that Benjamin, too, ultimately feels the need to exonerate dominators collectively as well as individually by turning 'domination' discursively into a thing, a given even if possibly changeable phenomenon from which both dominators and the dominated in their respective ways have to suffer.

As white moralists of the past tried to persuade white slave traders and owners that slavery ultimately was damaging to the white soul, and as some feminists today try to persuade men that oppressing women is ultimately dissatisfying for their own sexuality, so Benjamin argues that the subjugator deprives himself of a worthy other to recognize him. In fact she says that 'domination' deprives him of this possibility of being recognized by the other, and that 'gender polarity' deprives men of worthy others whose recognition might mean something to them. But the point is that her concern is with the powerful and dominant. Hence they must first of all be exonerated, so that we may then try to talk them out of practising slavery, dominance and oppression, and talk them out of it with their interests in mind: it is ultimately better for them too, ultimately they only have to gain – a pure soul, a more satisfying sexuality, or a worthy other who will recognize them.

Thus if violence or domination are to be given up at all, it is not because of any insight into what they mean for those dominated and oppressed – any acknowledgement of injustice or commitment to justice. It is because it ultimately does not benefit the subjects of domination, because according to the criteria of the analysis it is not in their self-interest. For the analysis assumes that a pure soul is ultimately of greater benefit than is the exploitation of slaves, that a satisfying sexuality is a greater pleasure than the pleasure of power over a 'sex object', and that recognition from a woman is more desirable than subjugating her. Thus it does not lead to any greater clarity if we talk about power and dominance as if they were phenomena in which somebody vaguely participates – if that participation is not analysed in terms of the power of agency and agents and in terms of actions and their consequences. If a change of perspective from the agent to the victim – 'he dominates her' – can equally yield a sentence 'she is dominated by him' or 'she submits to him', we have a linguistics in which 'he steals her handbag' is equivalent to 'she gives him her handbag.'

We are already familiar with this logic from a general public discourse in which the observation that 'men oppress women' has led to the conclusion that 'women allow men to oppress them.' Thus it neither contributes to our understanding of sexual violence, even less shows any, to talk of the man and woman 'involved' or even 'affected' by it,[45] as it cannot come out of a serious concern about racism to speak of white people (presumably as well as Black people) being 'confronted' by it. But since there is no shortage of publicly available insight, we have to see such discursive strategies for what they are, namely obscurantist manoeuvres in our own interest. Once again the discursive institution of a level of abstraction superordinated to the actual agents – the 'motherly' view from above – serves at the crucial moment to make even the 'agentic self' into an object and product of systemic mechanisms.

Thus Benjamin, too, leads her active agents into the hurricane of superior powers: the 'interplay between love and domination'.[46] She explores 'how domination is anchored in the hearts of the dominated',[47] and how domination comes into being: 'domination and submission result from a breakdown of the necessary tension between self-assertion and mutual recognition that allows self and other to meet as sovereign equals.'[48] Nobody dominates, nobody subjugates, above all nobody makes any decision to do so: domination 'results', and it results from a breakdown in the necessary tension between self-assertion and mutual recognition. Nobody unbalances this balance of a tense mutuality, nobody decides to be self-assertive and to deny recognition to the other. For nobody exists other than in the symmetrical equal participation, the equality of being subordinated to tension and balance. 'Mutual regulation breaks down', 'attunement fails', 'the fine balance of mutual recognition goes awry.'[49] Nobody makes possible an encounter between self and other as sovereign equals, say by meeting and recognizing the other as an equal; the necessary tension 'allows' self and other to meet.

Hence Benjamin's analysis, despite her embrace of theories which favour the active self, does not ultimately lead to an understanding, that is, an analysis of agency, of the will and decisions of persons. Nor does her attempt to break through the confines of a subject–object relationship, her sketch of a possible 'intersubjectivity', succeed in leading out of the 'vicious cycle'[50] of domination and the subject–object relationship. For her concepts of 'mutuality' and 'being with' – also known as 'togetherness' and 'sharing' – are based on the fundamental presupposition of the subject's self-interest and the resulting opposition and struggle of relationship. The possible space for an encounter between subjects consequently is the precariously balanced equilibrium between two opposed and competing self-interests. And even if mutual 'recognition' is the central factor in her construction of 'intersubjectivity', the recognition I receive from the other remains my gain, while my recognizing of the other is the price I have to pay for it. We are on familiar territory, the way to the Other.

The starting point for Benjamin is Hegel's conception of the self: 'In order to exist for oneself, one has to exist for another. It would seem there is no way out of this dependency.'[51] While it is obvious why this might be so in the case of an infant, it is not quite so obvious why it should also be true of adults – why in particular, it should become the chief problem of existence to exist 'for oneself'. All the more so since with ego and super-ego, unconscious and consciousness and consciousness about consciousness, the self seems to have been attributed enough instances so that one of them could take on the useful function of reassuring the self of its existence. My point, however, is not to argue for the self's self-sufficiency so as to liberate it from its 'dependency' as a social being; my point is, rather, that the conception of a self which needs to exist 'for itself', and which experiences its sociality as a dependency on others, is already based on the conception of the subject and the subject–object relationship.

Admittedly, Benjamin as ever is concerned about the independence of the 'active self' in relationship, a self which in her view even as an infant neither needs first to extract itself from a postulated total symbiosis of being one (with the mother) so as to enter into individuated isolation, nor first to come out of the cocoon of an original total internal subjectivity in order to enter gradually into relationship.[52] Yet we are less than convinced when she comments as follows on Winnicott's considerations of how the active self establishes its objects in the object world:

> Winnicott presents the idea that in order to be able to 'use' the object we first have to 'destroy' it. He distinguishes between two dimensions of experience: *relating* to the object and *using* the object. (These terms can be troublesome, for Winnicott uses them quite in the opposite sense that we might in ordinary speech: 'using' here does not mean instrumentalizing or demeaning, but being able to creatively benefit from another person ... 'Relating' refers to the experience of the 'subject as an isolate', in which the object is merely a 'phenomenon of the subject'.)[53]

The terms may indeed be troublesome if we wish them to mean the opposite of what they usually mean, but they are quite untroublesome in revealing what is at issue, namely the subject's exploitation of the object. While 'using' indeed does not as such mean 'demeaning', it does mean 'instrumentalizing', since it is by no means the case that we instrumentalize only what we have already mentally demeaned: usually we instrumentalize precisely what we recognize as being of value and use. Thus the subject, far from 'demeaning' the object, precisely perceives it in its richness, from which it wants to 'creatively profit'. Rather, it is demeaning for a person to be turned into an object and, creatively or otherwise, to be used.

And if the vital shift from 'relating' to 'using' in this transition of the infant's learning means to separate 'the object' out of its internal fantasy relation to itself and to comprehend it as existing in reality,[54] this nevertheless does mean, in Winnicott's representation, to regard 'the object' *as* an object in the object world, all the better to be able to use it: '[The subject] can only "use" the object when he perceives it "as an external phenomenon, not as a projective entity".'[55] And let us not forget that these 'objects' principally are people. Benjamin further explains: 'Winnicott is saying that the object must be destroyed *inside* in order that we know it to have survived *outside*; thus we can recognize it as not subject to our mental control.'[56] Many indeed seem to manage this step in early infancy, recognizing that it takes more than mental control, namely active violence in 'external' reality, to keep the 'object' under control.

Hence Benjamin, too, recognizes that any 'mutuality' and 'sharing' of equal subjects can be achieved only through a balanced struggle for power, a struggle in which neither achieves victory, and which hovers, so to speak, in a draw: 'The paradox of recognition, the need for acknowledgement that turns us back to dependence on the other, brings about a struggle for control.'[57] The encounter is a meeting of adversaries, a match between two approximately 'equal' contestants: 'To transcend the experience of duality [of subject and object], so that both partners are equal, requires a notion of mutuality and sharing. In the intersubjective interaction both partners are active; it is not a reversible union of opposites (a doer and a done-to).'[58] It almost looks as if Benjamin here is arguing against her own (earlier?) understanding of women as non-subjects and passive recipients of what others do to them, trying to convince herself of women's subjectivity. Yet, while a struggle is indeed an encounter in which both partners are active, that is, both are 'doers', this does not mean that therefore the doing of the one is no longer doing anything to the other. Rather, it seems that here the consequences of any doing (the done-to) disappear from view, are neutralized and made to disappear in the 'mutuality' of doing.

> The identification with the other person occurs through the sharing of similar states, rather than through reversal. 'Being with' breaks down the opposition between powerful and helpless, active and passive; it counteracts the tendency to objectify and deny recognition to those weaker or different – to the other. It forms the basis of compassion, what Milan Kundera calls 'co-feeling', the ability to share feelings and intentions without demanding control, to experience sameness without obliterating difference.[59]

We may ask from whose perspective shared states are judged to be shared and similar, and whether the experience of a state can be shared at all; whether to draw the fallacious inference that states are 'shared' is not precisely to obliterate difference, namely the difference that the other is indeed another and not the 'same' as me.

Nor is it the case that we objectify only what is 'weaker' and 'different', for objectification says nothing about the positive or negative quality of the 'object'. It is no less an objectification if we value a person highly, that is, as similar to or even the same as ourselves. Nor does it mean to deny 'recognition' if I judge the other to be weak and different: rather it is my 'recognition' of the other as weak and different.

As we have seen already elsewhere, the obligatory coupling into 'sharing' and 'being with' only serves to obfuscate the real relations so as to prevent an analysis of the actions of the individual partners. 'Sharing' and 'togetherness' not only linguistically overcome the oppositions 'between powerful and helpless, active and passive', they force the experiences of two people to be subsumed under a 'shared' experience, their variedness as people to be subsumed under the sameness of shared states. And even if here it is the eye of the theory and the theoretical discourse which construct this 'sharing' from 'above', it is no less a problem when it is the one or the other partner or both who construct(s) it. In that case, it is not only a matter of the violence of a discourse of power, but of the violence of one partner towards the other.

Hence it is neither a surprise that this fictitious 'sharing' produces no more than the old and notorious one-sided efforts of the subject, 'compassion' and 'co-feeling' – good deeds towards the other. As the conception of self and the other produces a 'humaneness' where 'humans' are everybody apart from myself, so compassion is the classic phenomenon of benevolence and charity. Not only are these forms of patronization and condescension – and an insult to the reality of the suffering (or 'passion') of another person – it is also a major self-deception if we believe that we really can co-feel the experience of others, and that this would in any way be helping them. A virtue in the eyes of the compassionate and detested by those who become its target, compassion satisfies the moral needs of the compassionate co-feelers rather than the needs of those 'with' whom they are feeling.

Instead, it would suffice to understand the other's suffering; there is no necessity to 'feel' it. For understanding the suffering of others, what has caused it and what the consequences are for them, would enable me to support them in their struggle to deal with the consequences and to liberate themselves from their cause. If on the other hand I am suffering and feeling 'with' them, I usually suffer so much myself in the process that no energy remains for any further support. In particular, however, it is a form of violence and an exploitation of the other's suffering and experience to reclaim it metaphorically as my own. Thus it borders on cynicism, for instance, when Western European women claim that the rapes of women in former Yugoslavia 'are rapes of ourselves',[60] that they constitute 'an international crisis for Women – not only Muslim women victims . . . but *all women*'.[61]

However, this linguistically enforced 'sharing' of experience and this rhetorical assertion of co-feeling are not the only forms of violence in Benjamin's scenario of 'mutuality'. For a struggle between two opponents by definition is violence and counter-violence. The 'struggle for recognition'[62] is not so much a struggle for this discursive object 'recognition', but a struggle to *be recognized by* the other; the struggle for love a struggle to be loved, the struggle of relationship a struggle to get the other to relate to me. That is to say, it is a struggle to determine another's actions towards me – not to leave it to the other to decide how to act. In this struggle I am using all available means of coercion, manipulation and blackmail: 'I was determined to make him love me back',[63] 'I made him tell me that he loved me, and I made him give me a hug . . . It never would have happened if I hadn't forced him.' To attempt to involve the other in a 'system of mutual dependency' means to instrumentalize the other's self-interest in my own, to use the other's desire for my recognition to fulfil my own desire for their recognition. It presupposes the self-interest of the other and imputes to the other the same political will to 'creatively profit' from others.

This explains why even in its most explicitly negative form of a quarrel and a fight the struggle fulfils its main purpose, namely to direct the other's actions towards myself. It explains why the subject perceives even in violence against itself a form of recognition, albeit a negative one: the other's recognition of the self as the other's opponent in struggle, and thereby the recognition of a relationship. And so we arrive at the most astounding revelation, namely that even an enemy is an adequate opponent, even an adversary a suitable antagonist, that even hostility and enmity enable a struggle, that is, the competitive partnership we call relationship. Whether the other's recognition of me is 'negative' or 'positive', it is a recognition of me as the other's opposite in a (still) continuing and above all 'shared' struggle.

Hence we also begin to understand why for the subject, the other's decision not to enter the struggle and to refuse counter-violence constitutes the greatest catastrophe of all, and is understood as the most deeply hurtful 'attack'. For the other's refusal to recognize the subject as an opponent means the rejection of relationship as struggle. And since the subject perceives a relationship by definition as an antagonism, its own enterprise of establishing 'togetherness', it cannot recognize the other's refusal to fight as an action in the continuous process of interaction between two people, understanding it instead as the 'end of the relationship'. In fact, a relation between two people can neither be ended nor dissolved, but merely changed; yet the subject only knows 'its relationship', and hence puts its own 'end' to it.

7

Ego-philosophy, or the battle with reality

We often hear it said – as for instance in the context of racism in Germany – that 'the opposite of love is not hatred, but indifference.'[1] From the point of view of the subject, indifference may indeed be worse than hatred, for with a conception of relationship based on opposition and a struggle for mutual recognition, 'indifference' signifies the refusal of any 'relationship' at all. But to rate hatred 'objectively' – from a standpoint apparently above and beyond those involved – as at least a relation and therefore as somehow preferable to indifference, is most cynically to underestimate what hatred and enmity mean for those who become their objects.

It would be cynical beyond measure to see in the Holocaust a sign that German Nazis at least were not 'indifferent' to the Jews, or in the Serbian onslaught on Bosnian Muslims a special, albeit negative, interest in the latter. While we mostly refrain from such crass statements in these cases, it is by no means unusual to view men's hatred of women in this manner, to consider their brutality and sexual violence as a sign that at least they are not indifferent to women – a helpless and perverted expression of their interest, to be sure, but a form of interest none the less. This is generally the case with psychoanalytic approaches – whether political, philosophical or historical – which in exploring 'why' the subjects of violence may have been violent, seek the answer in some qualities of those who have become the objects of violence – qualities which are then said to 'have roused' the subject's negative interest, whether envy, fear or anger. Like rating indifference as 'worse' than hatred, it betrays a preoccupation exclusively with the feelings of the subject, including the subject of violence and hatred.

Such a view of hatred, moreover, seems to correspond to a commonsense understanding of 'the relationship', where the crucial distinction seems indeed to be between 'a relationship' and 'indifference' – a relationship which means struggle and antagonism, and an indifference which means 'no relationship'. What kind of a relationship it is, whether of hatred or of love, is therefore of secondary significance: love and hatred are no longer opposites, they both are passions of the subject and thus the opposite of indifference. Hence popular wisdom assures us that a good fight or quarrel is a natural part of any love relationship. Conversely love, as we have seen, is a form of struggle, a fight with the other: a struggle for love, a battle for recognition, a competition of power that means violence. 'By means of physical contact I want to break the wall of glass which often stands between me and these women'; 'I as the one intruding from outside must make the effort to take down barriers . . . and the fear of contact.' As Jessica Benjamin writes: 'The underlying theme of sadism is the attempt to break through to the other.'[2] Or conversely, this attempt to break through to the other, in the name of 'love' to intrude and to penetrate, to break down the wall of glass between me and the other, is the sadism of violence. The discovery that a struggle motivated by hatred is a struggle too, that a quarrel is a fight too, and enmity a viable form of antagonism and violence too, is not really what we should marvel at the most regarding such a view of relationship and love.

In his book *La Sagesse de l'amour* (The Wisdom of Love) the French critic and philosopher Alain Finkielkraut is concerned about a conception of love which is neither unrealistically idealist, nor simply the kind of ubiquitous egoism which passes for love in our culture. The realism of modernity, so he argues, has meant such an absolute division between the ideal and the real – what ought to be and what is – that it has also split the notion of love right through the middle: 'In numerous languages there exists a word which at the same time designates the act of giving and the act of taking, charity and greed, beneficence and avid desire: the word "love".'[3] Extreme self-love and unconditional self-sacrifice or concern for others 'paradoxically converge in this same word'.[4] But since realism – or perhaps we should say, empiricism – has long won the day, disinterestedness is but a normative ideal in whose feasibility no one still seriously believes. Love of others belongs to the sphere of utopian idealism – how human beings will be once their history of oppression has been overcome. The human being as it really exists is the human being who does not give.[5]

> Since the beginning of modernity, all genealogies of morality have derived the generosity of love from greed, and noble deeds from the desire for acquisition: there is no self-sacrifice which does not eventually pay off for the self . . . no generosity which does not underhand and symbolically gratify the self, no sacrificial offering, in short, which does not betray the imperialist desire to affect the Other and own him . . . Astuteness to us means uncovering beneath the apparent sacrifice the ubiquity of egocentrism.[6]

Finkielkraut doubts, however, whether this neat division of labour between idealism and realism, in particular the relegation of any love of your neighbours to the realm of pure idealism, helps us to understand the real any better. Rather, he suspects that to understand the original relationship to others and hence the relationship of love as well as of hatred, we might not only require some old-fashioned concepts but in particular a conception of an 'involvement' which differs from possession.[7]

For such a conception he turns to the work of the French philosopher Emmanuel Lévinas, who made the relationship to the Other one of his principal concerns. As Finkielkraut explains, Lévinas, like Hegel and other modern philosophers, anchors his conception of the relationship to the Other in existence: 'Human existence is defined through two crucial implications: the encounter with the Other and the relationship to Being.'[8] Like so many other Western philosophers he derives the fundamental problem of (adult) existence from the experience of the infant: 'the fear experienced by the child when he is alone in the dark.'[9] This leads to a definition of existence which, while it has nothing to do with the attitude of children to existence, betrays all the more clearly the origins of Western philosophy in the power and privilege of the philosophical subject – white supremacy, male supremacy, class privilege and educational privilege.

For besides the infant, Ivan Goncharov's legendary literary anti-hero Oblomov, whose wealth and leisure as a landowner lead him to despair of waking existence and a nearly insurmountable desire to sleep, also serves to illustrate the difficulty of the experience of existence. Yet this is explicitly declared not to be a problem of class and leisure, but an 'ontological', that is, a universal and existential problem.[10] As Finkielkraut explicates, 'Existing, says Lévinas . . . is a burden rather than a mercy. It means being chained to oneself, the fact that the self is constantly overburdened with itself, is implicated in itself. Existence imposes itself with the full weight of a non-dissolvable contract. One is not simply, one *is oneself*.'[11] This is the 'fundamental tragedy' of Being: 'Tired or listless one recoils from existence, one drags one's feet, would sometimes like to shout "stop", but breaking out is impossible: man is wedged into Being.'[12]

What counts as the profoundest philosophical exploration of the 'human condition' in fact is the reflection of members of the ruling class who are beginning to be bothered by the conditions of their existence as rulers. For the struggle for power and domination engenders a self which ends up in the splendid isolation of the subject, a subject surrounded only by objects. In this loneliness the empowered subject reflects upon its 'existence', representing it, by means of the now familiar reformulations, anew and completely from scratch: having put others in chains in the process of empowering itself, the subject sees itself as 'chained to itself', victim of an 'existence' that 'imposes' itself with the stone weight of an indissoluble contract. 'One is chained to oneself, trapped like a bird in the lime of existence.'[13]

A subject who with its own ruling power indeed threatens the lives of other people, trapping them in economic and political dependence, experiences its own existence not only as a burden, but as a trap. 'Existence, says Sartre very similarly to Lévinas, means massive walls, from which man cannot escape.'[14] Just as the objectifying subject cannot escape from its 'prison of images', so the ruling subject cannot escape from its 'existence': it is 'wedged' into Being, caught in the trap of existence – in metaphors of violence which reflect, albeit with inverted signs, the very violence the subject exercised in the process of its self-empowerment.

The subject, making the world it lives in into an object world, in the course of its objectification and the mirror stage of its self-splitting also makes itself into an object: the privileged object of its subjective reflection. Thus it happens that, comparing its state as object with that of other objects, it arrives at the most absurd question of them all, namely whether it would like in fact to be 'itself' or perhaps rather something different. Just as the subject thinks it has a choice *whether* to enter into relation to others (the objects) at all, it calls its relationship to itself into question: does it even wish to be chained to 'itself'? And in doing so discovers a boundary to its freedom, a freedom which in its position of power it believed to be unlimited: the relationship to itself/oneself is an 'indissoluble contract'.

A subject whose relations are characterized precisely by the fact that the subject can call them off at any moment of its choice – whose cancellability is the very point of a conception of self as subject – now sees its project of power and domination reach a 'natural' limit, at least on the level of its own discourse: the split ego cannot think itself as pure and absolute subject, without its object complement. In the face of such 'superior power', the power of (its) logic and the grammar of being, the powerful subject makes itself into the victim of that 'power': the victim of a discursively thingified 'existence', an abstracted and autonomous 'Being'.

Hence the elites of the ruling classes of the world – the elites of white, Western, educated men – concern themselves not with the burning problems of the world – say the problem of domination and the massive subjection created by it, the exploitation of the majority of humanity and their consequent poverty and destruction, or the destruction and exploitation of their place of residence, the planet – they concern themselves with themselves and their problem of not really having any problems. Thus they create the most important and fundamental problem – most important in as much as it concerns themselves – by philosophically pathologizing their own existence as rulers in near-total supremacy.

What for other people are the real consequences of the actions of the dominant and the ruling – captivity, chains, servitude, the burden of an existence from which there is no escaping, to which there is no shouting 'stop', a social contract of power and domination which on the part of the dominated and oppressed cannot be called off or terminated – is turned, by means of rhetorical reformulation and metaphoric appropriation, into the grandiose problem of existence in freedom: 'More profound and perhaps more crucial than the wish to be oneself, to find oneself, to purify oneself from foreign dross, is the dream of being released from one's self . . .'[15]

Such a dream, rather than being the profoundest dream of universal 'humanity', is the dream of a subject living in the leisure and boredom of overabundance and superfluity, a subject which has depopulated the world around it, thus robbing its existence of any meaning and purpose beyond power. Hence there may indeed be '*ennui* of being oneself',[16] and satiety always to find but oneself. Under different conditions of being, the dream of liberating oneself from foreign dross and foreign chains may indeed be more profound and above all more urgent.

As the colleagues from psychology have recourse to 'original' needs and experiences of children in order to justify the claims to power of adults and to legitimate them as 'natural', so it is part of the stock repertory of Western philosophy to have recourse both to the child-hood of the subject and to a 'childhood' of humanity in order to legitimate the boundless, transgressive and exploitative aspirations of the adult philosophical subject as 'existential', 'universal' and 'onto-logical':

> When the child cannot find sleep, when all the lights are extinguished and he begins to listen to the impalpable murmur of the night, what he hears and fears is existence in its purity without the existing, the anonymous form of Being . . . there is nothing but Being as such, the inevitable murmer of *there is*. *There is* always, even if there is no particular thing – and this is precisely what the child grasps. Terror rises in him, because he feels as if sucked up into this amorph-ous existence . . .[17]

For 'the child' is a little existential philosopher, who even in the bed of his infancy is afraid of thingified abstractions, of the anonymous shape of shapeless Being or the vacant 'event of Being' – in short, who has a 'Heideggerian experience'.[18] Above all, he is a child who in his child's life has had no social experiences at all which might give him reason to be terrified of the dark – not of the 'shapes of monsters' and other 'fantastic images',[19] but of the experience of powerlessness and violation, or in other words the actions and the behaviour of powerful adults. Thus denuded of the social condition of his very being as a child, he may then serve as the *tabula rasa* of a human being in a state of 'nature', the philosophical subject in post-natal embryo.

Fear and terror, then, for Lévinas are the mark of the subject's encounter with the superior power of 'existence'. What in Finkiel-kraut's view distinguishes Lévinas from other great Western philo-sophers such as Hegel, Heidegger and Sartre, is that his analysis of social relations, of the encounter with the Other, is a matter neither of fear and terror, nor 'predominantly of struggle'.[20] While for Hegel the relationship between two subjects is determined by the dialectic of Master and Slave, the war between consciousnesses,[21] for Sartre the mere 'fact of the Other', that is, the mere existence of another, constitutes a challenge to the subject which Sartre calls 'violence'.[22] For the sheer recognition or consciousness that another exists suffices to catapult the subject out of the paradise of his singular existence – a perception of the other which according to Finkielkraut does not yet constitute a 'relation': 'No relation links me to this stranger.'[23]

The Sartrean subject's ability to reflect leads it to the alarming insight that this 'object', the Other, is himself a subject who in turn may reduce 'me' to the object of *his* sight: 'I am being seen, this is enough to transport me into a different world.'[24] To be precise, into the Other's object world. Looking, eyeing me, observing and appraising me, the Other is making me into *his* Other, fixing me in a mode of being, a 'nature', which I cannot reject, imposing on me, as we might say, an identity which is not of my making: 'the Other is for me at once he who stole my being and he who effects that there is a being which is my being.'[25]

While for Hegel the problem was that in order to exist, I need another for whom I exist, the modern existential subject has progressed so far as not to know any more if it even wants to exist, if it wants to have a 'being', dreaming indeed of detaching itself from its self and its 'being'. Hence the encounter with the Other no longer means, as it did for Hegel's subject, the troublesome yet necessary (and thus nevertheless wanted and 'needed') condition for existence: it becomes the violent aggression of an unwanted confirmation of one's existence and 'being'. This 'being', determined not by the self but by the Other, at the same time means the destruction of the subject's own (object) world, in which it was the sole and supreme ruling subject.

Sartre here is exploring the experience of being made into an object by another, facing the outrageous possibility that this might not just happen to the Other but to the subject itself. And as Finkielkraut comments, Sartre thereafter describes 'all forms of desire – from sadistic violence to the tenderness of sentimental love – as so many ruses or war stratagems deployed by the subject in order to free itself from such seizure'.[26] The most effective one is obviously for the subject to make the Other into an object instead, to enter into combat with the Other over who wins out as subject and who is vanquished into being the object: 'Caressing the Other, I make his flesh come into being under my caressing fingers. The caress is the sum total of the ceremonies which incarnate the other.'[27] As Finkielkraut explicates: 'An ambush for the other, so that, renouncing his own gaze and his own freedom, he may make himself an offered presence. An invitation to passivity, an attempt to stuff the desired being into its flesh so that it may not escape again, and I may cease to live under its gaze.'[28] It is an attempt, in other words, to lock the other into the status of object – the part from which the subject in its own case wishes to unchain itself – and to deny the other the status of subject, the role the subject aspires to in its purity.

Sight – the gaze, looking – for Sartre (as for so many others) is the determining structure of the encounter with the Other, what neces-sarily imposes the subject–object relation and the consequent battle between subjects for the dominant role of subject. Consciousness, in the sphere of the social (that is, where the subject does not simply reflect about itself) is thus identical with, is reduced to seeing: 'At the base of self-consciousness, there is not reflection, but the relation to the Other. Human reality is social before it is reasonable. Social and belligerent.'[29] Being social thus means (besides war) being reduced to the optics of our privileged sense organ, the lens, and its subject–object perspective. The sphere of the social, beginning with the singular Other – who at the caressing hands of the Sartrean subject is rapidly, and despite Finkielkraut's continuing male pronoun, turn-ing into the prototypical other, 'the feminine' – never so much as enters (the subject's) reason or reflection: it is banished to the sub-conscious, the pre-reasonable of a subject for whom reflection means self-reflection.

Far from being 'prior' to consciousness, however – more 'basic', more immediate or 'instinctual' than the subject's mature self-reflection – the social is, as the philosophers' own deliberations make abundantly clear, nevertheless secondary to the subject's self-conception: it is the subject's knowledge of its own structure (con-ceived in self-reflection), its own division of itself into subjectivity and an object-complement of whose desirability it is less than convinced, which moves, say, the Sartrean subject to perceive a like structure (and attitude to it) in the Other. It is the subject's projection of its own self-reflection into the Other which makes the Other such a fearful threat: a Subject who, like the subject itself, will attempt to constitute itself as pure subjectivity, devolving the role of object on to the subject.

It is a division of self, a splitting of the ego, which we may see as lying at the root of the Western subject's divisions into all its dualisms: the dualism of mind and body – the body the visual part of itself constituted as object, the object in the Other's sight and in its own – as well as of all its consequent divisions of labour which constitute the attempt to devolve the status of object on to the manifold definitions of 'others': the 'others' are bodies which can become property, bodies which produce labour, bodies which reproduce. Hence the social is reduced to and identical with the optics of the visual not because it precedes reflection, but because the subject's reflection has convinced it of the advantages of admitting no reflection beyond the optics of its self-reflection.

Lévinas's conception of the relation to the Other is said to stand in stark contrast to this belligerent tradition: 'it neither sets up a conflict, nor on the other hand an idyll. For in describing the encounter with the Other, Lévinas contests both the model of romance and that of a combat, rejecting both the silliness of an untroubled reciprocity and the merciless battle for recognition.'[30] The Other is not, or not in the first instance, that 'hostile power which threatens, which aggresses and enthrals the self'.[31] Rather, it provides the welcome chance for the subject to 'come out of itself' and to have its boredom and *ennui*, the burden of its exclusive preoccupation with itself, dispelled.[32]

'Before becoming a gaze, the Other is a face.'[33] That is, before the Other assumes his threatening role as a seeing subject who objectifies me, he is (to me) a 'face' – a kind of incarnation of the Other's personhood. For in Lévinas's terminology the face is very much more than 'what my gaze might obtain from it'.[34] That is to say, Lévinas is concerned first of all to relativize the subject's own perception, to draw a distinction between its habit of 'imaging' the objects of its sight and thinking it has seen what there is, and what he means by facing the face: what I see when I look, what I make myself a picture of, is but the 'aspect' of the face, which the 'face' always exceeds – the face 'is the one prey the image-hunter may never catch'.[35] For, in Lévinas's own words,

the manner in which the Other presents himself, exceeding *the idea I have of the Other*, we call the face. This *manner* does not consist of figuring as a theme under my look, of displaying itself like an ensemble of qualities that form an image. The face of the Other at every moment destroys and exceeds the plastic image which he leaves me, this idea of my measure . . . that inadequate idea.[36]

Put differently, for Lévinas's subject the Other, or more precisely, the face of the Other, constitutes the admonition that there is a reality exceeding the object world of the subject's perception. As Finkiel-kraut comments, 'there is in the Other a constant surplus or a devia-tion in relation to what I know of him.'[37] While we might have taken this to be the point of departure rather than the profound discovery at the end of philosophizing – the basic assumption underlying our relation to reality – we must remember that we are dealing with the advanced development of the philosophical subject of power. A sub-ject to whom this fact of a 'surplus' in the real, its 'deviation' from the subject's own image of it, appears as inordinate: 'This inordinacy, this constant excess of the being focused upon over and above the inten-tion [mine] which focuses on it, is called the face.'[38] While the Sartrean subject considers this inordinacy of the real, of the Other's reality, to be a veritable *aggression* towards the subject, Lévinas's subject, by contrast, considers it an entertainment, a kind of sport helping to dispel its tiredness: ' "To encounter a man means being kept awake by an enigma." '[39]

Finkielkraut's assertion, however, that this sportive engagement with the Other is not based on antagonism and struggle disproves itself even in his own explications. For it is the very language of power and of struggle which is used to intimate the alleged non-conflictual nature of this engagement. Thus there is talk of the Other's 'disobedi-ence' and 'resistance', the fact that he 'absolves himself from his image, and imposes himself beyond that shape, leaving but an empty shell in my hands when I thought I was holding his truth'.[40] The subject is so convinced of the reality of its own image world as to believe the 'image' to be the Other's, the empty shell to have been left by the Other, failing to recognize that they are of its own making. Just so the alleged 'inordinacy', the so-called 'surplus' of reality is judged and measured – that is, conceived of – from the subject's perspective: not as the fact of reality, but as its apparent resistance to my sight, an excess beyond it. Thus even if Lévinas posits the 'face' in the fullness of its reality, he does not succeed in making it precede the gaze, that is, precede and escape the subject's reducing it to its own objectification (image plus surplus). The face may be 'face' before it is 'gaze', that is, before the Other assumes the role of gazing subject, but it never precedes the subject's visual subjectivity, that is, the subject's subjective appraisal of it.

Philosophical analysis, in other words, has interposed a 'moment' between the Other as a reality, and his transformation (by the subject) into enemy – a distinction between the Other as he 'is' and the Other as (projected) hostile subject who may objectify me. But the analysis is apparently unable to interpose such a moment between reality and the self – a moment where the self does not (yet) constitute itself as objectifying and hence inimical subject. Thus Lévinas's analysis succeeds indeed in un-demonizing the Other for a moment, suspending the subject's presupposition that the Other is an enemy for the brief space of time when it recognizes him simply as being – before the Other begins to act (gaze, objectify) or, more importantly, is thought to do so by the subject. But the analysis does not un-demonize the self, does not, even for an abstract moment, suspend the subject's presupposition of itself as an enemy, enemy of the world and the Other.

Thus the difference between Sartre's and Lévinas's respective conceptions of the relationship is not that the latter's is not based on antagonism and combat: the difference is that for Sartre, it is a hostile, hate-driven belligerent combat which the subject conceives of earnestly, even hysterically, as self-defence, while for Lévinas it is playful and impassive, a game entered by the subject as a welcome distraction. Not being a certain enemy the Other is enigma, and for the sake of the enigma which may dispel its boredom, the subject affords itself this risk: an experiment with possible 'powerlessness', even 'defeat'. And lo and behold, this nonchalance, this unruffled philosophicalness (or is it self-possession?) in the face of an impending power struggle does indeed pay off:

> This disappointment [to hold in my hands but the empty husk of the Other, rather than his truth] is positive, the defeat salutary. For in order to be able to go out of oneself, it is necessary to lose power ... There is nothing in the world but the face of the Other that can really cut me loose from myself, introducing me to adventures which are not just Odysseys. I approach the face, but I do not devour it: marvellous impotence, without which even the most extravagant life would be monotonous, a journey of the self to the self.[41]

The point of the exercise, we are left in no doubt, is the value of adventure to a subject tired of its own company, who finds its own even extravagant life boring and so accepts an encounter with the Other as if for sport. Since the meeting is strictly voluntary, agreed to by the subject for its own reasons and hence could be called off by it at any moment, it reminds us of so many powerful men's visits to the prostitute, there to experience, for the short term of a contract, the 'marvellous impotence' of one 'dominated', the salutary 'defeat' at the hands of a 'dominatrix', without which even the most extravagant life of a judge or a manager, a politician or an industrialist or any member of the ruling classes of this society, would be monotonous indeed.

On no account, however, will the subject venture out of itself so far as to desist from a power struggle altogether, to give up its conception of the subject–object power relation: it comes out of 'itself' only on the level of its object-complement – the part it wanted to be unchained from anyway – never out of its role as subject. In other words, there simply is a controlled play with power, a temporary exchange of roles (under the subject's direction): there is no abolition of power, let alone a conception of a relation other than in terms of power. Thus the subject's voluntary reticence of not devouring the face of the Other, of not objectifying, dominating and appropriating it immediately, strikes it as positive and marvellous 'impotence', its decision not to exercise its power in the usual violent manner as veritable 'powerlessness'. Far from going beyond conceptions of struggle and power, the subject enters into a power struggle even with its own face, all the better to be equipped for the battle with the Other: 'Everyone wants to tame his own face, to be able to use it like a weapon, like a magic instrument, or to make it into an impenetrable surface.'[42] For like the Sartrean subject, this subject too is still haunted by the former's startled reflection that the Other may, after the manner of the subject, in turn want to penetrate the subject.

Hence the face of the Other is recognized as equally vulnerable as one's own – 'the most inaccessible part of the body and the most vulnerable'.[43] Like an experienced warrior, the subject sizes up its opponent's advantages and weaknesses: 'Being far above myself, the face escapes me . . . and very weak, it inhibits me as I gaze into its unarmed eyes. Separate from myself, it exceeds my power. Disarmed, defenceless, it exposes itself . . . It resists me and it requires me; I am not first of all its spectator, but its debtor.'[44] Seeing the Other's 'vulnerability' in the full knowledge of its own power, the subject is moved to a kind of consternation, as if unexpectedly seeing itself faced not by an equal or a superior, but by a potential victim: 'At my mercy, delivered into my hands, infinitely fragile, heart-rending like suppressed crying, the face calls me to its aid.'[45] The Other's fragility seems to appeal to a forgotton sense of chivalry, alien to the subject as such, which deems fighting a weaker opponent dishonourable.

Still, the subject does not wish to let go of its power and its power thinking. So that even this defencelessness, this heart-rending appeal for help, this perception that the Other is at my mercy, has 'something imperious' about it: 'His misery does not awaken my pity; in ordering me to come to his aid, it exerts violence against me.'[46] Unwilling to recognize that this perception – even this perception of the face supposedly prior to imaging it – is not the Other, but the subject's perception of the Other, that his alleged 'qualities' are not 'objective' or inherent qualities of the 'object', but aspects of the subject's appraisal of the Other, the subject is unwilling also to understand that the Other is neither inherently 'fragile', but fragile in relation to the subject's potential violence; that he is neither 'exposed' as such nor generally 'at mercy', but exposed to and at the mercy of a subject who is still deciding whether or not to use its own power, whether or not to exercise violence. Just so it also is the subject who imputes to the Other's vulnerability a capacity to exert violence, to 'order' and 'command' the subject to desist from its violence, when in fact it is the subject's own recognition of the damage it may cause – an intimation of its own power and violence – which seems to move it temporarily to desist.

Yet the subject clearly does not wish to take responsibility for such unwonted self-restraint, preferring to make itself, at the level of discourse, into the victim of another's power and command: the power of fragility and the command of defencelessness. Just as adults reformulate a baby's crying as its 'powerful demanding', in the face of which they are 'powerless', so the subject here redefines its own power and potential violence as the violence of its victim: the object's 'ordering' the subject to desist from violence. 'The humble nudity of the face demands, as if it were its due, my solicitude and, one might say . . . my charity.'[47] There could be no clearer indication of the subject's basic unwillingness to show any such consideration towards the Other's reality than this representation of 'enforced' solicitude and charity 'imposed' or 'commanded'.

So we are hardly surprised at the renewed insistence that 'it is thus not I who am being egoistical or selfless: it is the face in its nakedness which makes me forget my interest in myself.'[48] It is not I, in other words, that am responsible for deciding how I act, even if only to perceive the Other's vulnerability at my hands, for it happens to me as the case may be: 'The Good comes to me from outside, ethics falls on top of me, and it is in spite of myself that my "being goes out to another." '[49] From this it follows, presumably, that it neither is me if I turn out to be egoistical after all, if I fail to lose interest in myself – if the Good from the outside does not arrive and ethics fails to come all over me. In any case, it is despite myself if my self, my being, goes out to another, if I do recognize the other's reality. Hence it cannot exactly be because of myself if my self does not so go out and I continue to deny the other's reality. For my self is clearly outside my command and where my being goes is directed from outside myself.

'The Other's face orders me to love, or at the least forbids me to be indifferent to it.'[50] Since there continues to be a power struggle (albeit now with inverted power relations), there continue to be possibilities of self-defence: 'I can, of course, turn away, I can disobey or revolt against its prescription, yet it is not in my power not to perceive it.'[51] The ethics which drops on my head, it turns out, does not go so far as to direct or dictate my behaviour: I still may refuse to obey, I can yet choose to be violent or cancel the relation with the Other altogether. The authority of the 'prescription' to love turns out simply to be the authority of the real, a reality which I cannot overlook, which I cannot indifferently pretend not to have noticed. But once I have perceived it in its inordinate excessiveness and thus turned it into a formidable opponent again, I may continue to fight against it, defending my sovereignty as subject.

> The face harasses me, it draws me into making common cause with it, subordinates me to its weakness, in short, *orders me by law to love it*. And without a doubt it both is superior to me by refusing to be identified, and inferior to me because it is at my mercy. But humility and arrogance are the two sides of its supremacy, its ascendancy over my being.[52]

Since the face declares war on me, since I am at the mercy of its supremacy and ascendancy, no one will blame me for retaliating in self-defence. Moreover, rebelling against the arrogance of power and refusing obedience to supremacy appeals to our sense of justice and liberty, while escaping a face which harasses and subordinates me is but justifiable self-protection. So it comes about that the subject, despite strict orders, cannot love every face which by law orders it to love it, and that 'hatred is [also] one of the possible reactions to this order'.[53] Moreover, there is not just one such Other, and the subject may be harassed by a whole host of Others, their faces ordering it to love them. Hence it must needs choose which ones to love and which not to love – especially as those Others are also fighting amongst each other, thus obliging the subject to 'compare, measure, judge, reflect'.[54]

The point remains, however, to conceive of the subject as a victim of, and subordinate to, the reality constituted in the face – chained not only, it turns out, to its own self but also to the Other: 'From this Other, from whom I am separate and who escapes my power, I none the less cannot extract myself.'[55] I am as trapped by the bird-lime of this reality of the Other as I am trapped by the reality of my existence. Hence I do not really have any responsibility at all, excepting any I may within this basic non-responsibility decide to take on for one or another Other of my choice, for

> I live without my doing. To live may mean to develop or to remain the same, to strive for the useful or to desire power, to control one's impulses or on the contrary to give them free rein. Never, however, is opening to an other a basic given, like an instinct of my spontaneous existence. Morality, in other words, is a transformation whose origin lies outside myself . . . Something foreign – the face of the Other – comes to me and forces me to give up my indifference. I am being disturbed, sobered up from the delirium of my living, woken from my dogmatic sleep, expelled from my kingdom of innocence – called by the intrusion of the Other to assume a responsibility which I have neither chosen nor wanted.[56]

Despite all this intrusive reality, this merciless fact of the existence of Others, the 'reality' of the subject's subjectivity remains in place, unshaken and unmodified: it is the 'original' state of being, the 'natural' condition of existence, in which the unitary subject is being 'disturbed'. First of all *I am*: this is the kingdom where as subject I rule supreme, the paradise of my intact indifference and perfect unrelatedness. Only thereafter does the Other 'arrive', disturbing me in my peace, intruding into my realm, forcing me to recognize a reality beyond myself.

> Because of the Other, I cannot continue to exist naturally . . . He makes it impossible for me to exist naively, fully, be it as a hedonist self living in ecstasy, as a heroic self displaying his power, or as a bourgeois self devoted to the pursuit of his interests. The Other: the spoilsport of being . . . It is not I who naturally love the Other, it is the Other who falls to me, becoming my burden, who haunts me and overruns me – in short, who does violence to my nature by ordering me to love him.[57]

The 'advent' of the Other and (his) reality may indeed have disturbed if not destroyed the subject's indifference, its solitary autonomy. Yet this reality continues to be 'unnatural', against nature, a violation of my nature. In particular, it turns out to have been an illusion to think that this encounter with the Other might be something other than a power struggle, based on a relation other than conflict and antagonism. For if it is not conceived as the subject's relation of possession of the Other, it is conceived as the Other's violent attempt to take possession of me. The self, conceived of as the subject familiar from other philosophers, remains in struggle with its own existence and in struggle with the Other – that is, in struggle with a reality failing to conform to its subjective world of objects. A 'deposed king'[58] remains a king at variance with his lot, convinced of his righteous identity as king and of the inordinacy of his deposition. A subject steamrollered into assuming responsibility for a vulnerable Other, a responsibility it has neither sought nor wanted, continues to perceive itself as one violated, one done to against his will. The face of the Other, just like the sight of a stranger in the perception of Sartre's subject, continues to be felt to do violence to the subject – through its insistent and obtruding reality, its sheer existence.

The question whether some other relation might be conceivable – neither the subject's violent aggression in taking possession of the Other, nor the Other's violent aggression in subordinating the 'subject' – does not present itself, now that the possible permutations between subject and object, this 'radical' role-play with power and 'powerlessness', have been exhausted.

Sex and the intimate relationship

The subject's relationship to the Other, as represented and analysed in philosophical and psychological discourse, is often tacitly – or as with Lévinas, explicitly – assumed to be a prototype also of the subject's relationship to others in general, exemplifying in the singular a possible relation in the plural, the minimal unit, as it were, of the subject's sociality – or, as Lévinas calls it, 'pluralist existing'.[1] Yet this relationship to the Other, in particular the 'personal' or 'intimate' relationship, is also usually seen as eminently belonging to the private sphere, where any 'sociality' appears if at all in the form of a personal need or desire – a desire for 'closeness' or 'intimacy', a need for 'security' or for 'not being alone'. Rarely is the personal relationship considered to be part of the 'public sphere', or as Andrea Dworkin has called it, 'a society of at least two',[2] that is, as the political arena in which social life takes place. This suggests that the relationship to the Other, rather than being a miniature of sociality, in fact derives its structure and form from the prototype of the private, sexual and unique relationship: marriage.

Even where this is not explicitly stated, the analysis of the relationship to the Other invariably revolves more or less directly around the sexual relationship. Thus Finkielkraut explains how Sartre's reflections about the threat constituted by the existence of the Other led him 'to describe all forms of desire – from sadistic violence to sentimental love – as so many ruses and stratagems of war, which the subject deploys in order to liberate itself from this seizure' by the other.[3] The relation to the Other, then, is another name for desire, desire the dynamic of the relationship to the Other. Similarly Lévinas, in his consideration of the relationship to the Other, moves as if naturally to the erotic relationship, the relationship 'with the alterity of femininity'. For it is this relationship, together with the 'relation of paternity' – that is, the relations of a husband in the family – which he considers prototypical of 'relations to Otherness which distinguish themselves from those where sameness dominates or absorbs or engulfs the Other'[4] – prototypical, in other words, of the relation to the Other which he is trying to define and which is to distinguish itself from the usual struggle for power and dominance.

This only confirms explicitly what had already been implicit, namely that the philosophical subject, like the liberal 'individual', far from being a universal human subject, is fundamentally male in its conception: 'The feminine is other for a masculine being not only because of a different nature but also inasmuch as alterity [Otherness] is in some way its nature.'[5] Thus Lévinas joins the good old patriarchal philosophical tradition which Simone de Beauvoir has so thoroughly analysed, in which 'Woman' is the prototypical Other whose very 'nature' is 'Otherness'.

Yet if Lévinas finally names the subject explicitly as male, this does not mean that his analysis could simply and with inverse gender signs be applied also to a female subject. Male or masculine and feminine 'are not thought in the neutral reciprocity which commands their interpersonal commerce'.[6] Rather, it means that this 'erotic relationship' in its very conception is a sexual and a gendered relationship: not just a relation attributed to a subject which is male, but in being his relation to the 'feminine' (and not, *nota bene*, to a feminine being, let alone a woman) it is a relation which necessitates a male subject, is conditioned by and conditional upon a subjectivity which is male and an alterity which is femininity.

> In the erotic relation it is not a matter of another [different] attribute in the Other, but of an attribute of alterity [Otherness] in the Other. In *Time and the Other* [the relevant work by Lévinas], where . . . the subject's ego is posited in its virility, and also where the ontological structure proper to femininity is studied . . . the feminine is described as that which is *of itself other*, as the origin of the very concept of alterity [Otherness].[7]

What is required for an erotic relationship is thus not simply a 'neutral' subject and an attribute of difference in the Other, but a virile subject and another who by her very nature *is* Otherness.

There could hardly be a more explicit example of the androcentrism of Western philosophy, its definition of the subject as generically male and its definition of the feminine as the 'alterity' of 'virility' or subjectivity: not only is the subject male, it/its masculinity is the norm in relation to which everything is measured and compared. Even if the feminine is, in the English translation, 'of itself other', 'other' contains its relation of 'other *than*' the male: it is that which neither exists nor has significance in and of itself but only in relation to the male (subject), as the alterity of the male, as that which *is* its relation to the male. In particular, however, this means that the conception of 'the subject', like the conception of 'the individual', contains the feminine as an implicit attribute of the subject; the relationship of the subject to femininity is not a relationship between persons, but constitutive of subjectivity, constitutive of masculinity, the two being interchangeable. Thus the conception of 'the subject' subsumes the 'sexual', that is, the political relation between persons of male gender and persons of female gender, as a dimension of the (singular) subject.

Although Lévinas describes the eroticism of the male subject without a thought about women, this comes closer to the crux of sexuality and the erotic relationship than does the attempt, fashionable and widespread today, to treat them rhetorically as a matter of 'equal opportunities' and conjugate them simply with a 'female subject'. Not only is the concept of a 'female subject' philosophically a contradiction in terms: to consider sexuality as a gender-neutral phenomenon which could as easily take a 'female subject' as a male one corresponds to the logic of a verbal construction such as 'the pregnant man': it is a poetic possibility, like 'the river is flowing uphill', where a verbal 'equality' is created between 'up' and 'down' and gravity is declared a neutral phenomenon. It is a rhetorical possibility only on the level of vacuous grammar where nouns are combined with verbs and adverbs without regard to the reality of things, their meaning.

Yet this is exactly the level at which the attempt is being made today to democratize sexuality, as we might attempt to democratize gravity. Feminist analysis apparently has failed to lead to a general understanding of sexuality as fundamentally gender-specific, as a crucial dynamic in the oppression of women which not only takes place within a patriarchal social order of inequality, but which constitutes and maintains that order. Rather, it is beginning to emerge that for many women too, 'sexuality', like power or pornography, far from being the object of critique, is increasingly becoming the object of desire. Because men have them, (some) women want to have them too. Because they are the privileges of men, (some) women want to obtain them also for themselves. Little does it seem to matter what it is we thus desire, that we know that a privilege is not a right but an advantage predicated on another's lack of rights. That in particular the privileges of men depend on the oppression of women, and that gaining similar privileges means designating 'others' to take the role of the 'Other', to be dominated as women traditionally are dominated. Nor does it seem to matter what feminist analysis has shown sexuality to mean for women: that it is the medium of women's mistreatment, violation and exploitation in the 'private' sphere of men.

As feminist analysis has pointed out, the oppression of women and the division of humanity into two sexes differs from other forms of oppression precisely through the fact that the power relation at the same time defines sexuality:[8] men not only have power over women, they also desire them. Or to put it differently, the gender relationship is characterized by the fact that sexuality determines the power relation and defines the sexes: women are the group of people required for male sexuality to realize itself – they are the collective sex object of men's collective sexual subjectivity. As Catharine MacKinnon emphasizes, feminist critique 'identifies not just a sexuality that is shaped under conditions of gender inequality but reveals this sexuality itself to be the dynamic of the inequality of the sexes.'[9]

Hence the very concept of 'women' or the notion of women as an identity is not only a sexist construction, it is determined by sexuality itself, which defines women as a 'sex', the 'other sex', and thus specifically as the hetero-sex object of men. Under the perspective of patriarchy, or as Adrienne Rich has termed it, compulsory heterosexuality,[10] 'sexuality' equals male sexuality equals male heterosexuality. Since the norm never requires special qualification, it is superfluous from the point of view of the heterocentric norm to specify the sexuality as 'hetero', as it is superfluous from the androcentric norm to specify it as 'male', the lack of qualification as usual implying the norm(s).

A terminological distinction between heterosexuality and homosexuality moreover appears – together with the term 'sexuality' itself – only towards the end of the nineteenth century, when a newly emerging discourse of sexology sets about scientifically classifying types of sexuality. (Where a scientific discourse arises, so does an 'object' to satisfy it.) While previously the sexual was organized around a multitude of sexual practices and acts – sexual acts, sexual crimes, reproduction – the sexologists' radical reconceptualization of 'sexuality' relegates sexual actions, as is well known, to the realm of mere effects caused by a sexuality inherent in the subject: 'Sexuality becomes a property of the individual',[11] part of his personal identity. Henceforth the individual 'has' a sexuality (after it has evolved, as Freud has it, from 'bisexuality'): either a heterosexual one if all went well, and sometimes also a homosexual one if there were disturbances like, say, an absent father in the child's development (the child being, in the first instance, a male child, although the story is later adapted also to the female child). The sexuality one has leads to the corresponding sexual actions (if all goes well), although it may happen also that one acts against one's sexuality – as in the case of the relatively high proportion of heterosexual men who also engage in homosexual activities (and vice versa), or the large numbers of women who today identify as lesbians but who previously 'were' heterosexual.

Although there has been considerable critique of Freud and other sexologists, and although the options have since multiplied to a wide spectrum of 'sexualities', this notion of an inherent sexuality has solidified in the concept of a 'sexual identity'. This 'sexual identity' is of a consistence similar to a pattern of behaviour: sexual behaviour turns out according to the pattern or identity. In particular, one can recognize a person's sexual identity on the basis of their behaviour: the behaviour allows us to infer the identity. Even in the case of contradictory behaviour (see above) there nevertheless usually is a pattern which represents the 'true' sexual identity – at the very least a bisexual identity, if it cannot be decided.

Then as now the development of a discourse of sexology has been hailed as a first phase of the 'sexual revolution', and no doubt, as Sheila Jeffreys has argued, it has had its share in presaging the second 'sexual revolution' of the 1960s.[12] As radical feminists both at the beginning of the twentieth century and at the end of the sixties and the beginning of the seventies have analysed, however, this so-called sexual revolution has neither been propagated by political revolutionaries nor has it had revolutionary consequences – on the contrary and especially for women has meant a new wave of sexual oppression. For despite a scientifically 'frank' (even if mostly Latin or Greek) language about a multiplicity of lived sexual practices, conservative sexologists like Freud were more concerned about defending and scientifically reaffirming the old primacy of heterosexuality. With the influence of religion already on the wane, but above all with the new rights women had gained in struggles throughout the nineteenth century, which made marriage as a state-protected compulsory institution crumble a little around the edges, there was a need for new popes to defend compulsory heterosexuality. The popes of sexology have fulfilled their task more than admirably, building a church on the rock of Sigmund: sexological ideas have taken over the role of religion in providing guidelines for moral, personal and sexual conduct, creating a pansexual society that is truly ecumenical.

Granting indeed that homosexuality and other sexual practices exist in reality, the sexological perspective has nevertheless consolidated the hierarchy between heterosexuality and homosexuality (the androcentric hierarchy never having been in doubt): heterosexuality is the norm, homosexuality is the deviance. The ideology of the sexes has not been rocked. On the contrary, if it is a matter of sex and sexuality, the genders or sexes are already so firmly presupposed as to be subsumed in the prefixes – 'hetero', according to the dictionary, meaning 'the other of two, other, different' (*OED*): heterosexuality is sex with the 'other' sex (that is, sex with the Otherness, or women), while homosexuality is sex with the same sex or those who are the same (that is, men). Although the consequence is here turned on its head: instead of seeing sex(uality) as the dynamic which creates the so-called sexes, the sexes are presumed to pre-exist – according to empirical tradition are 'found' to exist and hence declared to be nature – so as then to define a sexuality between them, or else within each of them. Thus sexology presupposes both the duality of the sexes and two participants in a sex act – an idea which according to its own standards has long been outmoded – from which the first permutations can then be derived: man with woman, man with man, and reluctantly, but for symmetry's sake, woman with woman.

Even among many feminists this (mis)conception of sexuality as something which only follows on an already given (God-given or natural) differentiation of the sexes is often unquestioned. With the relative revaluation of the term 'women' in recent years, and as a consequence of feminist struggle, we have apparently become too attached to our 'gender identity', let alone 'sexuality' as a desirable good, to continue to question them. Thus we speak of sexuality and gender as if they could be separated from patriarchal power relations, filled with new and 'positive' meaning and put to new and positive uses. It leads into the dead end of an 'equal opportunities' politics as it is practised in many places today, which aims to make the rights and opportunities of women the 'same' as they are for men. Such a politics not only presupposes the sexes as given; it ignores the power relations between them which determine not only the rights and non-rights of the respective sexes, but the sexes themselves. Based on a sexist rather than a feminist analysis it posits the fallacious possibility of a society of two 'equal' sexes.

The ultimate consequence of a Marxist critique and class analysis is a society without classes, not 'equality' between the 'classes'. The consequence of a critique of racism likewise is not a society of 'equal races', but a society which has overcome and abolished racism and race ideology. The consequence of a feminist critique of gender is not an equality of the sexes, but the abolition of the political construction of sex and gender. This is not to say that existing differences are to be simply ignored, nor to postulate androgyny – the mixture of the two sexes – as an ideal. It is to say that the respective interests of the two sexes are not just different – that this is not a question of sexual difference – but diametrically opposed and mutually conflicting. While the interest of men is to maintain their power over women, it is women's interest to free themselves from this subjection. The way there necessarily means a political struggle between the sexes whose aim is the abolition of patriarchal power and privilege and thus the abolition of the sexes.

Notwithstanding, many women, too, take over from sexological science not only the conception of sexuality as a 'personal property' of the subject, but also the concepts of heterosexuality and homosexuality as the two main 'types' of sexuality, aiming to adapt them for the female subject. Even though we really know that there is no such thing as 'heterosexuality', that the heterosexuality of men and of women respectively is not only fundamentally different, but above all diametrically opposed. Since its beginnings sexology in its own way has taught us the complementarity of the two heterosexualities – has theorized the empirical findings of how sexuality is lived and exercised in practice and declared it to be the 'nature' of the said sexualities, or rather of the respective owners of these sexualities, the sexes themselves: male sexuality is active, aggressive, initiative and penetrative, conquest experienced as pleasure; female sexuality is passive, receptive, yielding and suffering. Havelock Ellis has already defined them respectively as sadism and masochism:

> While in men it is possible to trace a tendency to inflict pain, or a simulacrum of pain, on the women they love, it is still easier to trace in women a delight in experiencing physical pain when inflicted by a lover, and an eagerness to accept subjection to his will. Such a tendency is certainly normal.[13]

'Normal' for Ellis means in particular that this tendency persists 'even among the most normal civilized men and women possessing well-developed sexual impulses'[14] (remember the Western therapists). Today, in Western societies at the end of the twentieth century, we are reaping the full harvest of this theory: sadism, in hetero- as well as homosexual culture is legitimated and normalized, the latest fashion in 'liberated sexuality'. Although male sexuality, quite in accordance with its status as norm, still is the measure and model of how female sexuality is to be 'liberated' – if men want porn, the liberated female sexuality manifests itself in a similar desire for porn, if men want particular sexual practices, the liberated female sexuality proves its liberation by a corresponding interest in the same sexual practices – that is, although male heterosexuality continues to be the model of sexuality *as such*, the sexual role of women is becoming ever more clearly differentiated from the sexual role of men: through the differential between sadism and masochism, between His growing pleasure in exercising brutality and Her growing pleasure in pain and subjection. The two roles are strictly complementary, what is equal is but the pleasure to be taken in them.

From the sexual practice lived in reality scientific empiricism derives the 'essence' of the respective 'sexualities', and from these the 'nature' of the corresponding 'sex'. If we follow this construction in the opposite direction, we may begin to grasp its purpose: male sexuality 'is' conquering, initiative, penetrative and pain-inflicting, because men *do* conquer women, initiate this war, penetrate the conquered, intrude into her and occupy her; it 'is' pain-inflicting because men do inflict pain on women. Male sexuality '*is*' all these things, because men *do* all these things. Female sexuality 'is' passive, receptive, submissive and pain-loving, because women are the victims of men's sexual war campaigns, because they 'receive' men's deeds as a country being bombed 'receives' the bombs. *Women*'s sexuality '*is*' all these things, because *men do* all these things.

Woman moreover 'is' pain-loving, because the mere description of states of affairs and facts of the matter, without an analysis of who is acting and how they are acting – without an analysis, for example, of a transitive action – allows the empirical scientist not only to describe the facts of the matter 'neutrally', but to impute to the matter even 'pleasure' in the 'facts' of what is being done to it. Because animals are slaughtered by humans, it is possible not only to trace in humans a tendency to engage in slaughter or a simulacrum of slaughter; it is still easier to trace in animals a delight in experiencing slaughter at the hands of their slaughterers, a desire to submit to the slaughterers' will. Such tendencies are certainly normal: they are exhibited by millions of humans and animals daily in the most advanced and well-developed societies today.

Note that the action of the man inflicting pain is simply an empirically observable *tendency*, that is to say, a most common occurrence. When it comes to the research object 'woman', however, you may observe not only a complementary tendency which statistically corresponds amazingly precisely to the male action tendency: in the object 'woman' you can moreover clearly discern a 'delight' in the experience of pain and a veritable desire to submit to the will of the man. That is to say, in her case you can objectively trace a subjective motive. You could almost think that the man is simply and like a man fulfilling his duty to oblige the woman's desire and delight. The *active agency* of the man who initiates his undertaking 'sex', who pursues it aggressively, who penetrates, conquers and inflicts pain, is not, so it appears, in his case an expression of *his* desire and his decision to act. Rather, his delight and his interest are being projected on to the *passive, receptive, suffering* woman – are rhetorically simply imputed to her by the active, initiative, penetrating and violence-inflicting subject of a scientific sexological discourse. This 'neutral', 'objective' scientific subject, observing facts and stating matters as they really are, penetrating objects with his sharp sight to see their very subjectivity, shows a remarkable likeness to the sexual subject of the described sex scenario, just as his undertaking 'science' exhibits remarkable structural similarities to the undertaking called 'sex'.

This scientific empiricism, which infers from states of affairs and 'things as they are' not only their legitimacy, but moreover the will of the things and their consent to the state they find themselves in (never, however, the will of agents), is familiar also from other contexts, in particular the context of political argumentation. It is frequently argued, for example, that the fact that millions of women work in the sex industry (or rather, serve as the industry's raw material), clearly shows that these women *like* to do this work – else they wouldn't be there doing it. Rarely is it argued, however, at least in the sphere of paid employment, that the many women cleaning toilets are doing this work because they love it (although in the private sphere such a gender division of labour is probably determined by a similar opinion). Generally it is rare that it is thought that workers working on monotonous production lines or migrant workers doing the worst-paid, worst-status jobs allows us to infer their particular liking of such work, though we may indeed hear the old racist argument that the facts of such divisions of labour let us infer the particular aptitude of the people doing the work, that it corresponds to something in their 'nature'. If the area of work is sex work, however, it is not only women's 'nature' which is thought to make them particularly apt for it: the male subject's own pleasure in sex so infects his logic that he transfers this pleasure on to the sex worker – ignoring the fact of work.

Although heterosexuality defines two gender-specific sex roles, there is only one sex: male sex. Just as there is only one pain, the one the man inflicts on the woman he loves and the one the woman experiences. Male sexuality provides the dynamic (he is 'active'), woman is the medium (she is 'passive'). He is the sexual subject, she is object and means. Sex does not require two sexualities, it requires a sexual subject and his object. If a man rapes a woman, this is sex from his point of view. As MacKinnon comments, 'The male sexual role . . . centers on aggressive intrusion on those with less power. Such acts of dominance are experienced as sexually arousing, as sex itself. They therefore are.'[15] Moreover, contrary to the assumption that the kind of sexual object determines the kind of sexuality which is the 'property' of the subject – if the object is a woman, the male sexual subject is 'heterosexual', if the object is a man, the sexual subject is 'homosexual', if the object is a boy, the sexual subject is a 'paedophile' etc. – it is sexual *agency* which determines the 'sex' or sexual identity, in the subject as well as in the object. There are consequently only two sexual identities, that of sexual subject or agent, and that of sexual object.

As the term 'heterosexuality' suggests that 'heterosexual' men and women have the same sexuality, so the sexological division into two kinds of sexuality, hetero- and homosexuality, suggests that homosexuality or 'same-sex love' is *one* kind of sexuality. Yet even a cursory glance at male homosexuality and lesbianism reveals that they cannot have much in common besides the permutative grammar of 'same with same' and the heterosexist stigmatization as a perversion. While the male and the female sex roles of heterosexuality at least have in common that together they make up a 'complementarity', homosexuality and lesbianism are by sexology's own standards at opposite extremes, having a fundamentally different relationship each to heterosexuality. Male homosexuality shares both with (the postulated) female heterosexuality the desire for the male and his power, and with male heterosexuality male sexual agency as well as the contempt for women and the homosociality of patriarchal male bonding. Lesbianism shares neither the one nor the other, structurally has nothing in common either with male or with female heterosexuality. Indeed, as we shall see, it does not really belong to the realm of sexuality at all.

As political reality, for example, shows, the persecution of homosexuality and the repression of lesbianism in the European context have different histories and very different reasons: while male homosexuality in many European states has long been an object of legislative criminalization – as such, however, like for instance rape, in the realm of reality – lesbianism since the French Revolution has often escaped legislative regulation altogether. As Annabel Farraday and others have shown, it seemed more important to make it invisible and non-existent through non-regulation.[16]

In earlier centuries prosecution of 'lesbianism' had focused either on cross-dressing and deception (passing as a man), or on the use of 'instruments' to imitate penetration, both being severely punished.[17] While women's cross-dressing remained an offence in many countries well into the twentieth century, it was not necessarily thought to have sexual motivations – exemptions required (and often were granted) police permission, in Germany for instance as recently as 1923.[18] Thus what is threatening to Western patriarchy in lesbianism is above all women's usurpation of male social privilege and escape from male control, in particular the crucial sexual control through individual men. By contrast, the enormous significance of male homosexuality for the regime of compulsory heterosexuality lies, as Andrea Dworkin has shown, in the fact that here men are treated by other men like women. Yet 'Thou shalt not lie with mankind, as with womankind.'[19] (Just think of your own sons, who might experience what your daughters routinely experience.)

This asymmetry in the patriarchal meaning of homosexuality and lesbianism respectively also shows that sexuality equals male sexuality (that is, sexual agency). For it appears that from the perspective of patriarchy the problem of lesbianism is less one of sexuality than one of the social control of women, in that it constitutes a breach in the otherwise near-hermetic (hetero)sexual control of women by men. Moreover, it seems seriously to tax the patriarchal imagination even to conceive of lesbianism in sexual terms, since the absent penis, the power symbol of sexuality and the active factor and instrument of penetration, looms large. Thus a letter from the Association for Moral and Social Hygiene to the Law Lords in 1921, concerning the question of whether or not 'acts of gross indecency between women' should be made punishable, speaks of these as not only 'repulsive' but as 'indeed unintelligible to many people'.[20]

Since the constitutive element in the definition of sex is penile penetration (consummation of marriage as well as rape being defined on its basis, everything else counting not really as 'sex' but at the most as 'sexual'), and since 'woman' is equivalent to 'female sex role', there cannot be any sex taking place between two women: two passive, receptive, yielding and submissive sexualities together do not make sex; nothing at all is taking place. Only with Havelock Ellis and other sexologists of the early twentieth century does this problem finally receive a solution: with the invention of the 'masculine woman', the 'invert', whose sexuality is like male sexuality and who treats her sexual partner as a man treats his – as a sexual object subjected, as one who is done to. Only then does lesbianism have a sexuality – a sexuality corresponding to heterosexuality.

Conversely there is by the same accounting somewhat too much penis and active masculinity present in male homosexuality; for sex to be able to take place, therefore, one male sexuality must coerce the other into being a female, passive and receptive sexuality. The dominance of the one male sexuality defines the partner as 'woman' and sexual object. As we know, male sexuality, that is to say, dominance, can make anything, not just women, into women: every hole, every receptacle, every animal, and every child, whether male or female. And hence, theoretically, also every man. It suffices that there be male sexual dominance for another to be made into a 'woman'. And as we also know, it takes a man to make a girl 'into a woman'.

Even if under the normative auspices of compulsory heterosexuality the pre-existence of the sexes seems so 'natural' that we no longer perceive their construction through sexuality, the examples of male homosexuality and of lesbian sexuality clearly demonstrate how sex actually creates gender, that is, the sexes: it is the aggressive dominance of the 'active' sexual subject which makes the 'man', and which makes the victim of his activity a 'woman' and an object. The sexual action determines the sexual gender, which overwrites and replaces social gender identity: lesbian sex features the 'masculine woman' as sexual subject, while her victim simply remains (becomes) a 'woman'.

This is manifest in the sexological literature, which regards only the 'masculine woman' and active sexual subject as the true lesbian or 'invert', considering the other woman a 'normal' woman to whom it could equally well be done by a man. That is to say, the desire which is decisive is the active-male desire of the sexual subject; the so-called female desire of the sexual object does not really matter – else in the case of lesbians it would have to be considered equally 'inverted'. Yet it does not appear to be inverted since, assuming the desire of an 'object' exists at all, it is directed at sexual subjectivity, that is, as is proper in a heterosexual woman, at active-male aggressive and initiative agency. The social gender of the active sexual subject obviously is of secondary importance. Conversely, the 'invert' is less inverted in the sense that as a woman she has the wrong sexual object: she is 'inverted' in as much as she exhibits a behaviour which does not correspond to her social gender: sexually, she *is* a man.

Similarly, in male homosexuality the passive and penetrated partner becomes a 'woman', as can be seen also from the fact that a man raping a man constitutes a degradation for the man raped – his degradation to the sexual gender of woman – without his social gender, however, reflecting in the least back on to his rapist: the latter remains a heterosexual man, even if he rapes another man. That is, he is exercising his 'normal' sexual role, no matter whom he rapes. Similarly, men and society in general tend not to regard men who rape little girls as having an unusual sexuality like, say, a 'paedophile', nor do they necessarily regard men who rape little boys as 'homosexual'. Society's fear, rather, is precisely that the boy who has been raped might thereby become a 'homosexual'. 'Homosexual', like 'woman', thus tends to signify a gender of sexual object, a gender constituted by male sexual agency. This implicit recognition that it is sex (male-sexual agency) which determines gender can also be discerned in the different reactions of patriarchal experts to the sexual assault on boys and girls respectively.

Mainstream therapeutic efforts *vis-à-vis* girls who have been sexually assaulted by men aim at so-called 'heterosexual adjustment',[21] that is, healing them of their possible 'fear of men'. The fear of therapists is that girls might once and for all turn away from any 'normal' hetero-sexual aggression by men. Hence the empirical fact that many girls and women who were raped do indeed choose not to have any voluntary sexual relations with men, is regarded as one of the most deplorable 'damages' resulting from rape. Quite on the contrary in the case of boys, where it is hoped that they may have precisely this reaction and will in future eschew the sexual company of men. In the boy's case this is not a sign of damage and undue fear, but a sign that he has successfully overcome the experience. The fear of the sexperts is, rather, that the boy might – quite contrary to the tendency observable in girls – find pleasure in being raped and continue to look to men for the experience – which is a direct transference of their own sexolo-gical theory which imputes just such a pleasure in pain, and delight in being dominated, to the traditional sexual object, women. If a girl, after being sexually assaulted by a man, were still looking forward to sex with men, it would prove in the eyes of sexologists that after all she had, albeit precociously, become a true woman. All this shows that sexologists despite everything seem vaguely to know that sex or gender, far from being a personal identity, is constructed through sex. In the case of girls, their fear is that girls may rebel against being so constructed as 'women', in the case of boys their fear is that their own theory – that you just love being raped once you experience it – might be true.

It clearly shows, too, that sexuality means male sexual activity, and moreover, that there is no conspicuous difference between so-called normal sex and rape. From the perspective of the sexual subject it is the same activity in both cases – the will or unwillingness of the object not affecting the nature of the act. It is the (for a man) 'normal' and 'natural' act of constituting another as object, a belligerent expedition of conquest from which the subject necessarily must emerge victorious. The act itself says nothing about whether it is committed in love or in hatred: the male sexual subject does it equally to 'the woman he loves' and to his enemy. Moreover, he always emerges victorious: it is the woman who has been conquered, laid, had, possessed, and not the other way round. Similarly, it is the man who has been raped by another man who has thus been punished, made into a 'woman' or a 'homosexual'. The rapist himself was not involved in a homosexual act, the act does not make him a 'homosexual'. It is not the sexual object which determines the sexual identity of the subject, nor is it the sexual object's will or unwillingness which determines the nature of the act: it is the sexual subject's agency which determines everything.

Just so the identity of the sexual subject is in no way affected if, in the consciousness of his own racist ideology, he rapes a woman of a 'race' he despises, or if in war he rapes 'enemy' women: though the sexual subject 'defiles' these women, he himself is not so defiled by the association. It is not the 'association' which is defiling, it is the willed and initiative sexual aggression of the subject which defiles the object. Nor does it seem to contradict his racist and sexist ideology and hatred to engage in so-called 'normal' sexual relations with women of his 'own' or of any other 'race', since sex does not signify love for the class of objects. Nor does the fact that he may experience pleasure make violence into love or sex into an association. When men go to war they often also experience pleasure conquering and destroying the enemy, as the orgasmic descriptions of their military penetration acts impressively demonstrate.[22]

Nor does a man appear to humiliate himself if he rapes animals whom he rates 'sub-human': he does not thereby become 'animalistic' or 'sub-human' himself. Quite differently when he rapes women and animals in such a manner as to force them sexually to engage with each other: his understanding is that he thereby humiliates the woman even further than if he personally raped her, that thus he degrades her to the status of 'animal'. The postcards which by now are freely available on postcard racks for tourists, showing women with a pig or a dog between their legs, are not meant to imply an analogy between the absent sexual subject and the animal who has been made to take his place, it is meant to suggest an analogy between the woman and the animal. Yet it is less the status of the animal which degrades the woman than the (male) sexual agency which makes her a double sexual object: she is degraded in either case, whether she is raped by the man through an animal or by the man himself with his 'high status' of a human. All in all it is the self-initiated aggressive penetrative act which makes the sexual subject in every case a man, with the unimpaired status and dignity of a 'subject', the recipient of his action into the victim of degradation to the status of object – be it woman, homosexual, animal, child or enemy.

To consider sex a 'shared' act, a form of association in which two 'participate' and something 'mutual' is happening, or if it is not, something which could be 'democratized', thus seems to be considerably at odds with reality. Rather, the structure of 'sexuality' as of 'desire' seems to correspond to a transitive act of aggression, the subject–object structure of domination – a war campaign to conquer and occupy the living space of another. As Andrea Dworkin comments on this notion of hunt and conquest, 'The excitement is precisely in the nonconsensual character of the event.'[23] Nor can we view sexuality simply as a natural and existential physical activity like, say, eating, inflected only superficially by culture. Rather, sexuality (that is, male 'universal' sexuality) is deeply rooted in the history of the gender relationship, a political power relation of oppression, violence and exploitation. This means not only that it is a fundamentally antagonistic and hostile form of behaviour, but that the sexual 'object' by definition is a disempowered and disenfranchised opponent: only then is the subject guaranteed to emerge victorious.

This also explains why *vulnerability* is such a highly prized and 'stimulating' quality in the sexual 'object', to which the subject 'responds' with desire – why men love to assault children and child pornography booms, why childlike innocence, weakness and vulnerability are sexual ideals of femininity, and why women with disabilities are particularly at risk. Just so Lévinas's subject feels properly challenged only by the vulnerability of the face – its unprotectedness, its defencelessness, its being at the subject's mercy, its fragility, its helplessness and its crying, in short, its nakedness – feeling 'challenged' in a mixture of recognizing the other's 'misery' and a redoubled aggression towards that other. To stand powerless before the subject, so the philosophers insist, means to do 'violence' to the subject, 'ordering it to love'. Since the other's naked and defenceless face is doing nothing of the sort, it is more likely that this 'love' indeed originates in violence – not the violence of the powerless object, but the violence of the desiring subject seeing an easy victory close at hand.

Sexuality, in other words, is rooted in and determines the power inequality between the sexes, whose institutionalized and 'official' sphere is marriage. The historical significance and development of marriage, therefore, is decisive also for the development of the conception of sexuality and of the 'personal relationship'. In civil society – the blueprint of Western societies – men's marriage is the prototype of a relationship in the 'private' sphere which, unlike relations in the public sphere, is neither entered into by contract nor dissolvable simply by cancellation. What is nevertheless called the marriage contract is not a contract between the marriage partners; at most it is a contract between the man and another man, the woman's previous owner, or else refers to marriage law.[24] For contracts may be entered into only by equals, by legal subjects. Man's marriage, therefore, is originally uncancellable (by the other), and will be terminated through nothing but the death of the wife – it is guaranteed in its non-terminability. As such it is less a form of association than a possession. The man's ownership rights are constituted in his sexually taking possession of the woman – still reflected in the euphemisms for genital intercourse such as 'he possessed her', 'he took her' or 'she became his'. As Andrea Dworkin comments: 'he takes, he keeps; once he has had, it is his.'[25]

Thus in the history of Western democracy, and since the abolition of slavery and serfdom, men's marriage represents the unique model of a social relation which fundamentally and legitimately is defined as the possession of another human being (and which today has a parallel only in the relation of humans to animals as a relation of complete possession and control over another living being). Although a man's children are also his possession, it is in their case temporary and limited – until sons come of age and daughters are married off to become another man's possession. And it is an ownership which at least *de jure* does not anticipate his taking possession of the interiority of their bodies, though the history of legislation concerning incest shows that the law only reluctantly interferes in the private sphere of fathers to prohibit their sexual exploitation of their children.[26] Thus the crucial difference between men's relations to wife and children respectively lies less in men's actual practice than in the *de jure proscription* that in the case of his wife a man *must* take sexual possession of her. Marriage is consummated only with the first successful genital intercourse; without this the marriage can be 'annulled', that is to say, it was not a marriage without sexual intercourse, it was 'no marriage'. Marriage without sexual intercourse is a contradiction in terms: it does not exist (conceptually or legally).

In modern times, things have changed a little concerning the legal guarantee of men's private relations – besides the political emancipation of women perhaps most crucially on account of women having gained the right themselves to sue for divorce. That is to say, the legal and material framework of marriage may have considerably changed, so that men's marriage as a relation of possession at least theoretically is less absolutely secured. Yet in many Western states – wherever rape in marriage is not recognized as a crime – men's marriage relation, even in its temporary limitation until a divorce, basically remains a relation of possession, since he retains the right to decide over 'his' wife's body. And if the wife is of foreign nationality and without independent right to stay in the country, the marriage *de facto* remains safe from being terminated by her at least during the first few years, thus constituting an oasis of the old model of marriage in the midst of 'women's equality', which Western men increasingly take advantage of.[27]

Yet the original model of men's marriage survives in modern Western societies even without its legal framework – in the generalized ideal of and aspiration to a 'private relationship'. While it may less be the legal status of marriage which continues to be desired, it is the very conditions and structure of relation which marriage created for the man and subject of the marriage: above all the *security* and *durability* of the relation (the fact that it cannot be terminated by the wife yet can be left by the husband at any time), the *intimacy* of the relation, that is, unconditional access to the other, in particular the free availability of the body of the other for one's own sexual use, which often also means the *uniqueness* and exclusiveness of the relation. And it is the significance of marriage as a *right*, now of the partners to each other, originally the right of the husband to his wife without reciprocal right of the wife. That is to say, what constitutes the 'positive' values of the relationship ideal are precisely those aspects of the marital relationship which originate in a man's individual ownership rights over a woman within the institutionalized oppression of women.

Moreover, as recent campaigns for the institution of 'homosexual marriage' have shown, it is not only the essence of the marital relationship which is reclaimed for homosexual relations, but also what remains of its state protection and juridical framework.

While theoretically the subject might have several such 'private' relationships (even if the Western Christian state permits only one legal marriage at a time), it nevertheless must be obvious that this relationship cannot serve as the model for human sociality, let alone an egalitarian relation of humans to humanity. For the 'private' or 'personal' relationship defines individuals in their singularity rather than their sociality. Not only does it constitute – even in its modern variant – their 'private' and individual sphere, in which neither the state nor other individuals have a right to intervene. In the language of modernity it is moreover claimed as an aspect of individual *identity*. The right of the individual to privacy is not only the right 'to be let alone',[28] but guarantees, in the language of modernity, 'autonomy of control over the intimacies of personal *identity*' (my emphasis).[29] This transformation of a social relation into a dimension of the singular 'individual' is indebted to the fact that the prototypical 'privacy' of the male citizen's marriage in reality harbours a surviving form of slavery or serfdom.

All the more remarkable that today women also increasingly wish to define 'personal identity' precisely through such 'intimacies'. For, to construct such 'intimacy', another person is required, as a wife (who is there for nothing else) is required for a man's marriage. They are required to constitute a 'sexual relationship', that socially determined gender relationship which, in its individual form as marriage, makes the relation between a man and a woman a 'sexual' relation in every respect, even outside sexual activity. They are required as the 'object' of the 'sexual activities' of the subject, as a wife is required by a husband for sexual intercourse and reproduction, that is to say, as a body to which he has unique and exclusive access – that is 'his' body. Such 'intimacy' with one's 'own' wife or one's personal 'other' is what constitutes a 'feeling of selfhood' and 'identity'. All in all, such 'personal' identity is constructed by means of another person, who is necessary to it and to whom the subject tries to establish a 'right' on account of 'the relationship' as a husband has a right to his wife on account of marriage. This most personal individual identity, in other words, is two-personal. Or, to put it differently, the conception of 'the relationship' as the core of 'the intimacies of personal identity' programmes the control over and use of another person, that is, the subject's designed exploitation, abuse and violation of the other.

However absurd it may be to construct the 'private individual' as one person plus that person's intimacies with others, it is all the more naturalized in the modern relationship ideology. Thus contemporary feminist sexologists as a matter of course speak of the subject and its sexual object, of the subject's desire for the other and for control over the other. Far from questioning this concept of sexuality, this sexuality on the contrary is seen to be 'in need of reassurance through fantasies of control over others'.[30] But this claim to possession of and control over the other, this heritage from patriarchal male marriage, also looms large in the general relationship ideology. Thus it is not unusual to find that individuals consider themselves complete only if they are 'in a relationship', while a time without a partner is thought of as a temporary state of lack and an interim only between two relationships. Alternatively, individuals aspire to 'a relationship' without knowing of a specific candidate for the vacant post of partner. This in no way differs from the traditional search for a wife except in the formality of a church or registry wedding upon success.

The ancestry of marriage in the pedigree of 'the relationship' is perhaps nowhere more visible than in the homologous social, that is, 'public' role of this 'private relationship' and the attendant customs and expressions which have been seamlessly transferred to it from the former. Thus we speak of 'my partner' or 'my lover' as one used to speak of 'my wife', publicly characterizing a person as my possession and as lacking an identity of their own. If once this was a problem specifically with married men who, introducing 'their' wives as 'my wife', left us in the dark about the woman's name, it since has multiplied across the whole spectrum of relationships and partnerships. What is apparent is that through this statement of possession this 'private' relationship is made known to the public, who in turn are to give it 'public recognition', as a marriage entered in the church or state register has a claim to being publicly recognized.

Such recognition includes that the declared ownership is generally, that is, collectively and ideologically, respected (even if not necessarily in individual practice), in as much as any additional sexual partner is in principle acknowledged to constitute a violation of the rights of the other partner, akin to traditional adultery (by the wife). Even if this no longer entails the same severe social sanctions as in the past, the partner whose rights are felt to be violated may nevertheless count on the full understanding and sympathy of friends and acquaintances. In other words, the public declaration of the 'private' relationship, and its concomitant recognition by society, imply and realize the principle of monogamy peculiar to institutional (Western) marriage (which as sexual monogamy was enforced only in relation to the wife). Today, when sexual monogamy in many circles is no longer a moral ideal and multiple sexual relations may indeed be the aspiration, even this aspiration is expressed with reference to monogamy, i.e. marriage, namely as 'non-monogamy'. Marriage, in other words, remains the uncontested reference point both for relationships and for sexual relations, even in the attempt to escape its official form and to transgress its traditional structures.

Public recognition of 'the relationship' also means that society no longer treats the individual as an individual, but as a 'personal identity' whose 'intimacy' is acknowledged in the shape of the partner. Consequently, the individual is addressed as a relationship, in the plural of their intimacy, as a couple. One cultivates a social relation with this individual usually by cultivating a relation with the whole couple, addressing and inviting them together or at the very least asking after the other half. Similarly one identifies those participating in this relationship each as the other's partner or 'intimacy'. Thus if we ask 'Who is this woman Anna?', the response often consists in the disclosure of whose partner she is, as if we thereby knew more about who Anna is. Her personal identity obviously lies in her personal 'intimacy'.

Nor is there any doubt that the person who is named as another's partner is thereby designated as that person's *sexual* partner – whether or not there are sexual activities in the privacy of this relationship. Just so marriage signifies a sexual relation, whether or not the partners (any longer) engage in sexual relations with each other. Sexuality thus is constitutive of the relationship, whether or not the partners remain sexually active within it: it is what made the relationship (even if in the past) a 'relationship', as consummation of the marriage makes the marriage.

Conversely we may hear that the partners of a relationship have separated even though they continue to live together. That is to say, the public are informed that the relationship is no longer a *sexual* one (since it continues at the very least to be a flat-sharing relationship, the partners not being 'separated' in this respect). In other words, we are told that the partners are 'free' again and back on the relationship market, for what else could be the reason for making this private intimacy public? According to general relationship practice, society, in return for recognizing relationships, has a 'right' to know who is sexually tied and who is available, just as patriarchal society insists on knowing about everyone's marital or civil status. Sexuality thus remains a reference point also for non-sexual relations, even if only in that these are so defined, that is, through the absence of sexuality.

A further sign that the relationship derives from marriage is the common understanding of it as a 'bond'. We probably associate 'bond' in the first instance with something like an 'emotional bond', which is usually valued positively (although we may view it as an illness and specifically an addiction if we do not value it so positively).[31] Yet the terms 'bond', 'tie' and 'liaison' still betray a meaning which for most women for a very long time has been the reality of marriage and for many continues to be so today, namely that they are bound by this bond, as your hands may be bound by a rope, and as there is 'bondage' and chaining in the growing sexual culture of sado-masochism. 'Bondage', apart from having become a specialized term in the technical vocabulary of an international S/M culture, still means servitude, slavery, unfreedom.

What marriage and compulsory heterosexuality used to achieve as an institution, namely to bind women indissolubly to men and to a specific man, today other 'bonds' have to achieve, first and foremost the emotional and romantic bond. As Shulamith Firestone pointed out years ago, 'romanticism is a cultural tool of male power to keep women from knowing their conditions. It is especially needed – and therefore strongest – in Western countries with the highest rate of industrialisation.'[32] The industry of romance literature, which in the last hundred years has grown to phenomenal proportions, has successfully – and in a manner adjusted to women's economic situation – brought the romantic bond truly home to women. At a time when the institutional and legal bonds of marriage are slackening, it aims to persuade women henceforth to bind themselves for emotional reasons. As the parallel boom industry of pornography is confirming men in their sadistic sexual role, encouraging them literally to bind women, so romance literature defines and affirms women in their masochistic role, encouraging them to bind 'themselves' to men: to subject themselves to their will, to take over their will as (and instead of) their own, and to give up their own identity in favour of an 'identity' as a couple. In other words, it propagates women's voluntary mental bondage and servitude.

With all the contempt which cultural and political progressives usually have for cheap romance, Hollywood sentimentality and Mills & Boon melodrama, there nevertheless is even in such circles a considerable reverence for romantic ideals when it comes to relationships: uniqueness or exclusiveness, durability, and long-term security of the relationship are the uncontested positive values to which a 'relationship' aspires, as is accountability, a kind of voluntary mutual guarantee of the other person's right to oneself. That this is not just a matter of ordinary accountability as, say, in relation to other people generally or to one's principles, is evidenced in the fact that it has become a technical term of the relationship jargon. Similarly, the desire to accommodate the relationship in the domesticity of a shared home must be seen as a romantic ideal indebted to marriage. Generally, the growing 'intensity' and progressive 'intimacy' of a relationship follows the precise timetable of courtship for the purpose of marriage: from spatial as well as temporal distance during courtship and the time of uncertainty, through mutual avowal and the sense of security, to a temporal as well as a spacial maximum togetherness which finds its highest symbolic expression in the (prototypically marital) shared home – even if actual togetherness thereafter need not stay at the feasible maximum level.

These romantic ideals, not to mention marriage itself, are highly valued also in many homosexual and lesbian relationships – partly perhaps because marriage, being (as yet) unattainable, gains in attraction, partly because of a widespread assumption that a 'same-sex' relationship could never reproduce all the reprehensible aspects of marriage. Thus if two men or two women behave like a married couple, this is considered to be something completely different from a man and a woman doing so, and as having nothing to do with an ideology of compulsory heterosexuality. Alternatively, romantic ideals also count as progressive among some heterosexual men on the left or in green and peace circles, since they are deemed to be typically feminine and thus typically un-macho. For complementary reasons, pornographic ideals are attractive to women critical of femininity, because they are deemed to be particularly male and hence unfeminine. But pornographic ideals generally count as progressive in relation to sexuality, indeed, as the avant-garde programme of sexual liberation. Thus, if the issue is sexuality, pornography is the authority; if the issue is 'the relationship', romance is the standard.[33] Both romance and pornography are produced by the same capitalist film, music and publishing empires, which net some of the highest profits among multinational industries.

Finally, it appears that relationship romance feeds on the notion that the worst thing men ever did in patriarchy (in the long distant past) was to leave or abandon women. Hence the roving Casanova (though simultaneously admired) becomes the archetypal patriarchal culprit, while the faithful husband who keeps his wife ascends to the status of the progressive post-patriarchal hero. Women who, with or without children, were and are being abandoned – left in particular without money and opportunities to make a living – do indeed face formidable difficulties in a society based on the double standard and gender-specific discrimination regarding paid employment. Yet it does not follow that the absence of a man is the worst among their difficulties. Nor does it follow that a woman whose husband rules and abuses her in the sanctioned privacy of his home for a lifetime necessarily has the better lot. Rather, it shows that such a view remains indebted to the contradictory patriarchal double standard which for men simultaneously envisages marriage and roving Casanoving, reproductive monogamy and sexual promiscuity, thus instituting a division of labour between sex and relationship: 'sexual variety'[34] in the public private sector and relation of possession in marriage.

If 'the relationship', then, in its provenance as well as its structure, is a close relative of patriarchal marriage – the unique and exclusive relationship of a husband in his private sphere, for which sexuality moreover is constitutive – it should also be obvious that it cannot be 'democratized'. If there is a need for 'democratization', it means that the status quo is undemocratic and that undemocratic structures and practices need abolishing. However, the term 'democratizing' increasingly is used not in a political but rather a consumerist sense, meaning that a 'good' should be made available to the largest number of possible consumers. But even in this sense we would presume that something is to be democratized because it is desirable and positive – a privilege or a right or good which everybody ought to be able equally to enjoy. Yet the marital relationship, just like sexuality, is neither 'positive', nor 'desirable', nor a privilege – from the perspective of a wife who is required for and used in it. An analysis of this relationship and of sexuality which includes women's experience of them, reveals these not to be desirable goods which need democratizing, but structures of domination which need abolishing.

That there is nevertheless talk of it, that it is even considered a desirable goal, is due to the fact that this relationship – be it to the wife, the partner or the philosophical 'Other' – continues to be considered with unshakeable tenacity as a form of 'love', a good deed from which an optimal number of others should benefit. No matter that history teaches us otherwise, that experience shows the horrific reverse: both history and experience seem ineffectual in the face of the cultural onslaught of this ideology of love.

A relationship to the 'other' which is based on the uniqueness of the marital relation – a uniqueness which continues to be constitutive for the modern partnership in contradistinction to a multitude of sexual contacts – cannot be democratized in the sense of being multiplied to render a so-called sociality, quite apart from the question of its desirability. Universality cannot be made out of uniqueness. Rather the unique (even if multiplied) relationship of a man to a woman which is usually called love, far from being universalizable, stands in reciprocal relation to his general relations to women: his universal misogyny, not to say hatred of women, which is constituted in the social oppression of women by men. The romance of looking for a wife consists precisely in selecting from among the mass of despised and despisable women one unique one for private purposes, who will correspondingly feel flattered to have been chosen. As Firestone and other feminists have shown, what women consider to be positive in romantic love derives its value precisely from the comparison with the same man's negative relation to all other women.[35] This at the same time institutes the mechanism of 'divide and rule', since the woman chosen will not only not take her man's general misogyny personally, she will need it to assure herself of her position as the one and only 'exception'.

The 'personal relation', whether sexual or not, reproduces this structure of a positive choice before the foil of general negative relations: whether it is a partnership or friendship, its significance is that here we will not behave as we normally behave towards people, that the partner has a claim, if not a right, to be treated 'better' than we generally treat people. Such a relationship, therefore (even leaving aside the serious question whether 'better' really is better), is the worst possible model for a generalized relation between people, since it implies its own negative standard, and by the practice of exception fortifies the general rule.

Just as little can the fundamentally asymmetrical, transitive structure of sexuality, which is the defining dynamic of this relationship, be 'democratized' within the relationship or made symmetrical as a 'democracy of two'. The relation of serfdom cannot be democratized; if there is a critique of it, it can only be abolished. Neither can marriage, the relation of husband and wife, be turned into a pair of equal husbands, nor the sexual subject and his sexual object be transformed into two sexual subjects. It is not possible to turn a society of masters and slaves into a society of masters only, or a master–slave pair into a pair of masters. If they both become masters, they no longer are a pair, and others have been made to take the role of slaves somewhere.

Female desire, or the democratization of violence

The contradiction involved in wanting to democratize sexuality becomes most evident when women are trying to do just that: to become sexual subjects as men are sexual subjects, advocating women's personal sexual liberation after the model of the sexual revolution, and moreover mistaking it for a programme of 'women's emancipation'. This betrays a serious misconception not only of democracy, but also of the ideology of the 'sexual revolution'. For the aim of the latter is not to liberate women, but to liberate sexuality, which hitherto has been heinously oppressed. The characteristic oppressors are the personal as well as the cultural super-ego – an amalgam of external and internalized moral authorities like parents, church, education and the state, manifested in the average hegemonial morality and prudery, society's as well as one's own. It is from these repressive instances that 'sexuality' is to be liberated – there is no mention of sexuality itself needing to be revolutionized or even just democratized. The sexuality in question of course is male sexuality, which as usual goes without saying.

Feminists have extensively analysed the impact which this unleashing of male sexuality has had and continues to have on women: that the growing 'liberty' of the male sexual subject necessitates the growing 'availability' of women. It is the very reason why sexual politics has been at the centre of feminist politics: since the sexual constitutes the domain of the specific oppression of women as women, this so 'personal' and 'private' matter is political. Hence the political liberation of women from oppression necessarily also requires their personal liberation from the intimate oppression in sexual relationship:

emancipation from their status as 'other', 'otherness' and the 'other sex' to personhood.

Since it was moreover to be expected that the beneficiaries of sex and the sexual revolution would not be enthusiastic about a liberation project on the part of their sexual medium, feminists have emphasized from the beginning that the liberation of women, like, say, the liberation of workers, will require political struggle. The ideologues of the sexual revolution know this too, and have been at war with feminism ever since. It is only one of their many strategies to use the political vocabulary of women's liberation to camouflage their plans for women as a belated 'liberation' of 'female sexuality'. As we have seen, such liberation consists of women more freely indulging the sex role of masochist victim, to match the male role of sadist victor, as ordained by the sexologists of old and modernized only through an increased factor of brutality.

Since its eruption in the sixties the sexual revolution has gained substantial ground, sadomasochism rapidly becoming the norm of sexuality. Thus we may observe how a practice of so-called 'rough sex', to which a growing number of women are falling victim, is being confirmed as the new social standard of heterosexuality, with lawyers and courts helping to adjust the juridical standards of 'acceptable' brutality to an alleged norm in social practice. When in the USA Robert Chambers stood accused of murdering his sexual partner Jennifer Levin, his defence lawyer, Barry Slotnick, argued that this was less a case of murder than a mishap in the course of 'rough sex'. 'Sexual asphyxiation', so he explained, 'is a great hidden secret of this society.'[1] Asphyxiation, in case we are not so familiar with clinical Greek and Latin, means the transitive action of suffocating someone – in the words of the dictionary, to 'choke or kill by stopping respiration (of person . . .)' (*OED*). To call it 'a great hidden secret of this society' is to suggest that this practice forms a common part of the repertoire of 'normal' heterosexual activity. It becomes an open secret only if the partner happens actually to suffocate, i.e. when the secret leaves an unfortunate trace in the shape of a dead body. This may be a regrettable piece of evidence, leading to the lover being tried in court, but it is a happy circumstance in so far as such evidence is no longer in a position to give evidence. Quite on the contrary, authoritative experts may now impute to the evidence 'consent' to the very practice which turned her into evidence, that is to say, impute to the woman who cannot say otherwise that she consented to her 'lover' practising the 'rough sex' which killed her.

And indeed another client of the same lawyer and well-versed expert in matters of normal sexual practice, the nineteen-year-old Joseph Porto, accused of murdering Katherine Holland, is found guilty only of negligent homicide.[2] His lawyer apparently successfully argued that 'the young couple' were 'a pair who fell victim to a tragic accident that could easily have happened to anyone'.[3] As his client explained, retracting his earlier confession to have strangled Katherine Holland, he had been engaged in playful sex with her, and 'to increase her sexual pleasure', had 'put a rope around her neck' and 'inadvertently yanked it too hard'.[4]

To have shifted the issue from murder to sex means to have shifted it from an analysis of criminal action to the perspective of sexology, which conceives whatever 'happened' as by definition a shared event which allows us to infer the equal consent and shared experience of both partners – if anything, it is the 'pair' falling victim to the brutality of the 'sex'. But while Porto, like Havelock Ellis's loving pain-inflicting lover, is seen merely to oblige his partner's sexual pleasure, the sheer *presence* of the woman apparently allows us to infer her consent as well as her desire to submit to her partner's will – the presence of her corpse allowing the sexological jurist to infer her consent and her desire to be strangulated by Porto in a practice of 'rough sex'. If thus the alleged social 'normality' of 'rough sex' has helped to change juridical standards, the titillating court cases and their newly set precedents in turn help to normalize the 'great hidden secret of this society', that is, to legitimize the increasingly murderous sex practice of 'normal' men. The 'world's press' is in attendance at the Chambers trial at Manhattan's Supreme Court, to inform the 'world' of this momentous revolution in contemporary mores.[5]

What the sexual revolution thus has in store for women is not their accession to male sexual subjectivity, but the 'liberated' role of masochist and victim. The political vocabulary of women's liberation is humoured in so far as women are encouraged indeed to become more 'active' and 'assertive' – more active in seeking and more assertive in voluntarily assuming their preordained role. And if women perchance should fall for it and see no problem with such a notion of gendered 'liberty' – the liberty of voluntary subjection – the advocates of the sexual revolution certainly know that this complementary 'democracy' presents no threat to male subjectivity and no danger of a redistribution of power.

Rather, if women now aspire to sexual subjectivity as men do, this simply promises a more sportive battle of the sexes, on the individual as well as the collective level. On the individual level, since as a now open battle men will fight it with increased tenacity to ensure their continuing victory – a fact which has already seduced many a social commentator to blame the growing sexual violence of men in Western societies on feminism and the women's movement, as 'causing' or 'provoking' it;[6] and on the collective level, since the number of institutionalized 'victims' is objectively decreasing and 'victims' are therefore at a premium.

Thus the phenomenal increase in prostitution, in a society boasting apparently liberalized sexual relations among its members, is a sign that male sexual subjectivity is shifting to a context where both (male) subjectivity and (female) objectivity remain intact, framed and secured by contract. What 'woman' used to signify, today only 'prostitute' continues to signify with certainty (even if only on strictly limited and circumscribed terms). Similarly, the prevalence of child sexual assault confirms men's continuing predilection for persons of still disenfranchised status. While the growing interest of Western men in marriages with women from impoverished Third World countries (and the accompanying juridical framework facilitating the women's importation and ensuring their lack of independent rights) shows a strategic entrenchment of traditional male sexual subjectivity and privilege.

That the attraction of such marriages is precisely the increased differential of power between a male citizen and a 'foreign' woman is further evidenced by the fact that men pay an unusually high price for a 'mail order bride' who is also mute (the money of course going to her dealer, rather than the woman herself): 'Normally, a woman from Asia costs around DM 5,000 [approx. £2,000]. For mute women the demand far exceeds the supply. I have been offered mute women at DM 25,000 [£10,000].'[7] Yet the woman's lack of political rights, plus, as the case may be, her speaking a different language from her Western husband, already effectively guarantees her virtual 'deaf-muteness' – at least for the immediate future, and if she is carefully secluded, also in the long term. Her chances of self-determination, of articulating and asserting her own interests *vis-à-vis* her husband, are thus seriously impaired. Whereas the latter, as experience shows, may make himself sufficiently understood even without linguistic skills, that is, by the traditional means of battering and physical violence.[8]

So if female co-citizens – women with equal political rights who could at last challenge male subjectivity – not only do not do so, but instead aspire to such subjectivity themselves, it certainly constitutes no threat to male subjectivity. On the contrary, 'subjectivity' is thus 'democratically' ratified, 'women' and 'men' (that is, citizens of both sexes) now being united in a social consensus, sharing a common purpose, a common value, a common sense. For those continuing to be locked into social object status – 'mail order brides', migrants male and female, prostitutes indigenous and foreign, children and old people – do not count as part of the democratic 'society' which constitutes its consensus. The 'new woman' who co-determines the new social consensus of the new democracy is the woman citizen of (re)productive age in her capacity as 'private individual' – the embodiment of the 'emancipation of female pleasure'.[9]

As Ariane Barth informs us in an article in the German weekly, *Der Spiegel*, female emancipation, 'steadily as clockwork', is working its transformations, 'As the figure of post-feminism there appears the desiring woman, in theory and in practice. She is the completion of that cultural revolutionary who, in a process lasting over a century, has broken into the world of men and claimed her part.'[10] No longer satisfied merely to be desired, she also wants to have in her sexuality 'what used to be the epitome of the male role'[11] – although we might say that it is less a matter of something which may be *had* than of something one may *do*, and which so far mostly men have been doing.

As a shrewd social observer, however, Barth hasn't failed to notice that the first woman to do as men do has been the 'masculine woman', alias the 'invert' – even if Barth attributes her appearance to the women's movement (probably on account of the central role of lesbians in that movement) rather than to the sexologists at the turn of the century who invented her. For two decades there had been 'ideological shooting at the phallocrats' from the women's movement, and 'as a sign of the turning away from men' a totally different topic emerged 'from the depths of social repression': 'the female desire for the woman'.[12] Quite in line with the patriarchal and sexological perspective, women's struggle for independence – their political and ideological 'turning away from men' – is here equated with a sexual perversion or inversion: feminists are man-hating lesbians who turn away from men, not because of their critique of patriarchy and male behaviour but because really they are driven by a sexual desire for women. Yet this is ultimately of less interest to our social historian than is the 'gigantic de-eroticization' which by contrast has beset the relations between the sexes, at the same time as the cultural industry is signalling a 'hyper-sexualization' – producing a flood of lively 'sexuality' on dead paper and celluloid which, however, in Margrit Brückner's words, 'has left hearts and groins as living Eros'.[13] Hence, Barth claims, there is 'a yearning stirring in the women's movement' for the relationship between the sexes to be 're-eroticized'.[14]

The proof of such stirrings in the women's movement Barth finds in the texts of a sizeable collection of highly accredited female academics, professors from both sides of the Atlantic, all 'radical analysts of psychological and social phenomena, literature, art and cinema': 'American avant-gardists are feeling the "Desire to Desire" ', in the words of 'cinema theorist Mary Ann Doane, Brown University, Providence', while 'the psychoanalyst Jessica Benjamin, New York University, student of Adorno, admirer of Marcuse and feminism', speaks of a 'feeling of sexual subjectivity'. 'The sociologist Brückner', already previously identified as 'Professor of Sociology at Frankfurt', speaks of 'the social birth of female desire',[15] and all in all we may rest assured that these are not the usual plebs of the women's movement stirring, but a radical scientific discourse of renowned provenance.

'Never before in the history of the world has the female sex been as free as it is in our times',[16] the author continues, with a remarkably encompassing view of the world in our times, from which the millions of women victims and refugees of war, of women and girls living in abject poverty and famine, of women and girls enslaved in prostitution and the sex trade the world over seem to be wholly absent. The author's gaze is fixed on the free women who now are in search of their 'elementary wishes'.[17] One such elementary wish apparently is the wish to commit violence towards others, starting with the violence of objectification. For, as women have truly learnt from men, 'to desire means to objectify, means it even in a radical way', as Barbara Sichtermann elaborates in a collection of essays aptly named *Weiblichkeit – Zur Politik des Privaten* (Femininity – the Politics of the Private): 'How should women, burdened by their oppressing, centuries-old disadvantage, be capable of it overnight?'[18] A good question, though it is to be feared that power and practice will make perfect in the case of women as they did with men.

In the meantime an empirical survey of the state of the art may get us further: 'For the rising era of the erotic power of the female sex a certain look is symptomatic: direct, even aggressive, as if the women were penetrating.'[19] While 'the counter-image of the female trans-gressor/harasser has also been developing, although she [*sic*] is much rarer.'[20] 'Can a man be raped?' is the next question facing the serious student, and being rather difficult to answer, a male expert, the novelist Anthony Burgess, is consulted. Citing his fictional depiction of such a rape scene, Barth comments: 'Everything has become possible in this game of the sexes: promise as well as threat.'[21] What we therefore may learn above all from this male expert pleasurably imagining a man being raped by four 'unleashed' women who knew 'every trick of the brothel', is that rape is a jolly 'game' of the sexes as full of promise as it is of threat. Promise to whom and threat to whom remains unspecified, hence both remain 'qualities' of the thing itself, the 'game' of rape. Anyone claiming the contrary is but a spoilsport. The first two lessons on the topic of desire are thus: (1) aggressive objectifying and penetrating look, if possible accompanied by a bit of transgressive harassment; (2) rape.

There are complications, however, in the curriculum. For while the first two lessons proceeded on the basic principle of 'hetero' and its simple inversion – the inversion of the male subject to a female subject entailing a correspondingly inverted male object (even though the raping subject beyond inversion also requiring multiplication to four female subjects, plus the advanced competency of prostitutes) – the next step is a decided return to the 'normal' relationship between the sexes. After this brief practical field trip we return to the lecture theatre and the study of the great master – patriarchal culture. Since there is 'so little orientation' for the new women, we rifle the works of great men, in the hope that they may already have applied them-selves to the problem, creating some 'images and role models' for the new woman to follow.[22] Thus the Frankfurt literary critic Carola Hilmes investigated whether at least the *femme fatale* – from her biblical beginnings to her adaptation by great European writers as Penthesilea or Judith, Salome or perhaps Wedekind's Lulu – could not serve for the 'reconstruction of sensuality as female power'.[23] She could, but not sufficiently so. For although we find plenty of female figures of 'demonic power' who would do nicely, the problem apparently is that these are also invariably punished and ultimately destroyed for their power. That the aspiring female subject as a first step of her emancipation proposes to subject herself to the role model of a male fantasy does not in itself seem to pose any problem.

Because of this deplorable lack of pre-existing role models women resort to constructing their own cultural blueprint, be it Jessica Benjamin's 'psycho-utopia', Mary Ann Doane's 'artificial myth', or even 'female porn' or, more highbrow, the 'presentation of female bodies by female artists'.[24] Now the study of the art of desire no longer proceeds on the 'hetero' principle, but via the traditional object of desire, the female body. 'Women are thus demonstrating that they can define their own eroticism and oppose it to phallic desire.'[25] Whether it be their own or the phallic eroticism of men, its object remains a female body. Margrit Brückner explains: 'So long as the female body cannot be appropriated by women and women refrain from occupying their body positively, female desire will be stunted.'[26] So long as women do not appropriate the female body as men routinely appropriate it, that is, in an act of taking possession, women will not experience (male) desire. Women may *have* a female body, yet to learn to desire it in male fashion they will need to appropriate it like a foreign body, taking possession of it as booty in a crusade of conquest. This means, in the case of their own body, less an act of appropriation than the already widely current and culturally well inculcated alienation from their own body: not just the psychological splitting of the self into subject and object, but the radical splitting of the self into male subjectivity and a female body. It is a process whose harmful consequences for women are well known, as the manifold manifestations of a disturbed relationship to their own body. If the body in question, however, is not the woman's own body, but, as in the case of the female artists' presentation of women's bodies, *other* women's bodies, male desire is at last beginning to realize itself, predicated on a female subject: in the objectification of, that is the violence done to, other women's bodies and thus to other women.

What we are witnessing, then, is by no means a specifically female desire, but on the contrary, the sheer imitation of the old and familiar male desire for the object 'female body'. Similarly Lynne Segal's search for female empowerment, for 'women as empowered agents of heterosexual desire',[27] yields as its greatest success so far 'many young women presenting themselves . . . as sexual agents in ways not so different from men'.[28] The suspicion is growing that 'sex' means male sex, 'desire' means male desire, 'sexual agency' means male sexual agency; that the more closely any eroticism resembles male eroticism and the more closely any desire resembles male desire, the more certain they are to be 'real' eroticism and desire. And the more closely a female subject's behaviour resembles the behaviour of a male subject, the more likely the female subject is to be a sexual subject. In other words, we are dealing not with any democratization of sexuality and desire, but the simple attempt at a role change within the most undemocratic structure of traditional male sex.

Just as the experimenting sexual pioneers do not concern themselves with the existing problems of female self-alienation, so they do not seem to object to the traditional subject–object structure of sex and desire, nor to the fact that the role of object continues to be occupied by women. What seems of interest, rather, is the possibility of the pioneers themselves occupying the role of desiring subject – with a spectrum of diverse objects. Thus Jane Gallop's experiment first of all leads to auto-eroticism, that is, a relationship of the subject to its own art, the object 'desire': 'I animate it, and it animates me'[29] – in wonderful mutuality and reciprocity. By contrast, Gisela Breitling returns to the object 'man' and her attempt to utilize it for female desire: 'But can men stand up to such women's gaze? Can the sex, which for thousands of years has been holding the power of voyeurism, really bear to *be* looked at?'[30] No doubt they can, but do they want to?

While men, from the ideologues of the sexual revolution to the individual practitioner, seem to understand rather better that desire is a question of power and the will to power – that they neither want to give up power, nor aspire to being disempowered by women – these female ideologues seem to prefer to psychologize and sociologize men's behaviour, representing their not wanting to as not (yet) being able to, thus keeping them available for future experiments. An empirical survey apparently yields 'armies of men' avoiding women's penetrating look in 'deepest confusion', or leaving their place at the bar 'in flight'.[31] The conclusion: 'Fear remains an accompanying factor of desire.'[32] Whose fear and whose desire once again remains scientifically unspecified.

Under this psychologizing perspective, men are 'deeply confused' while the motive of their flight is fear. And while there is a certain

sympathy extended to them, a sensitive understanding of their 'fear' of
female aggression, it nevertheless is the aggressive women, and hence
aggressors in general, who appear as the ultimate victims. For as it
turns out, this penetrating gaze and this initiation of a transgression
towards another do not constitute a danger to the other, but an
'endangerment of the self '.[33] The aggressor 'exposes' herself through
her aggression: 'In the free play of forces this desirous exposure of the
needs of one's own body – its drivenness – seems to cause both sexes
equal anxiety', Brückner argues.[34] In other words, it is no longer only
traditional rapists, sexual harassers, molesters and abusers who thus put
themselves at risk and in danger; we now may count on women
aggressors similarly exposing themselves. Yet as the relevant science
also reports, men are still facing this danger in more manly fashion
than women, who 'fend off their own desire in panic and fright,
developing instead a hysteria of avoidance'.[35]

True female boldness is thus required to learn the art of violence:
'we need courage in order to desire' (Brückner); and 'we only gain
(or win) by objectifying' (Sichtermann).[36] For gain is the goal and
victory the purpose: gaining power over the other in order to profit
from them, to instrumentalize them for one's pleasure and use them
after one's will. 'The fact that the women's movement has devolved
the aggressive part exclusively on to men now takes its toll', Ariane
Barth exhorts. Now we have to win it back.[37] In fact, the women's
movement did not so much devolve the aggressive part on to the male
sex as find it there, that is, criticize that men freely choose it. But that
too, Barth argues, now takes its toll, since some men, taking the
critique to heart, apparently distanced themselves from the 'habitual
rapist' – 'and lo!, at the same stroke the force which once propelled
the conqueror was gone.'[38] That is, at the same stroke the violence
was gone and thus the sex was gone. What remained was 'infantile
snuggle-sex' (Ulrike Heider) and 'tender servicing',[39] which, the
scientists and pioneers are agreed, is no adult sex at all.

While mainstream ideologues still hesitate to equate sex with
violence, trying instead to differentiate between sex 'with' or 'without' violence, these radical analysts of psychological and social phenomena, literature, art and cinema are stating with unprecedented
clarity what before could be heard only from the radical feminist
underground, and then only amidst a clamour of opposition. Yet what
now comes as scientific truth even goes beyond what radical feminists

claim. Not only is the 'habitual rapist' clearly to be preferred over critical anti-sexist men, the unmistakable message is: no sex without violence, no desire without the lust for booty, no excitement without conquest. For without its goal of dominance and submission there is no motor and no dynamic for sex.

Since feminists, however, have been concerned with a critique of violence rather than with a search for sex, the emphasis, despite similar insight, has been somewhat different: if experience shows that sex indeed means violence and sexual excitement the pleasure of power – that sex minus the violence does not leave you with non-violent sex but simply with 'no sex' at all – it does not follow that we therefore must accept violence; it follows that 'sex' as such is unacceptable. It means to recognize the violence of sex, not filling the concept of 'sex' with 'new meaning' and rehabilitating violence. We neither attempt to give new and positive meanings to the concepts of 'war' or 'anti-Semitism' to rehabilitate them discursively. (Although with the notion of 'just wars', 'humanitarian interventions' and military alliances as 'partnerships for peace', a process of rehabilitating 'war' has clearly begun.) The critique of violence, of anti-Semitism, of misogyny, of sexuality does not call for a correction of these terms on the level of discourse, but for political consequences on the level of reality.

If your aim, however, is to rescue 'sex' – after this sobering lapse into insight to render Eros 'living' again – it means, in the words of one of its rescuers, 'a game of "destruction and survival" ' (Jessica Benjamin).[40] The distinction of this new eroticism, so Benjamin argues, lies 'in the survival of the other in and despite the destruction'.[41] In other words, it lies in avoiding the mishaps of a Robert Chambers or a Joseph Porto, whose partners transformed into corpses during destruction, failing to assert the crucial difference by surviving. For according to Benjamin, survival is 'the difference which the other asserts', that is, the one in the process of being destroyed; it is not the difference which rests in the hands of him who does the destroying.

Such survival does not look so very different from women's survival in sexual slavery and sexual violence, where the woman physically survives (if she does) in and despite her destruction as a person. Rarely do we hear it said in good company, however, that the small difference does indeed lie between sex and murder, with sex just this side of absolute destruction. 'The concept of destruction reminds us',

Benjamin continues, 'that a measure of aggression is necessary for any love life.'[42] Necessary certainly for saving this love life and for rescuing this sex. How large, though, is a measure of aggression? But this is precisely the thrill of the matter: the difficulty (or is it the danger?) of measuring the right dose. It promises most surely to remain but a 'measure', if we continue to regard it carefully detached from its consequence.

At what point a measure of aggression is a full measure becomes evident in those examples from literature, art and cinema that furnish the cultural ideals of our times, such as the Spanish cult film 'Matador', where the bull fighter Diego and the lawyer Maria 'kill themselves in the act' and 'Eros and aggression are one and the same.'[43] 'But in real life', the author deplores, we usually experience only a 'small death' – and, we might add, more often than the death of both probably the 'small death' of the partner. However, this must not be judged as a laywoman might do, for in sexuality, Sichtermann explains, 'aggression directly serves the peace (of satisfaction).'[44] Since the subject and the object of aggression as usual remain undifferentiated, there is only abstract 'aggression' and hence general 'satisfaction', spreading over the land like peace. Wars, too, have been fought for the same end of 'peace': the satisfaction of the conquerors' desires, their pleasure in expansion and domination, and for the deep 'peace' that comes over a country vanquished and occupied.

'There is a peace you can find after being handcuffed to the bed and whipped and then held, free and tenderly in your lover's arms that surpass [sic] all understanding', one advocate of sadomasochism writes about such peace from the perspective of the conquered.[45] 'Pain is so wonderful when it ceases', goes a bad joke about a man who hit his finger with a hammer to experience it. As pain is relative when it wanes so there is relative peace during a ceasefire. And freedom is apparently relative too, if after being handcuffed and whipped you are only being *held*, 'free and tenderly', in your torturer's arms. Yet even a small pain remains a pain, a little captivity captivity, and a ceasefire certainly is no peace. Occupation following a war may bring 'law and order', but it means domination established. Peace would require more than the relative semantics of war – but then, peace is not really the issue for our advocates of sexual warfare.

Rather, aggression, war and deadly intent are – even if it is no longer under the traditional circumstances where the (male) sexual subject's victory over an already designated sexual 'object' was ensured. In the democratic scenario of equal opportunities – where the roles of the dominant and the dominated are no longer given and the 'desiring (heterosexual) woman' has entered the scene – we have a 'battle between two desires'.[46] Male strategies to overpower meet 'female strategies to overpower', and 'male aggressor meets female aggressor.'[47] As Ariane Barth sarcastically comments, 'it is so beautiful you could die.'[48] And as we are obliged to add, no longer just for one: the chance of dying, too, has been (theoretically) democratized.

The theoreticians of the battle of two desires, however, remain silent about the outcome of the battle – how victorious, how satisfied or how surviving in the destruction both partners will be. Jessica Benjamin, as we know from the battle for recognition, is a passionate advocate of the suspended balance, the even match of two equal opponents. Yet even supposing that there was such a match, this would lead to a wrestling on end or the *détente* of a cold war, rather than the sought-after hot excitement, let alone the satisfaction which comes with victory. In other words, there no more would be any sex taking place between two equally balanced desiring sexual subjects than there was in the case of two passive and submissive sexual objects which so taxed the earlier sexologists' imaginations.

While the theoreticians nevertheless remain convinced that this is the way forward for the desiring woman, the practitioner with her eye on social reality remains sceptical. 'The artist [Gisela Breitling] doubts that she will find her "opposite" ',[49] doubts in other words that in reality men are going to play. The enterprise may be in the interest of the entrepreneuse, but apparently not in the interest of her 'opposite'. For even if the active desiring woman has long been playing her frolicking part in male pornographic fantasy, the pornographic moral of the story is no different from the high-cultural moral of the *femme fatale* stories: male victory is (must be) certain, the strong woman will (must) be subdued. Else it isn't the game we thought it was.

If thus the way to an actively desiring sexual subjectivity seems after all to be barred to women, there still remains a chance for them to realize their desire – as active, initiating and penetrating subjects of a scientific discourse. For on the level of discourse and theory there always will be a suitable 'opposite' who may easily be turned into an 'object', who will 'submit' to scientific subjectivity without resistance.

That it will turn out to be another scientific discourse about *women* –
the traditional 'opposites', patients and objects of so many a scientific
discourse – will hardly be a surprise. Nor is the fact that, on this level
of discourse, lesbian sadomasochism is being mobilized to the front
line of battle, as a sexual sadism of women also having women as its
object. For the science, like the art of desire, is being learnt at the
school of patriarchy, where it is taught on the traditional material, the
object woman.

As the literature of lesbian sadomasochism itself laments, women
abound in their traditional role as women, that is, as masochists and
victims, there being a pronounced lack (still) of candidates for the role
of sadist.[50] That is to say, the pioneers, be it of lesbian sadomasochism
or of female scientific discourse, remain a small – even if growing –
minority; they are a minority who themselves are ascending to male
subjectivity, while for their enterprise they require other women's
object status, requiring and thus cementing it in the very advocacy of
a 'female', that is, their own, subjectivity.

That lesbian sadomasochism, like the theory of female desire, fits
well into the programme of the sexual revolution and the battle
against feminist politics, may be seen from the fact that pornographers
support it and highbrow social scientists cite it. If we thought that
male academics and opinion-makers rarely read books by women, it
now appears that they do indeed rifle through them. Once women say
what they themselves have been saying, equality of the sexes may at
last be practised and a few women be given an opportunity: they shall
fulfil the promise of a democratized sexual revolution, the legitimation of sexual desire, of the principle of dominance and submission,
out of the mouths and from the pens of biological women.

There is no danger that women will thereby usurp or even just
decrease men's power: there are plenty of power structures all round
ensuring that they will not. In particular, it would require more than
the simple desire of a minority for equal opportunities, more than the
pioneering efforts of some women breaking into the hierarchy of
power, stabilizing it by taking their place in it. It would require a
political struggle for the liberation of all women, a struggle against
oppression of any kind, and hence against the pleasure of power and
domination, that is, against desire.

10

Relationship as trade, or the free market of bodies and services

If in practice there nevertheless exist relationships and sexual encounters which appear to be 'democratic' internally (even if they contribute nothing to the democratization of society as a whole), this does not mean that they are not based on opposition and the conflict of interests; it means, rather, that these relations, like the conflicting relations of the citizens in the state, are regulated 'from above' and by means of contracts.

As we have seen, 'sex' or a 'relationship' as the undertaking of two partners of equal rights is realized on the basis of a higher entrepreneurial interest, the interest in 'togetherness'. This interest is superordinated to the partners' individual self-interests, keeping their basic opposition in check. Unlike the citizen–husband of traditional marriage, the democratic subject does not require a disenfranchised 'object' (a wife), but a partner with an equal interest. The primary interest is in the relationship, for which a suitable partner is sought. Once the partner is found and the partnership founded, the business proceeds by and large like any other business relations – whether the habitual relations between firms or those of established business partnerships – on the basis of more or less fixed contracts. Consequently, the individual partner's actions relate not so much to the other partner as to the smooth operation and maintenance of the relation.

Thus the therapist Robin Norwood interprets the 'particularly good sex after a fight' as a 'tremendous investment . . . in making sex "work" ', a gesture 'to validate the relationship as a whole'.[1] Apart from the fact that 'the couple' is said to share an identical and common intention, this intention obviously has nothing to do with the interpersonal actions in question, neither with a decision to approach the partner sexually, nor with the satisfaction of sexual desire, be it one's own or one's partner's. Rather, the intention or desire is to validate 'the relationship' and to invest in making 'sex' work. It is a gesture, in other words, towards the protagonist, 'the relationship'.

In fact the fight already validates the relationship, but being validation of negative content, the partners now make a special offering to the relationship – through mutual surrender. Or to put it differently, through a sex act (by means of the partner), which is less a sign of love towards the partner than an affirmation to the self that the partner is still available for the relationship and willing to make it a common sacrifice. Hence it is not just individual transactions which are accounted in partnerships, but also the capital investments and the running costs of the enterprise, with any profits shared out *quid pro quo*. While investment in the joint venture is thus characteristic of partnerships, social relations in general resemble simple exchange trade.

This has all the more chance of success as in capitalist society not only economic production is organized along capitalist principles, but also the production of every expression of life on the part of individuals. Hence social relations structure themselves on the model of the relations between producers of goods. 'Private' individuals conceive of themselves as the private producers of their own lives, whose partial products acquire value from the work invested and may be exchanged with similar private products. Whatever we do, every 'productive activity' of daily life, does not just remain use-value as lived experience, but becomes 'useful work' and a product of labour which acquires the fetish character of the commodity. The daily products of living become commodities 'because they are the products of the labour of private individuals who work independently of each other'[2] and are exchanged with similar products of private labour. As Marx writes with regard to commodities:

> In order that these objects may enter into relation with each other as commodities, their guardians must place themselves in relation to one another as persons whose will resides in those objects, and must behave in such a way that each does not appropriate the commodity of the other, and alienate his own, except through an act to which both parties consent. The guardians must therefore recognize each other as owners of private property.[3]

Interestingly, Marx literally speaks of a 'shared act of will' ('ein beiden gemeinsamer Willensakt'),[4] rather than of two possible actions (and wills) – appropriating and alienating – to which each respectively consents. The joint act of will consists in appropriating the commodity of the other *by* alienating one's own ('indem er die eigene veräußert').

Nothing seems more natural to us today than to view social interactions in this light and to regard ourselves as the private owners of the property of our selves and all our 'products', and to behave towards others correspondingly, i.e. recognizing them as just such owners of private property. An encounter is seen as an act of exchange, the 'shared act of will' to exchange presupposed. The point of the encounter is exchange trade, the acquisition of foreign goods by alienating one's own.

For Marx, 'useful labour' is the 'eternal natural necessity which mediates the metabolism between man and nature, and therefore human life itself'.[5] It transpires that the useful and usable labour of living one's life has become the modern social condition which mediates the 'metabolism' between 'man' and 'man', and therefore social life itself. As producers we come into social contact with other producers only through the exchange of products and in order to trade. This is evidenced in the thousands of little calculations of costs and benefits by which we assess whether a contact is worth our while, how profitable it might be and how much we are prepared to invest. That is to say, the commodity another person alienates and which we regard as having been put on offer is assessed in terms of one's own demand and use. Conversely, it is on the basis of our own demand – our needs and wants – that we set out in search of a possible supplier of the desired goods. 'The persons exist for one another merely as representatives and hence owners, of commodities.'[6]

As we have seen already, in our advanced capitalist culture all and anything may be turned into a thing, a conceptual object, which one may 'have', that is, which offers the chance of acquisition, accumulation and private ownership. This starts with one's own 'being', which apparently is less a continuous process of living, experiencing and acting, a permanently changing personal history of present, past and future, than a thing one 'has', owns and hoards, but which may also, as philosophers have shown us, become a burden one might wish to get rid of. Moreover, one 'has' numerous qualities, even properties, which one holds on to as to other property and inheritance. In fact, such qualities usually are linguistic thingifications derived from actions and activities – we may for instance 'be' generous, because we have more than once behaved generously, although we might change such behaviour at any moment. Yet it suits our capitalist thinking to build a person a personality out of a collection of qualities and characteristics, so that clear property relations obtain. Everyone then 'has' a personality, so to speak their basic capital of accumulated history.

This considerably facilitates social relations, since one instantly knows who the other person 'is', thus being able to assess the other's behaviour in advance. Conversely, we know that the other 'is' as they behave at this moment, since following the same logic we may assume that they want to 'be' like this (rather than that they decide to behave like this, at this moment and in this situation). In other words, we can hold others to their personality and behaviour, and expect, if not indeed demand, similar behaviour in future. Such an understanding of 'personality' as a collection of (timeless and context-free) qualities, moreover, facilitates relations with oneself, enabling one to draw on one's stock of past behaviour, solidified into patterns and congealed to characteristics, without the trouble of adjusting one's own actions to the permanent changeability of life, reality and people. That is to say, it saves 'useful labour'.

It is a sign of this reorganization of social relations that we can hardly conceive of social behaviour, interactions, communication other than in the fetish character of commodities. Interpersonal processes and interactions are split into their (alleged) component parts, which then 'belong' clearly to either one or the other social agent (or the subject and its object). Thus thingified, they become measurable and hence permit proper accounting. For instance, rather than analysing the always restructuring power relations between people, we tend to attribute to individuals 'power' which they apparently, qua person or identity, invariably 'have'. Since they 'have' power, they may also share it or give a bit of it away. Thus power is turned into property, if not a property, ceasing to be a relation between people, groups or factors in specific situations.

Similarly, a conversation is split into the communicative elements of speaking and listening (not to say sender and receiver). Since speaking, as an obvious form of production, enjoys a very much higher status in our culture than does listening, and unlike the latter counts among the primary social 'needs' of individuals, it is subjected to rigorous accounting. This may mean that speaking, or speaking time, is carefully measured and equally distributed among the interlocutors, as for instance in group-dynamic therapy situations, where care is taken that everyone has the same number of turns with equal speaking time. Individual speeches are assessed not in terms of their contribution to the joint conversation and its goal of a successful communication among the participants, but in terms of quantity and ownership, whose speech and how much. Democracy and equal opportunity demand that we each have the same amount: one person's right to speak stands opposite another person's right to speak. Because of its tenuous link to listening, however, speaking is not just seen as a right but also as a privilege exercised at the expense of the listener(s).

Since there are rights, it is possible to establish equal rights. This is most simply achieved, as in the state, by regulation from above, say supervision by a speech umpire recognized by all participants. A relationship of two may also manage without an actual umpire – if both partners recognize the law and are prepared continuously to review their relationship and its distribution of speech from 'above', from the point of view, as it were, of an impartial court. Where there are rights as well as clear uses and clear costs, it is also possible to set up a fair and equal trade, so that the enjoyment of the privilege of speech incurs an obligation later to listen, and listening in turn entitles one later to speak – where, in other words, speaking is paid for by listening.

Such an arrangement is based on the assumption that all participants put equal value on the desirability of speaking, have the same urge to speak and to defend their right to speak. However, a relationship may also accommodate complementary needs and desires, say a partner who loves talking and one who loves listening, or does not like talking (the difference rarely troubling the account). If these predilections are mutually known, an unequal speech relation may precisely constitute an equal satisfaction of unequal needs and form the basis of a stable relationship. Not only does this confirm the old adage that opposites attract and suit each other; it also demonstrates the volatile nature of exchange-value, namely that it 'changes constantly with time and place'.[7]

The exchange-value of a commodity, say my speech, is thus on the one hand the 'quantitative relation, the proportion, in which use-values of one kind exchange for use-values of another kind'[8] – my speaking for the other person's speaking. On the other hand, the exchange-value is but the 'mode of expression, the "form of appearance", of a content distinguishable from it'.[9] That is to say, the exchange-value of my speaking is another form of appearance, a translation in a different medium, of the speaking of my listener, or indeed of her listening. The common unit which makes such translation possible is 'value'. Thus my speaking has no value as such, nor does it have a fixed price; its value is dependent on the values of the goods up for exchange and hence subject to the fluctuations of the market, the current situation of supply and demand.

Once commodities in the form of such 'things' and 'objects' have been created, their price or exchange-value is negotiated by means of the complicated procedures of estimation and market research; it results out of the balance between my own readiness to invest in the goods of the other and the investment the other is prepared to make for the commodity I am offering. While in the regulated business life of commercial trade such negotiations are relatively simple, there being occasionally fixed and known prices or else relatively open negotiations about them, the equivalent negotiations in social life rather resemble those of higher diplomacy, the 'black' market or Mafia deals. What one's goods may be worth to the other needs to be figured out, as in a game of poker, at one's own risk, and may mean the possible expenditure of an unprofitable ante. That is to say, a sample of one's own goods may be offered in order to discover (or raise) the trade partner's interest. Conversely, the value the other's goods may have to oneself must on no account be revealed too soon, since this might immediately lead to a rise in the price.

All the more restful, therefore, are so-called private relationships, those partnerships already entered into on both sides, since here the business interests of both partners are discussed or stated comparatively openly. Above all, their readiness to do joint business has already been established, a demand for the goods of the other having been acknowledged on both sides in the mutual agreement to the relationship. This constitutes as much as a mutual obligation to continue to do business. An engagement, or its modern equivalent, the mutual avowal of the relationship, corresponds as it were to the founding of a company or corporation, or the sealing of a stable business association.

In comparison to 'public' social life, the private relationship enables a relatively guaranteed trade and exchange of social commodities, that is, of the buying and selling of what are considered to be the social subsistence goods. These may include anything a person has to offer, or another may decide to be their need: communication, warmth, presence, interest, closeness, but also their capacities and skills, their thinking, their body, their social position, and many more. 'The commodity is first of all an external object, a thing which through its qualities satisfies human needs of whatever kind.'[10] Since human needs, in particular human-'social' needs or relationship needs – that is, needs relating to another person or person – are infinitely inventable and may take ever new forms, every and any aspect of a person may become a tradeable commodity.

By contrast to the free trading in 'public' social life – that is, with potential new trading partners whose business solidity is as yet unknown – the 'private' relationship provides added security that a contract may be enforced, and goods delivered or services rendered will be adequately compensated. For the risk of chancing upon a profiteer who disappears before both parts of the exchange are completed, that is, before the subject has secured the goods for which it alienated its own, is proportionally higher, the less the stranger is bound into the subject's own social network. A stranger may remain inaccessible to bailiffs or to possible sanctions such as trade boycotts by the subject's entire trading network. Conversely, the more firmly a relationship is established, the more thoroughly each partner is involved in the social network of the other, or the more deeply they are jointly anchored in a common community, the greater the possible social control and the greater the chances of enforcing contracts, or enforcing sanctions. This shows again the intimate relation between the 'private' relationship and the so-called 'public', that is, the extended social network of the partners in which the partnership is 'publicly' acknowledged, and its usefulness for the relationship.

Normally, then, the relationship is a mutual trade relation, where under optimal circumstances the needs of one partner are satisfied by the goods supplied by the other and vice versa. The needs may be similar needs, which are then satisfied alternately, or they may be complementary needs. What is important for the democratic relationship is that there be a relatively even distribution of needs, that is, that they occur on both sides, thus guaranteeing a mutual dependency. Hence the emphasis of the modern feminist relationship philosophy on *dependency* (and not, say, on autonomy), its vision of the ideal relationship of the future as the partners' growing and evenly balanced 'mutual dependency' or 'interpendence'.[11] For dependency is the *sine qua non* of relationship trade. Thus it is less one's own 'dependency needs' which are the problem than the necessity of creating a dependency in the partner.

The partner's dependency is a necessity for the subject, the precondition for the trade by which it secures the goods to satisfy its own needs, whereas a relatively undemanding or allegedly unneedy partner spells potential disaster. Since in fact there are no people without needs, the question is, rather, whether these are entered into the bargaining, are made over as the partner's competency and responsibility. What is considered to constitute an alleged unneediness is thus less an actual lack of needs than a person's old-fashioned decision to consider them a personal responsibility. Jessica Benjamin's struggle for mutual recognition is an example of a successful mutual dependency structure, as is Luise Eichenbaum's and Susie Orbach's vision of the ideal heterosexual mutual dependency of the future: 'One of the tasks in front of men at this point is for them to recognise their dependency on women, to take responsibility for it and for women to accept it openly.'[12] Of course, 'taking responsibility' in this context does not so much mean considering such dependency to be a problem of own's own responsibility, which would oblige one to decrease it; it means acknowledging that one *is* (however unduly) dependent on someone and 'standing by it', that is, keeping it so.

What selling and buying are to private commerce, giving and taking are to the relationship trade. Not only does it stand to capitalist reason that every giving necessarily means a taking, the inseparable twin of give-and-take has become the very emblem (not to say trademark) of successful mutuality and the motto of the democratic relationship: giving and taking are the staple of a healthy relationship, that is, giving and taking for the one as for the other partner. And they lived happily ever after, or as the modern version goes, 'and they were both able to enjoy the giving and receiving.' 'Each will have the ability to give . . . and the ability to receive.'[13]

Where once a man's marriage consisted of his taking, that is to say, his ensured exploitation of his wife, the modern democratic relationship aspires to mutually balanced exploitation. Each shall profit from the other, satisfying their personal needs by means of the other's goods. In the modern understanding this give-and-take has even become one of the many synonyms of love, as Alain Finkielkraut remarks: 'there exists a word which at the same time designates the act of giving and the act of taking, charity and greed, beneficence and avid desire: the word "love".'[14] Giving, therefore, does not really mean that a person decides to give someone something, which as far as the giver is concerned would be the end of the matter. Rather, the subject, like a trading subject, enters a complicated process through which its giving acquires additional significance, to be precise, the significance of the other's taking. Giving and taking are thus the basic metaphors of social relations, structured by the principle of exchange and equivalent to the commercial terms of 'alienation' and 'acquisition' or 'appropriation': commodities change their owners.

Above all, on account of a commodity being alienated, 'giving' acquires a *value*, namely the value the commodity has for the one receiving it – whence 'giving' no longer means giving, but through the other's gain has become the giver's equivalent loss. In other words, the subject of giving tends to be aware of the capitalist principles of exchange trade, according to which a thing (for example, 'giving') has no value in a social sense (even if as my own self-determined action it may have use-value for me), unless it also has use-value for others and is transmitted to another by means of exchange. Any *action* through which another may possibly benefit thereby becomes the agent's calculable 'loss' and may be accounted in the column of his costs. Hence one does not give in order to give, but in order through one's own loss to render the other person a debtor. In other words, it is not giving which is the primary motive, but the second thought that giving leads to debt and debt demands compensation. The measure of the debt again may be determined by the sacrifice made, the 'price' paid in advance. If this sounds somewhat abstract, it is all very familiar in the concrete form of daily life as we live it.

Thus a client of Robin Norwood's explains with what enthusiasm she used to cook meals for her friend: 'It was great. He let me cook for him and really enjoyed being looked after.'[15] We may assume that the client did not just cook 'for him' but also for herself, that is, that she decided to cook so that they could both eat – what would constitute a use-value. But her action apparently acquires its meaning not from her own decision and the action's use-value, but through the trade exchange of her relationship: she cooks 'for him', even if she joins him at the table. Under this perspective he becomes

the beneficiary (if not indeed the object) of her action, and as beneficiary simultaneously her debtor. That she does not simply cook
because she likes cooking (or even cooking for him) transpires from
her explicit mention of the success of her action, the manifestation of
the value it has for him: he really enjoyed being looked after. His
recognition of her labour as a use to himself not only valuates her
labour; it confirms the measure of his debt to her. Thus his benefit
from her cooking, as the client chooses to interpret it, is less the good
food he is eating than the fact that it had been cooked 'for him' – that
is, confirmation that she stands in a trading relation with him. Hence
the need which the client seeks to satisfy in her partner by means of
her cooking is not his need for victuals, but a postulated need to be
'looked after'. Her next step consequently consists not in the further
cooking of meals, but 'I pressed his shirt for him before he dressed that
[*sic*] morning.'[16]

Similarly, in the case of the mother of another client of Norwood's,
who would 'start making these wonderful meals' every time her
husband came home early and spent some time with the family. She
too, according to the client's account, did not do so because she liked
cooking wonderful meals (be it as such or for her whole family, which
also included two children), but 'to reward him, I guess, for coming
home to his family'.[17] In this case the mother's cooking is not an
attempt to render the father a debtor, but rather the settlement of a
debt of her own. For the father's coming home early to his family, too,
does not mean that he wants to come home early to be with his family,
it means that he is making a sacrifice and making the mother a present
of it. Her interpretation of it as indeed a personal present to her in turn
enables her to compensate him for it: her meal is the value-equivalent
of his coming home early.

The rhetoric of relationships abounds in expressions which betray
the calculation of actions in terms of their cost-benefit within the
frame of reference of the relationship, that is, its system of mutual
debt. Anything may be traded, alienated or acquired, so long as
accounts are pending and balances remain due, constituting a right to
settlement. At least, this is what honest traders expect, though they
may more than once have been defrauded by vicious profiteers. As
another client of Norwood's relates, 'I thought I was making him love
me, by giving myself to him. I gave him everything, everything I had
to give.'[18] The giving, that is, was anything but a gift; rather it was an

advance payment for which delivery of goods in return was expected: in this case, being loved. She gave him 'everything' she had to give, and apparently he took without giving back – a case of 'Loving the Man Who Doesn't Love Back', as Norwood calls one of her chapters. The client adds: 'Oh, but it hurts to know that I could do all that for nothing.'[19] That is, she did it 'for nothing', gratis – which usually corresponds to the sense of 'giving'. Yet this was obviously anything but an act of giving; rather, it was a delivery of goods which, through default on the part of the receiver, remained 'for nothing', that is, unpaid.

'All I ever cared about was making Jim happy and keeping him with me', the defrauded client continues. 'I didn't ask for anything except that he spend time with me.'[20] 'All I ever cared about was making him happy' is a construction akin to 'giving', denoting a good deed of a transitive nature, with a clear intention of its effect: that he may be happy. Yet this is contradicted in the same breath, since she did not just want him to be happy, but wanted to keep him with her (whether that would make him happy or not). Although her wish is expressed without reference to anything he might have to *do* – she wants to keep him – fulfilling that wish requires the presence of his person, that is, requires his person, and that he does as she wills. This wish that another may do as I wish is rendered innocuous, however, by preceding it with the generous intention of wanting to make that person happy. Which might allow us to infer that its illegitimacy – as a wish for possession of and control over a person – may nevertheless be dimly sensed. For once more it is presented as a mere nothing: 'I didn't ask for anything except' – read 'that trifle' – 'that he spend time with me.' Usually, I *have* what I am keeping *with me*, though perhaps without the 'with me' her meaning might be too evident: all I cared about was having and keeping him. That I may 'demand', that I may name the price, follows from the delivery of goods in advance, the client's aforementioned 'giving herself to him' – whether the goods had been ordered or sent in advance so as to make the beneficiary a debtor.

This may be one of the most pronounced differences between ordinary commercial transactions and relationship transactions, namely that goods are delivered unasked to a receiver of one's choice so as to extort a payment or return. Rather than a demand creating a supply to satisfy it, goods are supplied to create a demand – a demand for payment. Thus we are told of the same client that she had 'vowed she would never, ever be the kind of angry, demanding woman she saw her mother to be'; instead she would – no, not make her man blissfully happy, but 'win' him 'with love, understanding, and the total gift of herself'.[21] To demand, as she maintains her mother did, apparently means to demand something without having previously paid for it, whereas the daughter is opting for serious business relations: she pays in advance, 'with love, understanding, and the total gift of herself' – and with her own profit firmly in mind, namely to 'win' her man, to 'have' and 'keep' him once and for all. Loving someone, trying to understand another person and 'giving oneself' are evidently not things one does because one wants to do them (and with the consequences of these actions in mind). Neither are they actions which express the agent's 'personality' and manifest subjectivity and intent. Quite on the contrary, they are a means to an end, and therefore acts of self-damaging and self-dispossession, sacrifices the subject makes and losses she incurs in the secret or not so secret hope of later making good the damage.

Often it works, and the self-sacrifice pays off, yielding the desired compensation: 'In return, Jim gave her a great deal of attention and flattery when they were together.'[22] He did not simply pay her attention, he gave it to her 'in return'. The value of the compensation lies in the quantity: he gave her 'a great deal' of attention. Jim is not just attentive to her because she is there and he is relating to her: he makes her a present of a generous measure of attention (which he might as easily withhold). Nor does he flatter her, but he gives her flattery and she is given it (leaving aside what kind of gift this might be). Moreover, 'he managed to say exactly what she needed to hear.'[23] Apparently she does not wish to hear what he has to say, but wishes that he says what she wants to hear. Whether he says it because he wants to say it or because she wants to hear it, she interprets it in any case not as an expression of his will, but as the wonderful settlement of a debt in the currency of her choice.

Yet despite such successful transactions, this relationship ends in commercial fiasco and near-bankruptcy for the client, although her therapist sees this less as a sign of incompetent business management than an unhealthy 'need to give more love than she received, to give and give from an already empty place inside her'.[24] What is a fact, however, is that the accounts don't balance and the expenses by far exceed the incomings. That one loses by giving, getting poorer and poorer until one has nothing left to give, can be seen from the fact that the client has long emptied the place inside her – had overdrawn her account long ago. The cure now consists in no longer entering into business relations with men 'who have nothing to offer me, and don't even want what I have to offer them'[25] – in other words, checking rather more carefully both the supply and the demand, and no longer delivering goods where there is no demand for them. Conversely, it also means checking the goods, if any, being offered in exchange. Yet the problem was less that the men in question had 'nothing to offer', than that they were not, or no longer, or not to sufficient measure, willing to offer it. But that is already forgotten – moreover, an analysis which would reckon with the agent's will and with partners' freedom of decision would be detrimental to maintaining an unregenerate understanding of relationships as a jolly market life in which persons exist only as representatives and owners of commodities.

If we think that this self-sacrificial profligacy, this habit of paying in advance in the hope of returns which women report with such candour, might in fact be specific to women – perhaps the result of a socialization to care and nurturing, a form of female self-abnegation or even a masochist tendency – we are mistaken. It is a basic principle of relationship barter which men too have been using for some time, especially in relation to women they do not call their own. Every dinner at their expense, every invitation to the cinema, every lift offered in the car and every little favour rendered is thus considered, as we know from experience, as payment in advance for desired returns. Women have indeed criticized this practice most sharply, as among other things a refusal ever to enjoy a shared dinner or an invitation as a simple social use-value, regarding it instead under the perspective of its sexual exchange-value in a structure of debt and credit. Yet it seems that it was more the crassness of this barely disguised prostitution – the alienation of cash and cash-related goods on the part of men (who have tended to pay for dinner rather than cook it) in exchange for sexual services by women – which occasioned the objection, rather than the principle itself. For as it transpires, women do not hesitate to apply the same principle, even if it is less with cash than with everything else a person has to 'give'.

What tends to be gender-specific is the medium of payment rather than the principle of paying (in advance): that women, in accordance with their gender-specific economic situation, predominantly pay in goods of subsistence and substance, rarely with money. Moreover, as long as we do not buy a partner with cash, but try to 'win' them with the 'gift' of ourselves, as long as we do not pay for their attention and company with money but with 'understanding' or cooked meals, we apparently do not consider it to be prostitution but the 'natural' bartering of relationships. This corresponds to mainstream social morality which considers prostitution – sexual services in return for cash payment – a reprehensible trade, but sees nothing reprehensible in traditional marriage, where a wife may not be paid in cash for her services, but nevertheless in the commodities (it is hoped) of subsistence: a home, food, clothes and so-called coverture. This suggests that it is not really the trade in people's (women's) personhood – their behaviour, their will, their 'services' – nor the capitalist principle of debt and debt collection which have attracted critique, but alone the gender-specific role distribution in capitalist patriarchy which has privileged men as trading citizens. As the (once exclusive) subjects of the state and owners of private property, they have been able to determine commercial transactions, buying 'goods' from women which – in the case of the prostitute and the wife alike – are what the modern age calls 'property in the person', while themselves only alienating external property or money.

The modern democracy of equal opportunities and the emancipation of women to the status of trading subjects now seems to enable women, too, to buy such 'property' in a partner's person, that is to say, services rendered by another person that are a servicing *of* one's own person. Women may still not be able to match men's mode of paying in external goods and money, but the aim is less an equal mode of payment than the acquisition of the same 'goods' and services as men traditionally extort from women. Exceptions of course exist, for instance the experiments in setting up prostitution services for women punters (with male or female prostitutes), where women too may buy 'sex' for money. However, this constitutes a minor line of business in comparison to the cash-free relationship economy.

If we consider the mode of payment immaterial, however, focusing instead on the fact of payment and the nature of the 'goods' acquired, we might say that the modern understanding of relationships as trade constitutes a development of interpersonal relations towards 'universal prostitution'. The motive of traditional as well as universal prostitution is the buyer's free access to the acquisition of goods – even if the advocates of prostitution prefer to put the emphasis on the 'freedom' of the prostitute to put her goods on the market. As Carole Pateman shows, traditional (cash) prostitution is today being defended not only by contractarians but also by some feminists, as a form of commercial trade like any other and as a form of labour like any other – that is, as a supposed progress in women's right to enter contracts and to dispose of the 'property in their persons' as they wish. 'Freedom of contract and equality of opportunity', so the argument goes, 'require that the prostitution contract should be open to everyone and that any individual should be able to buy or sell services in the market.'[26] The universalization of buyers and sellers to 'individuals' and the presentation of the 'freedom of contract' as if it were a newly won right obscure the fact that the *prostitution* contract has never been closed to women (as sellers) – although more often than not they have then been appropriated by men taking over the selling of them.

As Pateman explains, the logical consequence of this vision of universal freedom of contract is that 'the final defeat of status and the victory of contract should lead to the elimination of marriage in favour of the economical arrangement of universal prostitution, in which all individuals enter into brief contracts of sexual use when required. The only legitimate restriction upon these contracts is the willingness of another party voluntarily to make services available.'[27] Of course it is not just a matter of sex: 'Other services presently provided within marriage would also be contracted for in the market. A universal market in bodies and services would replace marriage.'[28] The fallacy of this vision lies in thinking that such a free and universal market would dissolve the sexual division of labour and consumption – which makes women predominantly work in services and men predominantly appear on the market as consumers.

The conception of relationships discussed here is based on a similar universalization of the individual and a correspondingly fallacious hope for equality of opportunity. It similarly implies the elimination of marriage in favour of freely entered contracts which should enable individuals, women as well as men, to acquire the services of 'marriage' as required. Under conditions of universal prostitution, Pateman argues, 'the most advantageous arrangement for the individual is an endless series of very short-term contracts to use another's body as and when required.'[29] This is a situation which, especially with regard to sex, has already established itself fairly widely, even if the sex is not always paid for in cash. It is a development which is driven by the interest of 'buyers' and an arrangement which is also 'most advantageous' to buyers with potent purchasing power.

As we have seen, however, the relative durability of a contract and a long-term bond between partners also remains a widespread ideal. In other words, the advantage of marriage in providing ensured access to sexual and other services 'at home' rather than on the free market also retains its undoubted attraction. In particular, it informs the 'universalized' aspiration of individual women to equal opportunities in this respect: also wanting what men have been getting out of marriage. Moreover, there are sound economic reasons for this, similar phenomena being tried and tested practice in the traditional commercial world. Despite a free market in labour and services, firms are set up which, rather than buying services and activities of a long-term recurring nature, such as secretarial work, on the free market, secure them by integration into the firm's internal hierarchy.[30]

The fact remains, however, that the principle of relationship as a trade and the principle of equal opportunities together establish a universal market of bodies and services – whether the contracts be shorter- or longer-term, the services bought and sold on the open market or through fixed contracts within the same firm, and whether remuneration is paid in cash or in subsistence and substance goods. What is important is the establishment of 'contracts for access to sexual [and other] property' to be found in other people.[31] The private relationship democracy, in contrast to the public prostitution of the market, moreover envisages a mutuality where the latter is one-sided: a mutual or alternating prostitution within the partnership. This, however, is unknown in the realm of traditional enterprise, since there, hierarchical relations are rather more explicitly recognized and it rarely occurs to consider the employer's payment of wages a 'reciprocal service' to the worker. Nor does it often occur that employer and employee engage in 'role-play'.

That the core issue is indeed services – sexual and other – which formerly were provided prototypically by wives (but also prostitutes and servants of all kinds) can be seen from the fact that the relationship 'needs' most frequently articulated almost exclusively concern such servicing of one's own person. One of the most ubiquitous concepts in the context of loving relationships is 'care' and its relatives 'caring', 'care-taking' and 'nurturing': there is talk of 'his need for her caretaking',[32] of 'our own needs for love, attention, nurturing and security', and 'our own yearning to be taken care of'.[33] That is to say, we want above all to *be loved*, to *receive* attention, recognition, nurturing, to *be understood*, to *be taken care of* and to have someone standing behind us. Rarely do we hear needs mentioned that use the active form of these actions – wanting *to love* someone, *to understand* someone, *to make* someone happy, unless it be as a means to an end, namely to *be* loved, understood, taken care of, or, as the saying also goes, 'to take our turn', 'my turn to be on the receiving end'.[34] That is to say, loving as such, giving as such, or understanding as such do not seem to be an aim in themselves, being a mere step towards the real goal: to be loved.

This corresponds, of course, to the basic capitalist principle that paying, that is, giving, cannot be in our interest, except as a means to acquire desired goods; that the driving force of trade on both parts of the trade relationship is acquisition, that is to say, profit. While the term 'exchange' suggests a certain mutuality – both participants giving something the other wants and receiving something they want – we know the capitalist circulation of commodities to be a most asymmetrical affair: we only give in payment what we are willing to part with and what to us seems of lesser value than the goods we thereby acquire, so that the trade may be profitable and the costs worth it. As Carole Pateman reminds us, 'A contract of mutual advantage and reciprocal use will last only as long as it appears advantageous to either party.'[35] Since this assessment of one's own advantage and profit is by no means a 'shared' undertaking, but on the contrary is the subjective and self-interested judgement of each partner, not even a freely entered trading contract will guarantee a 'same' advantage on both sides, let alone a simultaneity of the duration of advantage. Hence, neither the wish to terminate the trade relation need occur at the same time on both sides.

Power, of course, is of primary importance also in exchange trade, for the one who succeeds in determining the price from their point of view is the one that wins and profits. This may explain the practice predominant in 'democratic' relationships (although unusual in commercial contexts), of paying in advance, for those who have paid in advance have fixed the price and may now order retroactively the

desired goods. Even though this may be a risky trade (remember the
frauds), it is also the case that the one who demands settlement of
debts has the moral advantage, and, in a relationship trade without
fixed prices, moral advantage is of primary importance. For now it is
no longer the need of the partner which is at issue – whether the one
supplied with goods even wants or wanted the goods received and
what, if anything, they might be worth to the recipient – but only the
fact that they *have* been received and now establish an outstanding
debt. In other words, the partner's need, though necessary to guarantee mutual dependency, has succesfully – and profitably – been
transformed into an obligation instead, in that needs which may or
may not have existed were prophylactically satisfied. Thus the 'democratic' mutuality of equal needs has been replaced by a structure of
indebting and debt collection which are both under the command and
initiative of the selfsame subject.

If the rhetoric of relationships and give-and-take thus also suggests
a certain symmetry, the democratic mutuality an apparently moral
balance between gains and losses, benefits and their costs, egoism and
altruism, or as Finkielkraut has it, 'charity and greed, beneficence and
avid desire', practice shows that the morality of the relationship is the
logic of profit, the ethics of relationship behaviour is the principle of
'fair trade', and the rationality of sociality is self-enrichment at the
expense of others.

If we take 'being loved' as the passive form of active loving, and
hence again suspect that perhaps there is a gender-specific distribution
of roles here, men preferring to love actively and women being
particularly concerned to *be loved*, we once again fall prey to patriarchal language use. For as the history of the relation between the
sexes shows, marriage (as well as sex within and without marriage)
corresponds to a structure of needs and their satisfaction which is
diametrically opposed to the cliché of male 'activity' and female
'passivity': the woman's role consisting of work, of active doing while
the man is the accumulated sum of needs which require satisfying. The
woman cooks, cleans, cares for and feeds the man as if he were a care-
dependent child like the children she really has. This has prompted
Marilyn Frye to speak of male parasitism, and other feminists of
cannibalism.[36] The power of a husband does not consist primarily in
his 'activity', but in his power to determine the activity of his wife and
channel it towards the satisfaction of his needs. That he may also resort

to active action towards her is a form of enforcing his power of being able to command her.

We may think, however, that care-taking is not really the core of love, and that active loving, if not care-taking, is none the less the prerogative of men, *being* loved the prerogative of women, all the more so as the patriarchal representation of sex – which after all is one of the most central components of the term 'love' and often designated by the latter – would confirm this. For in sex, this triumph of masculinity, the male role is 'active': he 'has', 'lays', 'takes', 'possesses' and 'fucks' a woman, in a multiplicity of linguistic alternatives of explosive hyper-activity, while women of course endure all this in the passive form, being 'had', 'laid', 'taken' etc. – and on occasion also 'loved'. Hence men are often called 'lovers', women their 'beloved'. Since the feminists critique of male sexual violence has also emphasized the active violence of men's behaviour, it might be thought to confirm the generalized ascription of activity to men and passivity to women.

Yet the 'active' part of men's role is fundamentally constituted through their position in the power structure, their institutionalized dominance in relation to women's institutionalized subjection, that is, their power and consequent freedom to exercise violence. The primary and decisive 'activity' lies in an active decision of will, for instance to have 'sex' with a woman against her will and to use her for his 'needs'. The role of the woman, with or against her will, consists in providing the service of 'sexual satisfaction'. Whether she is 'active' or 'passive' in doing so depends above all on the will and predilection of the man being serviced, but does not alter the fact that her role is one of providing satisfaction of his need. Prostitution also illustrates that the issue is the provision of service, regardless of the particular form in which the punter desires it to be done. It may be most difficult to perceive rape outside marriage as also a form of extortion of service, yet under the perspective of an analysis of needs and their satisfaction, here too the will, desire or 'need' of the rapist is determining, whether it be formulated as a 'need for sex' or a 'need for violence'. The role imposed on the woman, even in and despite her resistance, turns into a 'service' provided – her being raped serving the satisfaction of his will. But above all, we should remember that 'service' means work exercised in conditions of unfreedom – slavery, servitude, subjugation. Service means being at service to a master, while services are extorted from people dominated by people in a position to dominate.

Hence the distribution of active and passive needs and desires is not really gender–specific; rather, what determines whether 'passive' or 'active' needs are articulated is whether the context is that of 'relationship' or of 'sex'. 'Relationship' as the epitome of everything good and loving becomes the territory of care and nurturance, charity and beneficence, of altruistic good deeds and loving-kindness. By contrast, 'sex' is the territory of active desire, avid lust, pleasure and self-seeking sensuality from which, as popular wisdom knows, a measure of aggression must not be missing. Although, in public bourgeois morality, sex traditionally constituted the domain of evil, vice, depravity, and self-indulgence, the modern spirit is busy liberating it from this infamous reputation, launching it instead as a requisite form of egoism, a necessary self-seeking, a justified search for self-fulfilment – an imperative form of self-interest, which women in particular are exhorted to acquire a bit more of. Thus even in modern times we see relationships as fundamentally loving and altruistic, and sex as fundamentally selfish and egoistical – only that in this case the egoism is legitimate and therapeutically recommended.

Since 'giving' is thus constitutive of relationship and 'taking' constitutive of sex, we may begin to understand why in the context of relationship the subject prefers the role of the passive recipient – *being* loved rather than loving – in the context of sex, however, the role of the active agent. If it is a matter of giving, I would like to be the *object* of the giving; if it is a matter of taking, I'll be the *subject* of the taking. If the issue is altruism and love of neighbours, I'd like to be the neighbour; if egoism is called for, I will gladly be the ego. In this manner the subject gets the best out of both contexts.

Since relationship and sex are not absolutely separable – and especially in the democratic relationship tend to go together, so that sex, no longer just a matter of taking, is integrated into the care-taking, creating an additional field of sexual care-taking – the crucial difference ultimately comes down to the simple difference between good deeds and hostilities. As Lynne Segal has illuminated all the 'sorts of other emotional needs' with which 'sexual desire is knotted through', the issue is 'to *obtain* approval and love', but to '*express* hostility, dependence and domination', to '*relieve* [one's own] anxiety and repair [one's own] deep-lying wounds of rejection, humiliation and despair',[37] that is to say, to have them relieved and repaired (by the other). Approval and love the subject wishes to receive, hostility and domination it is prepared to 'give'. In fact the subject's self-interest is so pronounced that the figure of the other, so central to its undertaking, does not even once appear linguistically: all action processes are expressed exclusively with a view to the subject. The subject wishes to express hostility and domination – the other who is their recipient needs to be imagined by her reader. At least we may note it as progress that dependence, rather than being seen as the subject's neediness, is counted among the hostilities towards the other, that is, as something, which, like hostility and domination, one wishes to do to or inflict upon the other.

Beyond this, the subject aims to have its anxieties relieved and its old wounds of rejection repaired. That is to say, the partner shall heal my wounds, wounds which not she but others have dealt me in the past – shall compensate me for my experiences in the past by her care-taking in the present. Thus even dealing with my own past becomes the responsibility of the other; the losses I incurred in exchanges with others becoming a debt for her to repay. The fact that the partner so to speak by definition will have equal 'wounds' and 'anxieties', which the subject would have to repair in turn, no more appears as a suggestion than does the partner herself. Thus, where good deeds and healing processes are being mapped out, it is the subject who is their exclusive beneficiary; where it is needs and desires for hostile activity, agency is the subject's privilege. In short: the other must be nice to me, I want ('need') to be nasty to her.

Thus it is not just that give-and-take, or even love-and-hate, is a necessary constituent of a relationship (so long as it isn't indifference). Rather, a relationship requires that I am loved whereas I may hate, that I am given while I take. The modern relationship needs thus aspire without the slightest deviation to the privilege of the erstwhile husband of traditional marriage, his privilege of ensured exploitation of a disenfranchised wife in the 'private' sphere. In particular, they reflect that mix, so characteristic of marriage and 'love', between the exploitation of the woman's labour in terms of reproductive and emotional services on the one hand, and aggressive sexual exploitation of her on the other.

The desire to *be* loved while hating also reflects the apparent contradiction inherent in romance and sex: between men's fundamental misogyny on the one hand and their heterosexuality on the other, that is, their 'public' hatred of women on the one hand and their private predilection for one particular woman's 'love' on the other, one chosen to service their most intimate needs, especially to render the labour of love, sexual service. Just so the modern desire for a personal and 'private' relationship reflects the claim – originating in slavery and surviving in the marriage of citizens in liberal democracy – to possession of another person; that is, the desire to own a person which at the same time means the destruction of the owned person as a person. It is the interest in a profitable relationship for so-called private purposes, that is, to satisfy one's personal needs for 'sociality' by means of a chosen, now 'equal', single person, in the context of an apparently absolute unrelatedness and 'indifference', but in fact fundamental hostility, towards people in general.

It is of course partly due to our merciless cultural socialization in the ideology of heterosexual romance – now stylized as 'universalized' polymorphous romance – that we continue, against our better judgement and despite all evidence and experience to the contrary, unshakeably to consider such exploitative intents towards a partner as a form of love. Yet we cannot hold socialization alone responsible; if we ignore insight, judgement, evidence and experience so consistently, there must also be choice involved: a will to hang on, or ascend, to such power. It is a power which previously only men exercised over women in the sanctuary of their 'privacy', but which emancipated 'individuals' increasingly wish to exercise over other individuals, as their right to equal privacy.

In the subject's scenario of its relationship there is no trace of the famous democratic 'mutuality'. For contrary to what you might expect, it is not the subject's responsibility to establish it, say, by considering the partner's interests too. Rather, mutuality is guaranteed through the conception of the relationship as a trade, that is, the presupposition of an equally ruthless pursuit of self-interest on the part of the partner. It is for the partner to look after their own business, to assert their own interests and to maximize their own profit, as the subject looks after its own business and maximizes its own profits. Hence mutuality does not mean an evenly balanced consideration of the interests of both partners, but the 'evenly balanced' structure of opposition and competition, the equal conflict of equal self-interests. What is democratic about it is the freedom of access to the fight and the freedom to consent to fighting.

11

Needs, or the legitimation of dominance

Conceptualizing social interactions as an exchange of commodities also has the advantage, as we have seen, that the subject's designs on another person simply appear as a 'need'. What in fact is an act of violence, a bid for power and a planned transgression to manipulate another's freedom of action, is reformulated in economist terms as a factual demand for a particular service. Through the dissection of action processes into component bits – things and services – both the agents' will and their initiation of the action disappear. What someone 'gives' to another becomes a neutral transfer of the 'contents' of the action – the saying of certain words, the carrying out of certain sexual motions – without consideration of whose will they are and on whose initiative they occur.

Thus it was said of Jim that he managed to say exactly what his partner wanted to hear. There is then no difference between him saying what he says as a self-determined action and saying it to fulfil her wish: the same goods change their 'owner', the same words are said and heard. This focus on the desired goods cuts out the most significant aspect of any action – namely its meaning – reducing agents to suppliers of goods and sayers of words, negating them as persons. This apparent desire for the goods rather than the meaning of social interaction also explains why subjects consider it in their interest to *make* the other do and give what they want – coerce them, as it were, to hand over the goods, even if their meaning as a 'gift' is thereby destroyed.

This abstraction of social interaction to a simple transfer of goods is thus a first move to disguise the real purpose of relationship trade: power and control. For we are interested in the other's 'goods' precisely because the other's 'will resides in these objects', because in obtaining the other's goods we have made serviceable the other's will. The desire for 'relationship goods' is the desire for service(s), the pleasure in having one's needs satisfied by the other is the pleasure of the power to have bent the other's will. As Carole Pateman reminds us, men buying the services of prostitutes do not just want the empty 'goods' of sexual satisfaction – neither the gender-non-specific servicing through a 'person' nor a depersonalized commodified 'relief' (which they could supply themselves). They desire the 'use of a *woman* [or in homosexual prostitution, a man] for a given period'.[1] In the same way the subject does not just want the depersonalized goods, but the other's subservience embodied in these goods. What mattered to Jim's partner was less the words he said than the fact that he said what he knew she wanted him to say.

Reformulating this 'demand for goods' as a psychological 'need' not only further disguises the power relations involved, but in the now familiar manner even reverses them. The subject's claim to power turns into neediness and vulnerability, which the other has the 'power' to remedy. While it would be absurd to claim that servants have power over their masters, having the 'power' to satisfy their needs, it yet seems reasonable to say that women have power over men since they have the 'power' to satisfy their (sexual) 'needs'. Power, however, lies in the power to define both the 'needs' and what constitutes their adequate satisfaction. Psychologizing this power as 'need' and 'neediness' thus lays the ground for that staple of 'personal relationships': emotional blackmail.

Unlike with a gift, whose significance lies in the fact that the giver freely chooses to make it, the value of the satisfaction of needs derives precisely from the fact that it is the *subject of the need* that wants it and that the other is doing it because the subject of the need wants it. That is to say, both the need and the action of satisfying it correspond to the will of the selfsame subject. Psychologizing the rendering of this service as possibly also a need or even the free will of the person rendering it disguises the fundamental, and politically decisive, asymmetry between will and so-called consent. Women's history in patriarchy is a history of 'consent' – of disenfranchisement and the lack of freedom to have any will other than the pre-given will of a man, reducing their choice to a choice between 'willing' or 'unwilling' compliance. The patriarchal habit of representing women's *de facto* obedience as their free will or consent while ignoring the very power structures which constrain women's freedom, serves to disguise not only women's servitude, but men's will to dominate and command. As feminists have untiringly argued, where there is no freedom, there cannot be any consent, and 'where there is no consent, there is only violence.'[2]

The concept of relationship 'needs' thus hides the subject's claim to power, its desire for control over the other's actions. In the need to be taken care of – 'little-girlish' as it might sound thanks to the therapy discourse – lurks the original claim of the private citizen to his private relationship, that is, to his wife. It is the claim to the power to use another person's actions, and hence another's will, in one's own interest and to one's own will. It is a 'need' for obedience and compliance (on the other's part). 'Need' is another word for 'I want', with the added component of my endangerment if it isn't met, my 'need' for care-taking, nurturance, sexual servicing etc., an expression of my blunt will to use the other in my interest while denying any possible interest on the other's part. The pleasure of a need satisfied does not derive from the service acquired, but from the person having successfully been brought into service. For 'the delights of mastery, including civil mastery, can be obtained only from jurisdiction over a living man or woman.'[3]

In the democratic relationship of equal rights and needs, there therefore arises a competition on the level of needs: about who will manage more successfully to assert their own needs. This explains, for instance, the specific ways in which illness is traded in relationships, illness being understood less as a problem for the sick person to cope with than a particularly useful means – like Lynne Segal's old wounds – to prove a greater need for care-taking *vis-à-vis* a partner of otherwise equal claim to care-taking. This has led the partner of a woman who is HIV-positive one day to declare himself tested and found positive too – falsely, as it later turned out.[4] It was his attempt to re-establish equality in the relationship, seeing in his partner's threatening condition an unfair 'advantage' in the relationship economy. But even common colds, tiredness, overwork, and any other challenges of daily life may be used incontrovertibly to prove one's need for care-taking and to secure the other's services.

Even if the word 'service' has become so worn that we tend no longer to perceive its meaning of *ordered compliance*, it nevertheless is apparent in the context of a desire which is aimed at the other's labour of love. As Carole Pateman reminds us, Kant still regarded service as a servitude incompatible with the aspiration to freedom. Yet this did not lead him to challenge the legitimacy of service; rather, true to his own male and class interests he chose to exclude 'servants' from any claim to the political rights of citizenship.[5] A free citizen does 'not [allow] others to make use of him; for he must in the true sense of the word *serve* no-one but the commonwealth.'[6] This is an understanding duly reflected in the foundation of civil democracy and its axiomatic exclusion of women, as well as in the citizens' desire to protect themselves from being used by other citizens.

Just as it contravenes a person's freedom to be coerced to serve, so it contradicts the principle of democracy – that is, a freedom which simultaneously implies the freedom of all others – *to demand service* and obedience of another. If anything, however, we deem service and servitude incompatible with freedom, rather than the power of mastery which commands that service. Thus while Kant emphasizes that a free citizen must not allow others to use him, he fails to insist that therefore a free citizen must neither use others in service. Thus the 'freedom' which liberal democracy has aspired to and realized is not universal freedom for all, but the continuation of the 'freedom' of rulers and masters, now extended to a larger number of men. Or to put it differently, the foundation of liberal democracy has meant a wider group of men being enfranchised, without disenfranchisement fundamentally being challenged. On the contrary, mastery remains a constitutive condition of 'freedom' for those in a position to exercise it. Neither democracy nor the idea of freedom seemed contravened by women's continuing subjection, much less by men's continuing mastery, be it in the 'private' sphere of their family or the 'public' sphere of politics and the economy.

Kant was equally clear about the fact that the sexual part of a person cannot be separated from the person – that to acquire or use another's sexual property means to acquire or use that person. Being no more prepared to forgo male sexual 'right' than any other man, however, he grounded a 'person's' right sexually to use another 'person' in 'the sole condition' that he already has a 'right of disposal over the whole person' he is proposing so to use.[7] That is, he defined marriage as the sole legal condition under which 'persons' may 'reciprocally' dispose over each other's sexual property. This makes all the more sense as marriage is not a reciprocal association between two persons, but the association of a citizen with a *woman* who is both a person and a non-person, thus offering the unique situation where a 'person' has 'the right to dispose over the [other] person as a whole – over the welfare and happiness and generally over all the circumstances of that person'.[8]

Hegel in turn objects precisely to this 'degradation' of marriage to a contract of 'mutual' use,[9] preferring to argue instead that marriage is constituted in 'nature', marital association meaning that the partners become 'one person'.[10] Hence the question of mutual use disappears, since, as we would say in modern parlance, the 'couple' is but using 'itself'. The final solution to this dilemma, however – between the constitutive 'universal freedom' of persons on the one hand and the need to legitimate their use of each other on the other – is achieved only by modern contract theory, which sees in contract the apex of human freedom. The solution consists in that 'brilliant piece of political inventiveness', as Carole Pateman puts it, of giving 'the name of freedom to civil subordination', declaring a 'contract of subordination (sexual) freedom'.[11]

With the emancipation of women, however belated, to potential subjects of contracts, marriage may finally be defined as a mutual contract, a contract of mutual use: 'Husbands and wives contractually acquire for their exclusive use their partner's sexual properties.'[12] In fact this applies more directly to non-marital partnerships, which are exclusively based on mutual 'contract' and thus may be terminated also without state involvement. Anthony Giddens, too, sees in contract the key to a successful democratic relationship: 'All relationships which approximate to the pure form maintain an implicit "rolling contract" to which appeal may be made by either partner when situations arise felt to be unfair or oppressive. The rolling contract is a constitutional device which underlies, but is also open to negotiation through, open discussion by partners about the nature of the relationship.'[13] The fact that it is basically a contract of voluntary submission to and mutual use of each other disappears behind the rhetoric of contracts and constitutions.

Thus the argument comes around full circle to the critique of the economist concept of labour power, namely that the latter is just such an abstract construction as, say, sexual property, implying the separability of externalized action from its agent, of labour and labour power from the labouring person. A democracy which officially has abolished slavery (and which prefers to overlook its surviving remnants), may find it necessary indeed to speak of 'freely entered labour contracts'. Yet behind the abstract thingification of labour power hides the concrete thingification of labouring people. For as Pateman insists, you cannot hire or buy their labour without hiring or buying the whole person; the whole person, including that person's will, must follow the labour power to the work place. 'The fiction "labour power" cannot be used; what is required is that the worker labours as demanded',[14] that is, works to the employer's will. In other words: 'The worker and his labour, not his labour power, are the subject of contract', a contract in which, 'since he cannot be separated from his capacities, he sells *command over the use of his body and himself*' (my emphasis).[15] Conversely, employers do not just buy their workers' labour power, they are buying their *obedience*. As Huw Benyon sums it up, 'Workers are paid to obey.'[16]

The so-called free labour contract's ancestry lies in the contracts of slavery and domestic labour, from which it was properly differentiated only in the late nineteenth century.[17] What made possible the translation of *service* into the language of freedom and democracy is the concept of the 'individual' as 'owner of the property in his person': that most 'political fiction' that 'a worker does not contract out himself or even his labour, but his labour power or services, part of the property in his person.'[18] The answer to the question of how property in the person can be contracted out is 'that no such procedure is possible'.[19] What is hired or bought is a person − even if it is only for a limited time and not for a whole lifetime.

It is part of the brilliancy of this political fiction that its legitimizing thrust is aimed at submission − the allegedly voluntary submission of the persons contracting out their labour − with never a word lost about the legitimacy of mastery − the purchase and use of other people. It is not mastery which is the issue for the democrats, but service, and it is not mastery which needs legitimizing through contract law, but self-submission. Just so it is not the mastery of punters − their purchase of women − which is the topic when prostitution is being defended, but the freedom of the prostitute temporarily to sell herself. Neither do we seem to worry about the *appropriation* of so-called property in another person, but if anything, the 'right' to dispose of the property in one's own person. Similarly, we speak volubly about care and the labour of love, rarely of the corresponding mastery of love. In other words, the ideological legitimation of the remaining forms of civil mastery and subjection pointedly aims at changing consciousness about the meaning of *service* – what, because of the continuing power relations, is still the necessary reality for the majority of people. The aim is to undermine the resistance of those obliged to do service, to change their consciousness about the conditions of their reality. For once the oppressed cease to protest at their submission – their being used by others in service – no one will be left to challenge mastery.

If 'property in the person' cannot be hired out, no more can it be given away or exchanged. Or, to put it the other way round, just as the intent to hire the 'property in another person' is illegitimate, so is the intent to acquire 'it' free of charge. What is being exchanged, traded and appropriated is neither a service nor the labour of love, but a person who has been made to do as I wish, whose will has been brought into line with mine.

This is not, of course, a critique of those social interactions we generally consider gestures of love and friendship. The point is precisely not to consider actions as truncated external deeds which are either good or bad deeds, but to consider the agent's will and intent an integral part of every action. This means taking into consideration the conditions under which actions occur, and also recognizing violence, coercion and emotional pressure as factors of the context of action. That is to say, it should be of concern whether an action is the agent's free choice or whether it corresponds to the will of another person. In the integrity of action as the agent's free choice, as opposed to an action determined or commanded by another, lies the difference between freedom and service, between self-determination and obedience. And in the experience of a gesture of love as another's voluntary action, as opposed to the designed acquisition of this 'experience', lies the difference between freedom and mastery.

The violence of 'needs' and their 'satisfaction' begins with the intention: with a conception of relationship which degrades the other person to a representative of commodities and service, the source of the satisfaction of my needs, thus denying the other's status as person. As feminist analyses of the sexual enslavement of women have shown, violence begins with what Marilyn Frye has termed the 'Arrogant

Eye', the perceiver's arrogating, appropriating vision which excludes 'the possibility that the Other is independent, indifferent'.[20] This perception already significantly affects the other's context of action. As Frye describes the arrogant perceiver's action and intent, and the consequences for the one perceived,

> He tries to accomplish in a glance what the slave master and batterers accomplish by extended use of physical force, and to a great extent succeeds. He manipulates the environment, perception and judgement of her whom he perceives so that her recognized options are limited, and the course she chooses will be such as coheres with his purpose. The seer himself is an element of her environment. The structures of his perception are as solid a fact in her situation as are the structures of a chair which seats her too low or of gestures which threaten.[21]

That is, to ask whether the other consents of her own free will to a course of action which coheres with my will, is the wrong question. My wish and my expectation that the other may meet it already significantly change the situation in which the other has to make her decision. In particular, my 'wish' constitutes a perception of her which puts her into a specific relation to me (rather than leaving her free to choose how to relate to me): the possibility that she may be independent, indifferent, is thus precluded, the possibility that she satisfies my wish and makes my interest her interest pre-given. The other no longer may decide what she wants to do, only whether or not she wants to do what I want: she may assent (or not) to a given course of action, the options pre-structured by me – 'choosing' here means choosing between two options, one of which is strongly favoured by me.

It is often argued in the context of democratic relationships that a person who is coerced neither physically nor through a structural inequality is therefore free to consent. This misses the crucial point, namely the question of the political behaviour of the subject (ourselves), to whose implicit or explicit proposals the other is invited to consent. If we are concerned about relations of equality, the question of our own behaviour cannot depend on how the other responds – whether the other objects to it or lets it pass. The question is whether I am willing to exercise violence, including the violence of arrogant perception, thus to manipulate the other's situation and hence the other person. Violence does not just become violence if the other puts up resistance, nor does it cease to be violence if the other fails to object. The demand prevalent in social usage today that the *other* must stand up for her rights, that the *other* must 'draw her boundaries', that is, put limits on *my* behaviour, is an attempt to devolve the responsibility for my behaviour upon the potential victim of my behaviour, and to use the other's lack of resistance as a legitimation of my violence.

As the critics of slavery and colonialism have shown, and Kathleen Barry has analysed in relation to the sexual enslavement of women, the ultimate goal in the establishment of a relation of violence and slavery is to be able to exercise mastery without needing to employ direct force – to break the will and resistance of the oppressed to such an extent that they obey 'voluntarily'. As Marilyn Frye explicates,

> A system which relies heavily on physical restriction both presupposes and generates resistance and attempts to escape. These in turn exacerbate the need for bondage and containment . . . Efficient exploitation of 'human resources' requires that the structures that refer the other's actions to the exploiter's ends must extend beneath the victim's skin.[22]

Where the interest in the profit of exploitation exceeds the interest in violence as such, cost-effectiveness and saving expenses become the rationale. What the violent systems of slavery and colonialism eventually employed in addition to direct military and physical force, namely the ideological subjugation and inculcation of the subjected through the culture of the subjectors, becomes the primary means in political systems – including democratic relationships – which are obliged to renounce physical force. In either case, the aim is to weaken and ultimately dissolve the resistance of the subjected, so that 'the exploited are oriented . . . to the exploiter's ends rather than, as they would otherwise be, to ends of their own.'[23] Breaking their will – disengaging it 'from the projects of resistance and escape' and effecting an 'attachment to the interests of the exploiters' – means to transform a relation of conflicting interests into a system with but one – the dominant – interest. One might hesitate in this context to call it a 'shared' interest, for as Frye sums up, 'This radical solution can properly be called enslavement.'[24] We are familiar with this solution in the context of marriage, where ideologizing interpretations do not see two parties with interests of their own, but unification into a party of one.

While the democratic relationship, of course, fundamentally differs from systems of slavery, colonialism or sexual enslavement – physical force in particular having (theoretically) no part in it – we might none the less say that it (and democracy in general) constitutes a historically new and almost inverse situation: while slavery, conquest and occupation begin with violent physical subjection, followed by ideological subjugation, Western society today presents a situation where slavery, serfdom and colonialism are theoretically abolished and direct physical violence is officially outlawed, yet where the ideological subjugation of people, their inculcation with the values of dominance and mastery, seems well-nigh complete. Individuals of 'equal rights' encounter one another with interests and values corresponding to those of slave-holders, conquistadores, colonialists and husbands, without even first needing to reorient their potential victims to these values. The values of mastery and the interest in domination are not in question, only who will manage to assert these more successfully or how they may be evenly shared. For the culture that constitutes the ideological framework of our 'private' interpersonal relationships is a culture which celebrates mastery as 'democracy', and the individual's claims to power as universal 'freedom' and 'human rights'.

Accordingly, violence in the democratic relationship shifts to a power struggle of perception: the struggle to assert one's own perception as the 'common' perception, one's own interests as the 'shared' interests of the relationship. It begins with the mutual perception of each other as exploitable and usable for one's own needs, that is, as candidate for a 'relationship': supplier of satisfaction, minister of care, and generally as material for realizing my relationship and my interests. There is violence in the intention to commit the other to a frame of guaranteed mutual trade and to design interactions as debit and credit, considering neither one's own nor the other's actions as actions, but as sequences in a trade exchange. It is the violence of the arrogant perceiver not to see the other on principle as independent and 'indifferent', but as 'interested' in common trade and mutual exploitation, that is, mutual prostitution.

Refusing the 'personal relationship' and all its power and pleasure strategies might thus be a first step of resisting dominance and violence – one's own as well as one's partner's. It would mean parting also with that jewel of our identity, that source of infinite pleasure and satisfaction, our so-called 'needs'. These have no more to do with any elementary necessities of the survival of adult people than do consumer 'needs' created by production. The felt 'need' for the given commodities does not represent an elementary want or lack, but a will to have and a decision to want to have. However, representing the acquisition of consumer goods as the satisfaction of needs exonerates both the producers from the responsibility for their products – since they are merely supplying a demand – and the consumers from the responsibility for deciding to consume or acquire them. The mere existence of products and the standard of 'living' they create apparently render any desire to have them a natural human sentiment, and for sentiments and feelings we cannot be held responsible, for they come and go, as we know, without our asking. Their 'cause' lies, if anywhere, outside our (present) selves.

In particular, we tend not to differentiate between a feeling on the one hand, and its expression in the form of behaviour on the other: the feeling 'causes' its expression, without apparently any room for a decision whether to express it or keep it to oneself. 'I was so angry' is meant to explain why I chose to act out my anger in a violent stampede. Similarly, the urge and urgency of a felt need is to imply that we cannot but seeks its satisfaction. As a feeling it requires no further analysis; it suffices that it has been felt.

It is no different in the case of relationship needs. Humans may be social beings, yet this sociality is denied by every ideological means available, in order to postulate instead the 'individual', the one and only (nearly self-sufficient) subject, who shapes its sociality – if it decides to 'enter into relation' with others – out of its position of power and control. What this subject may experience as its need is less its immanent human sociality than what it decides it wants to have. It wants, for instance, to have company, but not just any company. It does not so much want company as particular people. Or it wants to be loved, but loved in the way it decides, and by persons of its own choice. As we saw in Katie's case, her partner's love was not enough; she wanted a sign of love which she, not he, had defined. Ideally the subject would write also its partner's part, the better to satisfy its own needs (being the one who knows them best). And if the subject decides to love, it will do that too only as it wants and whom it wants to love. Why it wants to do that we have already seen: in order to *be* loved in return. On no account will the subject love at its own peril, that is, leaving it up to the other what the other will do. For this would mean reckoning with the other's will and the other's freedom of choice, which to the subject is as good as acting against its own will and sacrificing its own interest.

Like consumer needs, relationship needs derive from the consumption of commodities. It is goods that the subject has already experienced — another has already once offered — which the subject wishes to have delivered again; the taste for commodities comes with their consumption. Thus a man describes how his first encounter with a woman left him 'wanting to see her again, wanting to feel the way she had made me feel: *appreciated*'.[25] He does not so much want to meet that woman again as re-experience the way he had felt with her. His interest is not in the woman as a person, but as a means to the production of certain feelings, a supplier of desirable goods. Hence the woman must be manipulated in such a way that she may produce the same feeling in the subject again. Even where a need is formulated abstractly, that is, without reference to a specific person — say a need 'not to be alone' or to be taken care of — that need also derives from commodities consumed before, that is, from a conception of relation which is the product of the subject's experience and fantasy, and is independent of a particular person.

As we saw with the psychological justification of needs as allegedly deriving from infancy, such needs in fact reflect the current wish to reproduce past experiences (or fantasies) *as* experience. These are, in particular, experiences of pleasure and profit, of being given and of taking, of power and the service of others, and altogether experiences of suspended responsibility towards others. Infants do not, of course, have any experience of irresponsibility or of lack of consideration towards others, since they as yet largely lack any conception or means of responsibility and consideration. Rather, their experiences become such in the fantasy of adults, whose desire is focused on precisely this aspect. Alternately, the experiences which the subject wishes to reproduce may have been genuine experiences of love, which the subject however, in deciding to acquire them on its own initiative, transforms into experiences of power and manipulation.

If it seems, therefore, that feelings and 'experiences' form the core of relationship needs, they too are conceived as consumer goods which can be 'had' and which one wishes to 'have' again, satisfactions corresponding to needs. Hence an experience is less a historically specific process of actively experiencing, perceiving and understanding a unique situation; rather, it is the detachable *effect* of a situation on the subject, so to speak the service rendered to the subject by the situation. Hence the 'same' situation is to be reproduced in order to reproduce the desired experience. The experiences sought are 'being taken care of', being loved, receiving attention and flattery – that is to say, actions on other people's part. The specific co-ordinates of the situation – including its participants – are as secondary as is the partner in the relationship: they are at best ingredients in the production of the experience. To the extent that my 'needs' concern the actions of other people, they are a matter of these people's obedience, their degradation to a mere function. This becomes most obvious where the experience concerns 'sex', which apparently is infinitely reproducible, independently of time, place and person, and yet is the 'same' ever-recurring experience for which there is an undoubted demand.

Thus a client of Norwood's reports: 'When I was drinking I went to bed with lots of women, and basically I had the same experience many times.'[26] In fact there were different women involved, on different occasions and in different places, yet what the subject defines as the relevant 'experience' is the same every time. Even if the need consists in having sex 'again' with the same person, it means instrumentalizing the person to re-produce the desired effect. The question remains why it is perceived so readily as a repetition of the same experience. Yet there is no doubt that it is, since it is its repetition which makes a relationship a 'relationship', and its absence which defines a separation. Nowhere else perhaps is the expectation that an action be repeated, indeed become a 'quality', more pronounced than it is in this case. As a person who repeatedly acts generously becomes a 'generous person', so a relationship through the repeated sexual interaction of its participants becomes a 'sexual relationship'. Logically, the partner thus also becomes a sexual partner, in contrast to all other persons with whom the subject interacts and who – in spite of Freud and postmodernism – remain asexual.

Even where advocates of the democratic relationship insist that sex must cease its long tradition as consumption and self-gratification and be structured instead more like communication – 'In the realm of sexuality, emotion as a means of communication, as commitment to and cooperation with others, is especially important'[27] – it helps little if communication, too, is already subject to the laws of capitalism and consumerism. While we might have thought that in the context of communication, the idea of repeating the 'same' experience – say a conversation – might still strike us as absurd, it is not unusual to encounter the wish to have 'another such talk' with each other. The conversation has been experienced as a 'good' one, an experience whose repetition is not only desirable, but apparently viable. What has been 'good' about it, therefore, is less the conversation itself than the communicative relationship, that is, the fact that it has occurred with the said participants. The point is to repeat the arrangement – the reason for and point of the talk being secondary factors.

Even if the invitation to a repetition of a 'good talk' may appear to some as a compliment, it is nevertheless a negation of the interlocutor as well as the conversation, and a valuation of the person only in so far as that person is being 'wanted' again. Similarly, people increasingly meet each other in order to have met, and write to each other in order to have written – without apparent awareness that this reduces the actions in question to relationship trade. For from this perspective one talk is as good as another, one action (nearly) as good as another, one letter as good as another, so long as they have occurred or been sent. The relationship has been reaffirmed, even if the interactions are thus devalued.

Hence 'communicative sex' may indeed not be so very different from commercialized communication trade: 'Eroticism is the cultivation of feeling, expressed through bodily sensation, in a communicative context; an art of giving and receiving pleasure.'[28] It corresponds to the cultivation of a comparable feeling, expressed in the context of conversation: an art of listening and speaking, of giving and taking, where listening is a gift to the other through which the other receives pleasure. It neither constitutes a dissolution of sex (or talk) as a form of self-gratification, nor the establishment of communication. Rather, it seems to represent the familiar democratic solution of evenly alternating pleasure, evenly alternating (self-) gratification.

As opposed to actual communication, where both participants realize their interest both in speaking and in listening, the interest in this so-called communicative sex is in 'pleasure', while pleasure is the profit resulting from exchange. Pleasure, this highest value of consumer culture, is either given or received, is received *because* the other is giving. Pleasure is no more 'shared' than the need or its satisfaction are shared, or than sensation is a form of expression. As the need remains the subject's need, and its satisfaction the subject's satisfaction, so pleasure is the profit of the subject. The profit of one is the loss or gift of the other – the structure is complementary. Hence the ever more widely used 'Thank you for listening'[29] (not to mention thank you for the good sex), indicating an understanding that in listening, another has made a sacrifice from which the beneficiary profits.

Hence the language of sex and the conception of sexual behaviour remain true to the understanding that one receives pleasure while the other at that moment gives it. So Norwood's client, who also used to cook for her friend, says of herself that she had 'always been very sexually responsive', so much so that in high school she thought she might be a 'nymphomaniac'. 'They say that guys are supposed to be the ones who always want sex. I know I wanted it more than he did.'[30] Shortly after, she explains that in her later relationship with Jim, she tried hard to 'thrill and delight him'.[31] If in her first statement sex was something that she wanted to have and was getting something out of for herself, in her account of her relationship with Jim she emphasizes that this time, she was dedicated to the task of providing thrill and delight for him. That this is arduous work indeed transpires from the fact that she bought special lingerie 'to wear just for him' (where usually one wears it for oneself, as simple use-value), studied books on lovemaking, and 'tried everything she learned on him'.[32]

Despite her pronounced liking for sex and the gratification she derives from it, she here renounces it in favour of servicing her partner. 'It wasn't her sexuality she was expressing', but work she contributed towards his, as she apparently also was 'much more in touch with his sexuality than with her own'.[33] Why she does it we already know: in order to 'win' her man and keep him. What is important in this context is that sex and sexual activity, despite all professions of 'togetherness' and 'sharing', obviously mean pleasure for one and work for the other partner, and vice versa if it alternates. For satisfaction is locked indissolubly to its need, and hence may occur only where there is a preconceived need.

A conception of sex – or indeed of any social behaviour – as not divisible into the twin constituents of giving and receiving, satisfying and being satisfied, seems beyond the capitalist imagination. For one thing, it would make it difficult to keep accounts. Especially where the pleasure of the other is obvious, the subject would get suspicious that the other might be profiting 'more'. So we are hardly surprised that, where the subject is most acutely aware of its own pleasure, its desire for accounting slackens and the possibility of an automatically 'shared' satisfaction decidedly gains in attraction. This may be seen from the following formulations, which are a standard in democratic romance and the goal of many a therapeutic programme:

> During love-making they were so utterly engrossed with each other that they remembered not knowing whose body was whose; and the intimacy which crossed physical boundaries created new psychological states in both of them and between them. They felt physically fused and totally absorbed by the sensuality they were creating together. Their sexual relationship became a means of communication for them.[34]

Absorbed by the experience of sensuality, one's own subjectivity is raised to the status of 'the couple's subjectivity', the psychological states in both of them willed and linguistically forced to be a psychological state 'between them'. It is an alleged togetherness and identity of experience, two being 'fused' to one. Not just one soul and subjectivity, but also one mixture of two bodies. The appropriation of the other's body, so central to the conception of the 'intimacy of one's identity', is at last completed, as is the invasion of the other's 'mind' – at least in the perception of the representing subjectivity. If I no longer know whose body is whose, nor that the sensuality experienced is mine; if the physical intimacy crosses boundaries and so does my psychological state, I clearly no longer need to worry about possible transgression, about potential violation of the other. The other is territory I walk, body I occupy and psychological 'state' I inhabit.

It is more than doubtful, however, that such fusion and confusion constitute a 'means of communication'. If I pretend not to know who I am nor who the other is, there is no I and no you who could be communicating – no understanding of mine and none of the other's that would enable us to come to an understanding *between* us. The entire unison is a willed self-deception, a pleasant representation to oneself, after the familiar model of the patriarchal union of husband and wife: the subjection and annihilation of the other by and in the dominant subject's subjectivity.

While the apparent 'gain' of the other raises the spectre of the subject's possible exploitation, thus necessitating accounts and trade agreements, the subject waives accounts in the face of its own ecstasy. Just as it is the citizen's sense of democracy to be protected from being exploited, with no proviso that he will not exploit others either, so the subject knows of the fundamentally exploitative nature of the relationship and seeks protection from being exploited – having no objection to doing the exploiting wherever it may get the chance. Thus the democratic relationship seems to reflect the development of patriarchal capitalist democracy from its inception to 'gender-equality'. Not only are the aspirations of the emancipated subject inspired by the power of the erstwhile husband, the ruler over his non-enfranchised wife, but self-prostitution and servitude also seem to have their pride of place among the newly available liberties: as a means to manipulate and as the price for one's own right to mastery.

Not only have we internalized the values of dominance and exploitation, making mastery our own aspiration, we also seem to have understood the functioning of dominance and submission, be it through experience or the incessant cultural propagation of the masochism of 'voluntary submission'. Most people's experience of democracy includes experiences of power as well as subordination. In particular, we seem to have understood that ascending on the ladder of the power hierarchy must be 'earned' by accepting subordination. Socialization in the sadism of power necessarily means socialization in the 'inevitability' of masochism.

Choosing a democratic 'personal relationship' over autonomous and independent social relations means choosing of a democratic mixture of sadism and masochism – of self-subjugation in the interest of exercising mastery, of masochistic payment in the interest of sadistic appropriation.

12

Identity, or history turned biology

In the age of leisure and entertainment, 'topicality' has usurped the place of historicity; moments no longer follow one another according to a sensible and recountable order; they succeed one another like meals in an unending cycle. The world having become a multiform and permanent object of consumption, its destiny is to be continually gobbled up by its consumers.

Alain Finkielkraut, *Remembering in Vain*[1]

The reorganization of human living as the production and circulation of commodities not only displaces reality, it also dissolves any sense of the historicity of (one's) life. For despite all emphases on 'experiences' one wants to have and events one wishes to consume 'live', the underlying urge is less to experience reality and to understand what is happening, than to get the imminent future under control: to shape 'events' after the pattern of previous events and to perceive in new experiences what is familiar, thus facilitating the search for profit and pleasure without the cumbersome adjustment to the nuances of the ever new. Time thus loses its reality and significance: if anything, it is a necessary component of labour as a productive activity 'within a given period of time'.[2] That is to say, it too is carved up into measurable pieces, amounts of time which one invests into products.

It is part of basic capitalist thinking to compare things and to measure them against each other. Since in historical social reality nothing is like anything else, but on the contrary, everything is historically specific and thus unique, certain mechanisms are required to enable us to compare what is actually incomparable. 'Value' is the abstract element by means of which comparability is established. Exchanging commodities creates a relation of value between them – a relative value of each, expressed by the other as its equivalent. In other words, an equation. We have seen this construction of 'value' play a vital role in social relations, so also for the client of Robin Norwood's of whom it is said that 'She interpreted the time he stole from his other life to be with her as the validation of her worth.'[3] That is to say, the client does not seem to have any recognizable worth in her own eyes except for the value which her lover's stealing time from his other life constitutes for her.

As Marx says of ordinary products, we may also say of these life products, substituting people for 'men':

> [People] do not therefore bring these products of their labour into relation with each other as values because they see these objects merely as the material integuments of homogeneous human labour. The reverse is true: by equating their different products to each other in exchange as values, they equate their different kinds of labour as human labour. They do this without being aware of it.[4]

Although the client indeed thinks that her lover's visits bestow value on her – that she is receiving her worth from him – and correspondingly will feel devalued if he fails to come, it is in fact her own equation which equates the value of his brief visits with her entire worth as a person. If women like her, then, suffer from 'low self-esteem', it is less because someone has taken it away from them than because they set their own value on the basis of self-chosen equations and exchanges: the other shall prove my value.

Even though women (for instance) have the collective and personal experience of being deemed by men to be of 'lesser value', this is no reason to give up responsibility for our own judgement. The problem of women's lacking self-esteem (as it is raised in the therapy discourse) is not that men do not value women highly enough; the problem is granting men in our own minds the authority to put any value on us whatsoever. Even if they valued us more highly (being able to lower their estimate at any time), this would lead not to more 'self-esteem' but to dependency. Rather, a sense of oneself derives precisely from taking responsibility for one's own judgement. In the knowledge of one's own judgement and the responsibility for one's own thinking, the collective devaluation of women in patriarchy is a cause for outrage – a political problem which requires a political response: a feminist critique of sexism and the patriarchal power structure, and a political liberation struggle aiming to change it. Without this consciousness, moreover, men's undervaluing of women could not even be perceived as such: we would merely 'have' the value we have (been given). And if we have also internalized our cultural valuation as a consequence of our socialization, this does not necessitate a man who temporarily bestows a dubious value on us; it necessitates freeing ourselves of this internalized male judgement, say, by the practice feminists call consciousness raising (whether it be in CR groups or otherwise).

If 'validation' in some quarters has become *the* proof of a positive relationship, and the experience of validation, appreciation or recognition *the* commodity for the individual subject to strive for, we should not only question the principle of validation by others, but equally the construction of this estimation on the basis of 'value'. Similarly, it should make us pause for thought when arguments in favour of others' right to life and integrity are based on the notion of 'equal value'. Not only do well-meaning xenophiles explain to us that other cultures are 'equally valuable', but many animal rights advocates plead for the animals' right to life by attributing comparable 'value' to their lives. This in turn allows, for instance, Helga Kuhse and Peter Singer (and a host of enthusiastic followers) to value the (future) life of disabled children (at the stage of the embryo or shortly after birth), or the future lives of old people and people with illnesses or lasting injuries, as lives lacking in value and not 'worth living' – and to recommend eugenic 'solutions'.[5] Nor does it help if we call the value an 'intrinsic value': the perception of the object's 'value' remains as subjective and dependent on the valuer as does its perception as 'beautiful' and 'pleasing'.

Value is a fundamentally relative category, deriving from the economic calculations of the judging and valuing subject. It is a subjective judgement which, through the process of exchange, seems to slip into the object as its 'objective' or 'intrinsic' value. The ability to enforce a valuation as a value (that is, a price) depends on one's power and influence over the exchange. The objective is to put the 'value' of the other's product as low as possible, to keep down its price. Moreover, 'validation' itself becomes a commodity, a gift made by the subject to the other (in exchange). If I 'value' and 'appreciate' another, it not only betrays the arrogance of my position of power – evaluating not just a person's 'goods' but the very person – it simultaneously implies the possibility that I may find them of no value. The other 'acquires' her worth thanks to my generous estimation – thus she will need me if she wants to keep it. Through periodic validation I will ratify it (as the case may be), thus keeping her informed of any fluctuations in the exchange rate.

These mechanisms of evaluation and equation, then, are based on a primary restructuring of the real into a judging subject and a judged object, into I and the 'other'. Only with the (subjective) category of the 'other' does it become viable (for the pivotal subject) to make a comparison – to divide into 'same' and 'other', 'like' and 'unlike'. It is a concept of 'difference' that has nothing to do with the constitutive uniqueness of everything real (what the subject calls 'variety'), and is incapable of encompassing it. It is 'otherness' and 'difference' constructed on the basis of criteria selected by the subject and constituted on its implicit norm, from which everything 'other' and all the 'others' are first of all judged the 'same' among themselves, equally 'other than' the norm. We know this to be the case with the 'otherness' of race, sex, etc. Once everything 'other' is potentially the same, an object of otherness in the subject's sight, comparison between these objects becomes possible. As we know, this may even include comparison between objects and the self (as object).

Just as value is a subjective category deriving from the subject's arrogant power, so experiencing something becomes an experience on the basis of a subjective selection of criteria. If sex with many different women on different occasions is always the 'same', it is because the women are not a relevant factor. Similarly, one experience is 'like' a previous experience because the specificity of the situation, the people involved and the historical time, do not play any part. Thus Katie's therapists explained that the 39-year-old Katie was 'reliving' with her partner the very experience which, aged three or four, she had with her mother. The feelings she felt were not just like the feelings then felt, they *were* the old feelings, re-evoked from where repression had stored them. They were not current feelings about a past event, but the 35-year-old originals.

Similarly, in our self-psychologizing accounts we may claim a tendency to construct the 'same' situations, to form the 'same' relationships time and again, and generally to display the 'same' behaviour. Yet it is not the same but new behaviour, occurring in a new context and following a new decision to act (even if it is a decision to act 'as' one did on a past occasion). And it is based on a new assessment of the current situation, which at the very least includes one's knowledge of the last situation in which one is said to have done the same. To speak of the same behaviour and the same situation in this context not only degrades the current situation and its participants, reducing them to mere irrelevancies; it also means regarding one's own historical existence and development, including one's consciousness, as immaterial – considering oneself instead as the timeless and experience-consuming subject of a continuous present.

With the subject thus losing its sense of history, time loses its historicity – its relationship to historical reality – turning instead into 'time off', the 'free' or leisure time of the civil individual dedicated to the pursuit of consumption and the satisfaction of needs. That is to say, the subject seems to divide its own living in its 'private' sphere (that is, its 'social' life apart from economic activity) after the model of capitalist production into the time of 'productive labour' on the one hand (the production of 'private property' for exchange), and leisure time devoted to consumption and reproduction on the other hand. The latter is less a time in its historical sense than an 'eternal present',[6] the infinite sequence of infinitesimal moments of the subjective 'I' reproducing itself.

This also expresses itself in the subject's need to construct itself an 'identity': an understanding of itself as remaining the 'same' in and despite the current of changing reality and time. Not in its change – its growing and changing understanding of its own history and experience – and not in its current behaviour as an expression of who the subject has become today does it see its significant 'personality'. It is in the same, the unchanging or hardly changing that it seeks and anchors its 'identity'. It is a constantly self-reproducing (albeit ageing) body on the one hand, and an (equally self-reproducing) psychological constellation rooted in infancy on the other which are the primary loci for self-identification: a biologism on the one hand, and a barely de-biologized psychologism on the other.

It is not what a person *does* that constitutes the personality, but what a person 'is' that constitutes the identity. It is not the person's (historical) action that we are interested in, but their 'being' reproducing itself as eternal presence. Hence any question concerning identity tends to be answered with the words 'I am'. Correspondingly, it is the phenomenon of a person's change in the course of time – a change of mind and a change in the course of action during a person's lifetime – which seems to require explanation, whereas treading a fairly straight line of 'consistent' behaviour, unmarked by any learning and unruffled by any insight, generally counts as exemplary strength of character. Such an understanding of identity means not only declaring oneself (and people in general) incapable of learning from experience; it also means placing the responsibility for one's decisions and actions not in oneself (or people themselves), but in a conglomerate of self-reproducing behaviour patterns and early childhood influences – facts of 'nature' which others and other things have caused – that is to say, in a form of history which, seen from the point of view of the eternal present, takes on a quasi-biological function, the ideological function of 'nature'.

Similarly, the new trend in identity politics shows a development towards forms of newly clad racist, sexist and nationalist biologisms: not only a parallel interest in the 'being' of specific groups or their members in preference to their activities, but also a biological construction of the relation between the individual and the group. What originally made its appearance on the political scene as a *political consciousness of identity* – a consciousness of the specific collective history of oppression, accompanied by a corresponding self-naming, say as Blacks or Women in the Black and Women's Liberation Movements – today is turning into a pretext to reconstruct identities of race, nation, ethnicity, sex, and their subgroups. Since a political consciousness of 'identity' is eminently historical – deriving from an analysis of the historical past with the aim to intervene politically in the present, thus to create a different future – 'political identity' necessarily implies its own changeability and eventual supersession. The goal is to make such political 'identity' redundant – to create a society (a material reality) in which it has no more relevance. But even in the present, where it is a necessity, consciousness of the history of oppression is continually growing and changing, most of all through the political activity and experience in the present, which add to the original consciousness of historical oppression the current consciousness of resistance and change. Hence 'political identity' means anything but an unchanging sameness, much less a state of being marked by past oppression, but, on the contrary, the collective consciousness and self-confidence of a group in resistance and in the process of historical change.

Yet political practice increasingly shows the phenomenon of an 'infatuation' with one's own oppression (or rather, the identity which bears its name). Audre Lorde (back in 1981) refers to it specifically in the context of white women's reaction to Black women's feminism and critique of racism, yet defines it as a general problem of power relations between women: 'What woman here is so enamoured of her own oppression that she cannot see her heelprint upon another woman's face? What woman's terms of oppression have become precious and necessary to her as a ticket into the fold of the righteous, away from the cold winds of self-scrutiny?'[7] Similarly, Cherríe Moraga writes in the preface to the second edition of *This Bridge Called My Back* (back in 1983):

> I worry about the tendency in the movement where women of color activists seem to become enamored with our own oppression . . . I worry about the tendency of racial/cultural separatism amongst us where we dig in our heels against working with groups outside our own particular race/ethnicity. This is what we have accused white people of, basically sticking to their own kind – only working politically where they may feel 'safe' and 'at home'. But the making of a political movement has never been about safety or feeling 'at home'. . . Cultural identity – our right to it – is a legitimate and basic concern for all women of color . . . But to stop there only results in the most limiting of identity politics: 'If I suffer it, it's real. If I don't feel it, it doesn't exist.'[8]

As Lorde and Moraga both indicate, it is a phenomenon of relative privilege: the use of an 'identity' in cultural-political situations which precisely exclude the danger of the particular experience of victimization that has given the identity its name, situations in which cultural self-representation moves to the foreground, ready to become an activity and an end in itself.

Thus an infatuation with the victim status of 'women' is particularly manifest among white women in situations with other women, especially Black women (and also in situations with relatively gentle and critical men) – rarely in situations with sexually exploitative and violent men. Similarly, Moraga sees a problematical attachment to oppression status in the tendency to cultural separatism *vis-à-vis* women experiencing different oppressions – that is, not in the politically necessary separatism *vis-à-vis* white people and men as a form of effective political organizing, but in the voluntary exclusion of women of different ethnic origin. We exclude where we have the power to exclude.

Oppression identity becomes problematical, if we follow Moraga, when it becomes a new home – a 'homeland of the mind', as Jenny Bourne calls it:[9] a symbolic country where we 'belong', where we feel safe and at home, being among our own 'kind'. Our own 'kind' are not those with the same political aims, but women with the same oppression status. Yet a political movement, Moraga insists, cannot be about safety and feeling at home. Feeling at home and safe, we may equally insist, is not about building a political movement. In particular, we gain this home and its safety by fighting against those less powerful than ourselves, those underprivileged in relation to ourselves, however underprivileged we may be, over whom we are exercising power and privilege – it is our heelprint in other women's faces, it is other women we dig in our heels against. And we feel finally 'at home' where we neither are struggling in a political struggle against oppression, nor are personally in any danger, but where among our 'likes' we feel 'understood' in our suffering – our ticket to the fold of the righteous.

By insisting that cultural identity is indeed a legitimate concern, while at the same time criticizing the use of oppression status as new home country, Moraga highlights the importance of considering power relations: 'cultural identity' in the sense of a political consciousness is appropriate as a means of resistance in struggle, not as a state of being (far from the struggle). Multicultural oppression identity as new homeland is a form of exclusion on the basis of criteria of race, ethnicity, class etc., exercised from a position of power over those excluded. That is, the identity where we feel 'at home' is constructed on the dominant principles of inclusion and exclusion on which home countries and nations are formed.

Kathleen Barry in her analysis of female sexual slavery describes *victimism* as the practice of treating women *as* victims, thereby 'creating the role and status of the victim'.[10] This in turn may lead women to hold on to that 'status', as their only supposed chance of finding understanding and support.[11] Victimism 'extends the terrorism of the act of sexual violence [against a woman] by continuing to rob her of her humanness'.[12] Since Barry's analysis it has become apparent that the practice of victimism is by no means restricted to patriarchal institutions (police, social workers, medical and psychiatric personnel etc.), but is current also amongst women of the women's movement. Not only do many women treat other women as victims, considering it a special form of 'caring' and 'understanding'; they also treat themselves as victims. As bell hooks has argued, 'the vision of Sisterhood evoked by women's liberationists [primarily bourgeois white women, both liberal and radical in perspective] was based on the idea of a common oppression', a 'shared victimization'.[13]

While thus many women, rather than rejecting the status of victim, are celebrating it as a source of identity, this may partly be due, Barry argues, to the heritage of 'the political and academic left-liberalism of the late 1960's when the cult of the victim was the liberal's answer to urban racial violence'.[14] It is a heritage which also seems to inform the 'answer' to the pervasive sexual violence in our society, including the answer of parts of the women's movement. It is an 'answer' on the level of culture to a problem of oppression in the real: the offer of a cult as compensation for oppression. After twenty-five more years of this particular heritage, the cult not only continues to be offered, but increasingly is being accepted, cultural representation of oppression identity being regarded not only as an adequate compensation for, but an adequate response to, oppression. If its 'offer' is made in lieu of political support in the real, its 'acceptance' similarly is in lieu – a renunciation of resistance on the level of oppression, in favour of the cultural construction of elective home countries.

Alain Finkielkraut also analyses this infatuation with one's oppression status, subjecting it to probably the most self-critical and uncompromising scrutiny. Not only is the *absence of danger* its condition: 'through the proximity to the [Second World] War I was protected from any anti-Semitic violence, so that I could identify with the role of the victim without personal danger to myself.'[15] But to adopt a collective 'victim identity' is above all to *appropriate the suffering of others* for one's own personal identity: 'Being a Jew to me for a long time had meant a right: the right to appropriate trials I had not suffered . . . This enormous suffering, however, which through proclaiming my Jewish identity I had thought to be able to acquire, cannot – so much I know today – be appropriated.'[16]

Claiming a collective victimization for one's individual identity thus means exploiting the victimization of others, in a situation different from the situation of victimization, where on the contrary it becomes an advantage – be it in a political scene which attributes cult(ural) credit in the form of attention and recognition on the basis of suffering,[17] or as Finkielkraut also describes, in one's own consciousness, where it lends a 'touch of suffering and tragedy as a spice' to the banality of one's everyday life.[18] If this sounds hard on one's own psychology as well as one's own relative suffering, it has to be remembered that this insight is due not only to unconditional honesty (the 'cold winds of self-scrutiny'), but also to political necessity: 'For, if authenticity today means no more than not to be ashamed of one's origins, it is but another form of forgetting. If being a Jew is reduced to the little bit of courage it takes to call oneself a Jew, Judaism has the choice only between two kinds of disappearance.'[19]

Presenting this 'self-image' to oneself and to the general public means disparaging reality, seeking to gain value in the eyes of the public (or oneself) which is based on a reality other than one's own. It means constructing a self-image with the material of the reality of other people's suffering. Nor does this abuse of historical suffering contribute to preserving its memory, but on the contrary helps to annihilate it. As Finkielkraut says with regard to Judaism, 'I have understood that Judaism is not simply a matter of expression of personal sincerity, but that it exists outside my person – indeed that it precludes any definition *in the first person*.'[20] Just so the collective history of the oppression of women exists outside the person of individual women, and precludes any definition in the first person, any representative appropriation by individual women. Rather, the representation of identity wrought out of collective experience – the so-called personal 'political identity' – is a form of self-posturing: 'To say "I" already means to pose. But the problem is that one is continually starting again from this self-satisfied, seductive and voracious "I" which usurps the history of an entire people, annexing it to its need to be loved.'[21]

In particular, it is the mere (perverse) reversal of the identification underlying the collective power bonding, say, of nationality or masculinity, where individuals appropriate the collective historic and cultural deeds of their 'kind' – which they have not accomplished themselves – thus to dress their humble persons in the glory of national or sex pride. What applies to the collective suffering of others also applies to one's own suffering in the past, which can no more be 'appropriated' for the present, no more permits a definition in the first person and the present tense.

Moreover, it is no longer only the cultural or political 'identities' of resistance (oppression) which are being cultivated as collective and personal home countries: there is a gradually emerging 'victim status' of the oppressors similarly serving as material for the construction of identity. That even the status of the oppressor may acquire special victim identity we owe to an oppositional 'political culture' which makes oppression into a cult, where 'oppression' is traded as accumulated credit and multiple oppression (as a status, never of course as lived experience) has degenerated to a desirable exchange-value.

Hence, if the oppressed appear to derive a 'positive identity' from the biologist, racist, sexist, nationalist, eugenicist criteria of their oppression – defining themselves as Blacks, Migrants, Jews, Muslims, Cripples, Women, Lesbians etc. – it must be possible also to construct an identity out of the 'negative' criteria of the status of dominance: a sad and painful identity, to be sure, yet a home of sorts, a refuge of 'being' (which is none of our fault).

So it happens that the virtually unchanging and usually unchangeable data of our biological and social biography – sex, nationality, race/ethnic origin, religion and all the other data which we usually find on forms issued by local and national authorities – are employed not only by ruling groups and institutions as a means of discrimination and social control, but are chosen by individuals and groups of the movement culture as the defining reference points in the construction of their so-called political identity. In other words, the ruling criteria of the *norm(s)* which define the 'deviance' of all 'otherness' are becoming fit again for good (political) society.

Thus women of the women's movement are exploring the significance of their multiple being ('What is the relation between our being lesbian and our being white?')[22] or inquiring into the 'identity components "German" (and "white") as well as "socialized as a Christian" '; or pondering the question: 'Who then is speaking when I say "I am . . . "?'[23] White feminists of anti-racist intent recommend that we locate our identity in the categories of power and dominance, say as white Christian heterosexual middle-class women without disability – thereby not only confirming and strengthening dominant ideology, but once more making colour, nationality, class, religion and physical symmetry the factors defining *other kinds* (also called 'difference'). That is, despite protestations that 'Black' is conceived as a *political* term, it is becoming a criterion again of skin colour.[24]

Thus Black people are no longer those oppressed by white people's racism, who could do with our solidarity in the struggle to abolish racism; they apparently are people who *are* black and thus really *are* 'different'. No matter that it is precisely such an alleged identity of otherness, of *being* 'different' (from the 'norm') – whether of women as a sex or of Africans, Indigenous people, Jews, and many more as 'races' – which was the basis and legitimation of the historical atrocities of systematic slavery, persecution and murder (and continues to be in the present), or that it was, in Finkielkraut's words, the Jews' 'being, not their actions, [which] had led them to Auschwitz or Buchenwald'.[25] There seems no recollection, in other words, that it was and is a racist ideology which defines the 'being' or 'identity' of people, classifying them as *kinds* of people, to be done with as the definers see fit – to be murdered, enslaved, exploited, persecuted and displaced the world over.

Similarly, it no longer seems to be a collective (even if differential) history of oppression and resistance which defines 'women' as a group, but increasingly (again) a common theoretical reproductive capacity to give birth. The concept of 'identity' is stripped of its historical, political and liberationist significance, to be used once again in its original oppressive racist and sexist sense: to designate multiple 'kinds' of people. The term 'race' may, as Finkielkraut comments, be largely taboo today (at least in French and German), yet 'typological thinking and the fetishism of differences establish themselves under the aegis of the irreproachable concept of culture.'[26] Multiculturalism and the multiplicity of 'cultural identities' take over the function of race typology.

The apparent irony that whites, in response to the political self-naming of Blacks, Christians in response to the self-naming of Jews or Muslims, nationals in response to the self-naming of migrants, and men in response to the political self-naming of women, today define themselves as 'other than' Black, ergo white, and 'other than' female, ergo male (etc.), we owe to the same cultural scene in which politics is but radical chic, feminism and the critiques of racism and anti-Semitism no more than trends on the level of discourse. On the level of a left-liberal intellectual discourse, the concepts 'Black', 'Jewish', 'migrant', and 'women' etc. are found simply to be *dominant* concepts, political values which are in fashion, *in relation to which* whites and/or men now 'need' to define their 'identity' – as Black people or women defined theirs at the time of their emerging resistance movements – in 'resistance' to the 'dominant' fashion in discourse.

Hence masculinity studies are booming with the justification that 'there is a need for a reassessment of masculinity in response to the feminist reinterpretation of women's identity'.[27] Were it in response to feminist critique rather than an alleged 'reinterpretation of women's identity', students of men's studies would realize that feminism already *is* a reassessment of masculinity. Yet by reducing feminism to a mere reinterpretation of women's identity, the parallel project of 'reassessing men's identity' acquires a spurious political status, on a par with the radical project of feminism. Similarly, women try to reassess their 'national' 'white' 'Christian' 'middle-class' identity, thus assessing it as of old. The critiques of racism, of nationalism and Eurocentrism are reduced to the mere renaming of 'identities', identities created by structures of oppression, but now subject to the volatile valuation of fashion.

That such reassessments turn out to be like the original 'assessments', in the old and intact categories of dominance, follows from the application of the double negative, the doubly deployed dualism of the dominant culture: women are those who are 'other' than men. Men are those who are 'other' than those who are 'other' than men. Ditto white, Christian, German, etc. Rather than being due to a political necessity of resistance, however, this 're'-assessment offers yet another chance for self-representation and self-realization, that is, for occupying oneself with oneself, maintaining a position of power and self-interest, now clad in the glamour of a 'political' activity.

However, it is no longer just men of discourse who see in feminism no more than a reinterpretation of femininity. Increasingly, many women also see 'feminism' if not indeed 'post-feminism' as a chance cosmetically to revamp the cultural image of women and to reclaim biological sex as a factor of personal and collective identity. What the repressive measures of patriarchy have for centuries been forcing on women, namely their identification on the basis of their reproductive capacity, ideological persuasion seems finally to have brought to completion: namely that women – especially women with education privilege and thus highly trained in the culture of patriarchy – are now claiming it voluntarily and without direct or physical coercion.

Such enthusiasm at the reappearance of the reactionary and positivist concept of 'identity' can be explained only by the profit it promises the subject. Identity offers, as we have seen, a refuge of 'being', from which historicity and action have been banned. If 'Black people' have become, once again, those who *are* black, then white people, too, are simply those who *are* white – and less those responsible for racist oppression, who are exercising, profiting from and maintaining it. 'Identity' no longer refers to historical and political doing, it is a mere statement about people's *being* (which they cannot help). Equally 'men', rather than designating those responsible for exercising and institutionally maintaining the oppression and exploitation of women, who are collectively and individually benefiting from it, increasingly is meant to designate people who *are* biologically (and culturally and socially) male and thus different from what women *are*.

Hence we may own not only a white, Christian, male etc. identity, but own up even to being 'bearers of a racist identity'.[28] 'Being racist' thus becomes something we no more can help than we can help being white or male. Generally, the politics of difference offers all of us equally – be we oppressors or oppressed – the democratic opportunity to define ourselves from our own point of view, and in relation to an 'opposite' of our choice, as 'different' and 'other' – thus to affirm this 'relationship' as an eternal (ahistorical) actuality.

Moreover, this preoccupation with cultural or 'political' identities pre-empts any serious discussion about political activity. For what determines political activity is less the political necessities of action than who we want to be doing it with. What the activity is about is discussed, if at all, after the question with whom we are doing it has been resolved. The highest priority is the community, that is, the social and political elective home country, with political activity its by-product. This is how the well-known separatist political groups are formed to which Cherríe Moraga refers, and it is how coalitions, once the groups exist, are to be made between them.

What white 'anti-racist' women today know for sure is that white and Black, Christian and Jewish, nationals and migrant women shall 'come together', the analysis concentrating on why it is 'so difficult'.[29] The 'lack of contact' and connection between white women and Black or migrant women is now being experienced as a lack, to be overcome by increased contact.[30] The goal is 'togetherness', whose advantages are extolled while the potential disadvantages muted by other white women are systematically denied.[31] What is clear is the desire for 'coalitions' and 'bondings' – communities we want, encounters we seek and associations we regard as desirable – and less the political necessities calling for political solidarity. That is to say, for many white women, working together with Black women has become a veritable need – and a condition for any anti-racist commitment on their part.

We will even work on recognizing and overcoming our own personal racism, *so that* we may successfully work together, rather than the other way round:

> Coalitions demand that we inform ourselves about the needs and goals of different groups of women and on the basis of this knowledge formulate our own aims. Only then can a joint discussion begin . . . Coalitions require even more . . . Successful coalitions presuppose . . . Albrecht and Brewer see the key to viable coalitions in the development of credible leadership qualities . . . This means that feminists, in order to be able successfully to work together, must go beyond the boundaries of the horizon of their own experience and be able to deal constructively with differences.[32]

Note that 'feminists' in general need to do all this, that 'we all' need to explore the others' differences, there being no particular power disequilibrium that would necessitate a particular effort on dominant women's part. The point is, however, that we take on this burden of working on our racism *in order* to be able to have a viable relationship with Black women; we do not enter into political coalitions in order jointly to fight against racism and sexism – that is, fight racism (and not just our own) because we recognize the political necessity of fighting it. Rather, if we want coalitions – and it is obvious that we now do – we need to take all this upon us.

Going beyond the horizon of one's own experience and dealing constructively with differences (whatever that may be) are thus not political necessities themselves – a standard we aspire to even without the promised reward, which we might even regard as prerequisite in relation to any people and hence does not require special mention. Rather, they are a necessity in our own interest, a means to fulfil our wish for successful coalitions with Black, Jewish and migrant women. That is, we are really in search of friends, in particular, friends defined *qua* their particular (racial) identity.

A friend, thus, is not somebody with the same political ends; a friend is somebody who belongs to the right identity. Similarly, 'enemy' does not signify a political adversary but a member of an identified collective identity. This saves much political analysis, since to know friend from foe we do not need to analyse their actions and the political implications and consequences; we only need to consult their identity. What is a matter of course, say, for nationalists or racists, namely that Germans love Germans, the English love the English, the French love the French and so on, is becoming a matter of course also for 'political identities' – 'lesbians love lesbians'[33] – and we behave altogether as if identity were the relevant criterion, be it for political association or for friendship (if any difference is made between them).

This means that friend and foe, too, are categories of identity, no matter how the people in question behave: we love them or hate them not because of what they do, but because of who they are. We deposit our love or our hatred in their persons *as* a friend or a foe respectively. Thus we may continue to love individual people even if they fight us, beat us, degrade us, because we once designated them as friends, thus because they *are* friends. We love them 'despite' their behaviour, for we do not see people as their behaviour, but as identities inscribed in their bodies *minus* their behaviour. In this way some women explain that they do not leave a violent partner (even if they could) because 'I still love him. I want him, only I want him to behave differently.' 'He' is apparently everything except his contemporary behaviour, a fictional identity consisting of his embodiment and the memory of his having behaved differently in better days. It is a construction which is apparently more 'real' than his real behaviour today, and which we insist constitutes the 'real him', with which his current behaviour is merely inconsistent.

If we manage this contradiction in relation to friends – loving people who are behaving towards us like adversaries – we succeed even better in relation to foes, whom we hate on the basis of their identity and at a distance from which we do not even know of their behaviour. Thus what we regard as a radical identity politics is an exact replica of national war-and-peace politics: we make coalitions and alliances with people wholesale, people about whose behaviour individually we know nothing, inversely declaring war on people in similar bulk under the same conditions. This not only constitutes an injustice – in the 'positive' as in the 'negative' case – towards the individual people concerned, whom we treat as representatives of a given identity rather than as persons. It also prevents us from forming political alliances on the basis of people's politics and behaviour, that is, political conviction expressed through, and proved by, action. For in the case of 'friends' we abstain from analysing their behaviour, and in the case of supposed 'enemies' do not even get to know it.

'Politics' thus becomes equivalent to knowing who is our enemy or ally respectively – certainties based not on politics but on categories of identity: people's 'being' or belonging to ethnicities, races, nations or sexes and their subgroups, our 'natural' community being our 'kind'. This leads to conventional warfare – say, with the tribe of patriarchs or 'fathers' – and to the accompanying problems of a militarized community: 'Our efforts to create lesbian community were in serious jeopardy both from without and from within.'[34] From outside 'we faced outright violence . . . penetration and disruption, and all manner of other male sabotage', while inside the members of the community 'attacked each other far more vehemently than [they] ever dared attack men . . . we were using our survival skills against each other.'[35] No matter, for we know who our friends are, however violently they may attack us. What are called survival skills clearly are methods of fighting or beating anyone threatening our interests, if they can be used just as well against each other, that is, regardless of whether it is a matter of survival. They are 'skills' of martial self-defence (attack), learnt in the war with the enemy: 'We had most of us learned well to survive in the patriarchy . . . We'd learned to survive on the street, on the job or through the welfare office, in the bedroom.'[36]

The aim seems no longer to change a society which is patriarchal – to abolish the power structures and fight sexist oppression. The aim is a territorial war with the tribe of the 'fathers', with a view to establishing a nation of our own. For lesbian identity is a home, a country where we are among our own 'kind': 'Coming out was, for me, coming home.'[37] It is an experience of 'landing',[38] of touching ground as much as of entering safe land, and 'lesbian community . . . a ground for be-ing'.[39] Just as patriarchy has become embodied in the tribe of the 'fathers' – identifiable people of a kind – so the ideal community aspired to (as an alternative to society) is a community consisting of people of one 'kind'. Having declared war on the tribe of the 'fathers', what can our goal – to abolish patriarchy – mean?

Even where it seems, at least rhetorically, to be an issue of politics – of racism, sexism or patriarchy, what in relation to people concerns political behaviour – we tend to biologize the political, so that we may fight against (or avoid or exclude) *people* – patriarchs, sexists, racists etc. – who supposedly personify the politics. That is to say, we opt for war with particular people, in preference to resistance to the political order and to racist and sexist behaviour, whosesoever it may be (though on the principle of identity it rarely is one's own). If the ultimate consequence is not the extermination of sexists and racists, the implication at least is territorial segregation and the creation of 'pure' communities, on a principle of exclusion (after the motto of 'fascists out'), or else a retreat into niches of separatist living space. It is a version of 'ethnic cleansing' and the nationalist claim to an exclusive territory of one's own, there to realize one's 'national identity'.

Lesbian ethicist Sarah Lucia Hoagland writes of the incipient lesbian revolution:

> During the emergence of the u.s. women's liberation and gay libera-tion movements . . . we turned our backs on the fathers' categories and began to focus on each other . . . hundreds of lesbian projects began: collectives, newspapers, record companies, bookstores, presses, film companies, schools, lesbian community centres, libraries and archives, credit unions, magazines, healing centres, restaurants, radio stations, food co-ops, alcoholism detox centres, rape crisis centres, bands, womyn's land, music festivals, more bars, and on and on.[40]

In other words, everything you need to live – a lesbian republic nearly ready to declare its independence. As Hoagland also emphasizes: 'I do not believe oppression is going to be lifted from us . . . If oppression is going to end, we need to move out of it.'[41] Although this must be a metaphor, the metaphor bespeaks a conceptual framework, for we also 'created conceptual frameworks *outside* the values of the fathers' (my emphasis).[42]

Oppression thus is no longer what in our society we need to fight against, or patriarchal values what we oppose where and when they are realized: they are like an untoward climate we turn our back on and 'move out of', to an 'outside' we make into our own space, from which in turn we exclude and include whom and what we see fit. For territory is the basis on which political power rests – the material range of its jurisdiction. Hence the attempt in the centres of power to extend its range – say, to unify 'Europe' or ultimately create a 'global village'. Conversely, however small (and powerless) a minority may be within a larger community, with a territory of its own it will be the majority, with power and jurisdiction over its space.

The territorial metaphor of 'space' with its geographical borders ('within and without') is paramount in identity politics, as is the notion of a community of one's own 'kind'. This 'community' needs adequate living space, that is, needs to *expand* its territory: 'We were (and still are) boundary dwellers. Atravesamos fronteras. And the first task at hand was developing lesbian space.'[43] Like a settler community building a future state in what it considers to be a 'void' in the 'wilderness', 'lesbians were going to forge something within a void', wanting to 'create what we'd imagined and dreamed'.[44] Spirits are correspondingly high and full of the promise of the future state: 'We focused on ourselves. We told our coming-out stories. We celebrated lesbianism. We began many different lesbian projects. We created space in which we could develop a new context and build collectivity. This was an exuberant time . . .'[45] There may be setbacks of course – the dangers of 'sliding back or being undermined', 'we have suffered many internal defeats' – but 'we have made lesbian space credible to ourselves', 'our work to date has also been successful . . . we have been growing, healing, learning, and changing despite the dominant society all around us and the wars between us.'[46]

After the heady days of pioneering and conquest, now is a 'time for deep reevaluation'. With the territory (space) staked out and the borders more or less fixed, there is no need, apart from vigilance towards ever hostile neighbours, for any further political work: the community can go on living in the eternal present of its being. 'I want to suggest it is also a time of lesbian celebration', writes Hoagland at the end of her book; 'we have accomplished as much as we have because we believe in ourselves – we have believed in ourselves and each other . . . Can we take time out, heal, recover, learn to play, and come back?'[47] Having needed 'sufficient time and room to create [something new]', space where 'we focused on ourselves',[48] we now need 'time out' to heal, recover, play.

Identity politics thus replicates the very principles on which nations are built and new-found land is settled, the racist-nationalist and inter-nationalist principle which organizes supposedly homogeneous peoples – people of a 'kind' – within their respective own countries, each a people of 'friends' surrounded by enemy peoples. For even if there are differences within the community – 'we have been exploring our differences'[49] – there nevertheless is something specific which unites it making it into a community within society. And it seems that all our political efforts concentrate on not referring to people's behaviour (or else to excuse it), so as to save ourselves having to respond to it politically. Instead we distinguish between people on the basis of their 'being', their incorporated identity.

Even where we seemingly approach questions of behaviour, for instance our 'treatment of the Others', this too is abstracted to a new kind of 'identity'. Thus Christina Thürmer-Rohr writes:

> Subordinates, too, tend to project themselves as masters as soon as they get the chance. This chance occurs most readily and most safely in the treatment of the Others – in and outside one's own country. Our relationship to the Others is the test case which shows in how far white people are bearers of a racist identity. Here it will show [be decided] whether they know their own boundaries and where they know them to be, whether and how they accommodate the Others and whether they accept them as Others, whether they are capable of taking responsibility for their own history and the present and, on the basis of understanding [their] errors, will be able to change themselves.[50]

The test case seems to concern people's behaviour – accepting and welcoming or accommodating others, accepting them as they are, or not doing so. Yet if they do not accommodate these others, and if they do not accept them as they are, this does not show how they are *acting*, it shows in how far they are 'bearers of a racist identity'. White people's relationship 'to the Others' is thus, even in the test case of 'their treatment of the Others', not a question of their behaviour, but of their 'identity'. In this case it is not an identity as whites or Germans or Europeans, it is an identity of 'being racist'. Nor of course do they themselves create this identity, but as is the case with identities in general, they are 'bearers' of it. In particular, this relationship of white people towards the 'Others' does not concern behaviour *towards others*, with consequences worth mentioning *for those others*: it means that subordinates 'project themselves as masters'. It may be an unpleasing image that they are thus projecting, one which in current political culture is negatively valued, yet it remains the mere projection of an identity, behaviour on one's own behalf which if anything is damaging to the projectors. Hence the 'Others' indeed do not suffer from our behaviour; they 'are suffering from Western culture'.[51]

Moreover, it appears that such 'treatment of the Others' refers not so much to the personal behaviour of individual people as to the collective 'behaviour' of the nation they belong to. Although there is mention of people in the plural, they seem less a multiplicity of individuals than the single entity of a collective. It is the 'relationship of white society to the *Others*' (emphasis in the original),[52] and a question of 'white women being bound into their own racist society'.[53] Thus, if it is a question of whether they know their 'boundaries' (*Grenzen*), in the test case of their 'treatment of the Others within and outside their country', it seems as much to concern their country's national borders as any potential personal boundaries.

'Directly or indirectly, white people have in the course of their relationship to the Others developed a consciousness of normality which includes as a matter of course' a whole number of 'claims' and 'rights'.[54] White women are also 'bearers of the problem, belonging to the culture which *is* and *creates* the problem'.[55] But they are bearers of this culture and members of this society through no personal fault or responsibility of their own; they are bearers of it *qua* their identity, through an accident of history and birth. So presumably they cannot really be responsible for being bearers of their consciousness, a consciousness developed by their 'race' over centuries.

For they are bound not only into their contemporary society; they are bearers of a *historical* identity, heirs to a European legacy left not only by fathers to their sons but also by mothers to their daughters: 'The racism of the Christian-occidental culture is not only a question of a 500-year-old history of individual colonialists, but also of a prehistory of European men and women.'[56] In any case, however, it is a question of *history*. And if this history is 'full of examples of women who actively supported the hostilities of their men',[57] the present seems peopled by no such examples.

Racism is thus a problem principally of historic events going back up to 500 years, passed on as the sins of the fathers and mothers to the umpteenth generation. Our problem as contemporary Europeans is simply that we 'cannot sneak out of this history', that 'elements of Western European identity . . . obviously remain effective into the present time.'[58] Just as Katie can see herself in the past as a little girl who was an active agent, yet in her adult self sees but the passively suffering bearer of a personal identity in which elements of her personal-psychological history are still effective, so Europeans in the past used to be active agents, participants in the political events (for example, racism) of their time, while contemporary Western Europeans simply suffer the effects of a Western European past, a historical identity.

History and the past are thus really a biological inheritance, on the personal as on the political level. That is to say, we psychologize the history of 'nations' and continents (not to mention 'races') after the model of the (biological) theory of the psychology of individuals. The point in the one as in the other case is to banish action and behaviour into the remote and inaccessible past, rendering the present a state of pure being, troubled but by the interference of particles from the past which refuse to pass, following us into the present. Thus in an editorial entitled 'The Past does not Pass', in the renowned weekly newspaper, *Die Zeit*, it is said of Germany that the past has 'burdened our people with a particularly heavy inheritance [*Erblast*]':

> What during the time of Hitler the Germans in cold blood brought upon the world in terms of cruelty and pain exceeds every measure of previous mistakes [*Verfehlung*]. It is painfully brought to our minds time after time on ever recurring anniversaries . . . This past does not pass. It will persecute us with biblical force unto the seventh generation.[59]

Once again an entire people becomes a victim of persecution, this time the contemporary German 'people': not just racism and anti-Semitism persecute us as our pain and our misery; the past is also persecuting us with biblical force. 'To be sure, the generations which have followed are free of direct or indirect implication, free also of any personal responsibility or guilt.'[60] All the more so are they truly victims, being persecuted for no fault of their own.

If we think, however, that the author is challenging the law of 'blood and soil' relation, which alone visits the sins of the fathers upon the sons – that is, the racist, nationalist biological construction of an extended national family as a historico-biological organism – we are mistaken. For though responsibility is said to be specific to the context of action, thus absolving contemporary Germans from any guilt and responsibility for the Holocaust, their blood relation with those responsible is reaffirmed in the very same breath: 'Three things nevertheless are imposed on them. First, the burden of insight: so low may Germans fall, so low may people fall.'[61] The tragedy (or 'mistake') of the National Socialist past is not that millions of Jews and other people were murdered and tortured, and many countries brought to ruin; the tragedy is that Germans sank so low. Hence it is 'painful' for 'Germans' to be reminded of it on successive anniversaries: this history was and remains a blow to German national consciousness. For secondly, the editorial continues, it imposes on Germans 'the continuing duty to be ashamed of monstrosities committed half a century ago in the German name and by German hands'.[62]

It may be a 'painful history', but it is none the less the Germans' history, their property and possession. It has been made by German hands, hence it is their prerogative – however negative it may be – in all innocence to be ashamed of it, to be ashamed *of* the Germans. This history does not, apparently, impose any obligation to reflect upon any connection between this understanding of national identity and the historical understanding of it in that National Socialist past which so burdens us today: an understanding of the national identity of the 'Germans' as a transhistorical 'blood and soil' organism – which not only brought the National Socialists to power, but was the basis of a politics of 'race' which culminated in the murder of millions of Jewish men, women and children as well as of other people considered to be of 'inferior race' – and this understanding of 'Germans' today who, however painfully, nevertheless identify with this 'master race', with the German name as well as German hands. The principle of identification is the same, whether it fills those identifying with pride or shame. Yet this biologist principle of biologically national origin remains unchallenged – the principle according to which we *are* 'the same' as the generations of people of the same 'nationality', the same 'blood', who lived on the same soil before us.

Thirdly, the past imposes on the Germans 'the task of seeking the lessons of history by continuously remembering it in the present'. Why the task specifically of *Germans*? Because it is the history of 'the Germans', their national heritage, their inheritance? What about the history of the Jews? Of the Europeans east and west? Of the Soviet Union and so forth? Have they all their own little national histories, which it is their task to come to terms with? Does no one else have to think about race ideology, about national pride, about the notion of a 'master race', about mass murder and war, about the Holocaust, and to draw lessons from the history of this century – because it was 'German hands' that made 'the history' of half a century ago? Just because we do not hold a German passport, enjoying citizenship of a different national state (an accident of history and birth), do we have no responsibilities concerning this history of 'the Germans'? Nor for the history of the Khmer Rouge, the history of millions of murdered Cambodians, the history of the Serbs, the Croats, the Bosnians, the Somalis or anyone else? Even less for the history of any multinationals and transnational capital and their exploitation, say, of 200 million children? Because despite fine-sounding words about universal human rights and about crimes against humanity, we do not really feel responsible for any humanity, but if anything for 'our own kind'?

It appears so. It appears that we are carriers of history as we are carriers of bad (or good) hereditary factors, of congenital diseases passed on through blood relationship to innocent victims of future generations. Thus the social philosopher Norbert Elias writes in his *Studien über die Deutschen* (Studies about the Germans):

> In the German tradition we can quite clearly note both a habituation to strategies of commanding and obeying, often enough also by means of direct or indirect use of physical force – and, until recently, a comparatively low degree of skill in strategies of discussion, as the heritage/inheritance [*Erbe*] of a long absolutist and near-absolutist rule. Displeasure in relation to the relatively complicated control of emotions required for resolving conflicts exclusively by means of discussion, or conversely, the pleasure [taken] in the simpler command and obedience strategies may still be observed in Germany today.[63]

That is to say, the pleasure taken in giving orders or in obeying them, or the displeasure experienced in controlling one's emotions, and conversely, the pleasure of indulging one's emotions, which all may be observed in people living in Germany today, are not, as you might think, a matter of their personal interests and their personal political will – say, a question of certain advantages they can see in such behaviour, or indeed, the pleasure they are thereby experiencing. Rather, the cause of such behaviour is to be sought in the history of Germany, the 'blood and soil organism's' collective experience of long absolutist rule. For as a people 'you' get used to absolutist rule as a rat gets used to the systematic manipulation by a laboratory technician. Whereas a skill in discussion strategies can be learnt only 'in the course of a long series of generations'[64] – who will pass on the fragments of their learning in the form of hereditary cultural factors to future generations.

In particular, there exists a 'typical' behaviour of Germans, if not indeed a 'national habitus of the Germans'[65] – a 'character of the people' or a 'national character of the Germans', similar, say, to the 'sexual character' of women.[66] Citizens of the United States or of Switzerland, say, have been much luckier in this respect, democracy having been practised a lot longer by the predecessors on their soil – be they blood relatives or 'elected relatives' acquired through immigration. It is so also with Britain and the Netherlands: 'Members of these states possess as part of their national heritage a choice of behaviours which allow them and at the same time oblige them to keep their feelings – more or less – in check when resolving social conflicts.'[67]

As Alain Finkielkraut describes his construction of a Jewish identity as an attempt to usurp and claim for himself the history of an entire people, so the construction of a 'national character' is an attempt to usurp the experiences of previous generations for the benefit of individuals today. Although Germanism, like Judaism, precludes any definition in the first person, today's Germans seem to consist of individual Germans whose pleasure and displeasure, whose explosive emotional behaviour and whose reluctance to engage in discussions (where they display it) we explain by a national collective character developed 'on German soil' and passed on through German blood.[68]

Even where it is not a matter of virtues, heroic deeds and cultural achievements, but of centuries of absolutist rule, these may be appropriated and annexed by contemporary individuals – as an 'explanation' of unacceptable or reprehensible behaviour in the present. For 'in Germany one did have too little time and too little opportunity to develop the kind of self-control, the kind of conscience, which makes it possible individually, out of one's own strength, to check hostility against other groups and classes of one's own society – even if insight makes one see the necessity.'[69] One hasn't been around for the centuries it takes to learn to control one's emotions or to develop a sort of conscience individually.

Although Elias wants to challenge explanations which see, say, 'civilized behaviour' as a 'genetically inherited attribute',[70] his drawing of an analogy between the psychological individual and the collective 'organism' of a 'people' leads him to a theory which biologizes 'cultural heritage'.[71] Not only do 'members of [national] states or other social units' share a common 'psyche', they also share a common, transhistorical 'life' and 'experience': 'Members of a state . . . often take a long time, sometimes even centuries, to come to terms with [a problem like their reduced sense of self-worth].'[72] And they also share a common 'feeling' or 'sense': 'People who form nation-states with a relatively long tradition usually have a certain sense of being dependent on opposing groups within their nation, of being joined as heirs to the same community, a community sharing a fate and the struggle for survival.'[73]

What could be discussed precisely as a question of *culture* – say, how a shared sense of nationhood is created not only through national literature, art and history,[74] but also through the constitution of the nation-state itself, together with its civil and military institutions – is turned into a matter of 'feeling', a collective psychological heritage. Thus even culture, which is consciously produced by people and disseminated with the material support of the state and private industry, turns into a psychological state of nature – an expression, if not of human nature, still of the national people's 'nature'. What is to be found in the cultural products of the nation, including its national institutions, is located instead within the emotional household of its citizens. Hence it is treated as an individual's emotions are treated by psychology, for which there are no actions in the present, but only the effects of actions in the past. Feeling a feeling in the present is therefore no action in the present – say, an interaction with the current state of reality – but the effect of a past stored in the collective national organism.

Since a 'people' has a collective 'psyche', 'it' also draws upon itself the psychological understanding which sees the individual primarily as a recipient of traumata, that is to say, as a victim. Thus Elias 'has for a long time had the conviction that there also are collective traumatic experiences in the life [*sic*] of peoples and indeed many social groupings, which sink deeply into the psychological household of members of these peoples and there create enormous damage'.[75] Hence we are hardly surprised that for Elias, too, the National Socialist past becomes a 'trauma' in the 'life' of the 'German people', which has damaged the German 'soul': 'the traumatic experience of National Socialist rule and the terrible consequences which it has had for Germany'.[76] Was it traumatic for the 'German people' to exercise this rule, or did 'it' itself have to suffer under it? If the latter is intended, who then was 'the German people' who elected Hitler to power and helped turn its state into the 'Third Reich', to separate the 'Jews' out of the 'people' and deport them into the camps, there to be killed? Which part of the 'people' is 'the people', which experience is 'the people's experience', and which is the 'damage' that scars 'the people's soul'? Yet the objective is hardly to analyse the 'people' of the past, which in the past had still been acting. The concern is with 'the people' of today which, despite its transhistorical incorporation as 'a people' with a 'life' of many centuries, has nothing to do with those actions in the past, yet has the psychological inheritance of past 'experience' in its bones, and hence is damaged in its soul.

There are therefore no lessons to be learnt from other people's history; nor apparently may ideas such as democracy, non-violent behaviour, controlling emotions or skill in discussion and the like be learnt or acquired by persons living anywhere in the world, on their own initiative and within their own lifetime – unless these happen to have been practised on the same soil by their local predecessors. It appears that we are anything but Hannah Arendt's 'new arrivals' in this world who may 'renew the world . . . *because* we all at some time come as new arrivals into this world, which was here before us and will be here after us' (my emphasis).[77] Hence we neither can, as she envisaged, temporarily take on the material estate handed on to us, cultivate and renew it to the best of our ability and conscience, and pass on, if possible, a better world. On the contrary, we seem to enter the world genetically afflicted, as people suffering from their respective national diseases. Our contribution to the world, if any, will be towards a deeper understanding of the symptomatology and a more differentiated aetiology of these illnesses, comparing our national genetic defects (and strengths) with those of other nationalities, the national characters of the British, the Italians etc.[78] Thus it is doubtful ultimately whether we may learn any lessons even from 'our own' national history, or whether it is worth our trouble and effort, since an improved national behaviour may simply develop in the course of history and centuries of practice. If not – 'poor self-destructive Germany'.[79]

As the biological/psychological understanding of identity ultimately declares the person incapable of learning, so this national Darwinism declares so-called 'peoples' and communities of people collectively (and individually) incapable of learning, handing them over to a behaviourist cure of centuries-long drill-training and conditioning. It constitutes a justification for coercive measures of political and social control – presumably through advanced specimens of the species (or foreign nationals of better disposition) – in order slowly to breed the gradual progress of humankind. At the same time it serves to excuse, explain and exonerate the behaviour of people living today, ascribing their behaviour not to their own willed decisions, but to a 'national character' which they cannot help. In any case, however, their behaviour – be it violent and murderous or controlled and 'civilized' – is a question exclusively of their own interest, with consequences worth mentioning only for themselves: poor, self-destructive Germany.

'What is Ideology?' asks Alain Finkielkraut, and answers:

> According to Hannah Arendt, it is 'the logic of an idea', the claim to explain history as 'one consistent process' whose conclusion is the perfection, the production of humanity itself. . . For what Ideology calls law is the formula of evolution and nothing else. Whether it speaks of the 'law of history' or the 'law of life', whether it refers to Marx or Darwin, Ideology subjects humanity to the same regime as nature – that is, to an order that knows no commandment; the goals people set themselves and the imperatives they impose on themselves dissimulate, in the eyes of Ideology, the causes that make them act. In short, Ideology substitutes necessity for obligation and the scientific law of 'becoming' for the transcendence of judicial or moral law. While using legal terminology, it excludes the law from its vision of the world.[80]

The scientific perspective on humanity and history sees in these only the law of becoming which 'knows no commandment', making any question of people's moral or indeed political decisions, of the goals they set themselves, or the principles they elect for themselves, superfluous. The scientific perspective renders people the mere material through which the gigantic and suprahuman 'force of nature or of history' is realizing itself, racing through them.[81] In this ideological sense of a 'law of nature', Arendt argues, 'law' is first of all the 'expression of motion itself', that is, the motion of cause and effect. In the interest of mastering, of getting a grip on this law of becoming, we – the subjects of ideology and the scientific perspective – deny people's will and their responsibility for their own actions, 'disclosing' instead the 'real causes' of their behaviour – by means of sociobiological, psychoanalytical, ethno-psychoanalytical, national-Darwinist, or as Elias says, 'human-scientific' explanations.[82]

It was just such a scientific understanding, Finkielkraut argues, which found its most totalitarian expression in the ideology of National Socialism, or the Pol Pot regime, where ideology was pushed 'to its ultimate consequences', where it was ' "science" and not nature [which] stifled the voice of conscience', where it was 'the idea which conquered the instincts and not . . . the instinct which broke through all barriers'.[83] Nevertheless, 'Ideology is being reinstated in all its honours.'[84]

It is an ideology which may purport to distinguish radically, that is, dichotomously, between 'scientific idea' and 'instinct', between a 'thought' and a 'feeling'. Yet it is a science in justification *of* instincts, and a science *of* feeling and emotion. The problem of our new sentimentality with regard to scientific ideology, Finkielkraut argues, is that 'the critique of ideology, despite its vehemence and radicalness, has missed the main point, namely that Ideology is paved with the best intentions and the most noble sentiments', promising the coming of one harmonious, happy and perfected humanity.[85] A homogeneous super-nation of 'friends' on the territory of the 'global village' – an end which obviously justifies all means, making any further critique redundant.

Resistance and the will to resistance

War – attack, conquest, domination – seems to be the guiding principle of human interaction, in our modern 'cilvilized' times as much as in a projected 'barbarian' past. Nation-states, our chosen (or accepted) form of organization into communities, are built on their right to wage war, militarism being a central feature of civil society in 'peacetime' around which the *civil* as much as the military order are built.[1] The achievement of European/Western 'civilization' seems to consist in the successful exportation of war and militarism to the 'rest' of the world, and in having kept military conflict away from home territory since the mid-twentieth century. Its second major achievement is the successful naturalization of war and martiality as a '*civilized*' way of being.

This means that Western society has become thoroughly militarized even in its 'civilian' outfit, martiality having been internalized by 'individuals' to such an extent that they 'naturally' constitute themselves as subject – an entity in opposition – each a warrior at war with an enemy world. Hostility has become the basic constitution of self, not just in relation to recognized enemy forces – an oppressive state, systems of oppression, threatening individuals – but equally in relation to those we consider our nearest and dearest. Hence even resistance tends increasingly to be conceived under the aegis of martiality – a possibility within it rather than a radical refusal of it.

Today, if people are against anything they consider themselves to be in resistance to it. Thus the racist and neo-fascist group of whites in South Africa responsible for murdering Chris Hani call themselves 'resistance fighters', a term duly repeated by Western commentators, who merely point out that Black people had given no cause for this

particular outburst of anger. The implication is that there might have
been a cause for such a murder, only in this case, there happened to
be none.[2] If white fascists are against the rights of Black people and
thus against *Black people*, we seem to think it fit to describe them as
being in resistance to them. Resistance is demoted to a mere synonym
for opposition – aggressive enmity – ennobled by the positive
connotations of a beleaguered fight against oppression.

A political concept of resistance implies a struggle against a force of
power and violence by those who suffer under it, that is, it includes an
analysis and recognition of the superiority of that power, and the aim
to dismantle that power. Much of what today goes by the name of
resistance, however, is retaliation against the enemy (if not indeed
attack, as in the example above), a counter-move in what is seen as the
chronological sequence of (violent) action and reaction, attack and
counter-attack between designated opponents. The aim is not to
dismantle power, the aim is victory over the enemy, that is, gathering
enough power on one's own side to overpower the other side.

Hence the crucial question is less what the power relations are than
where the consideration of history begins, that is, which is the 'original' action to which there is re-action, 'who began' by making the
first move, to which the second is but a counter-move. Thus it was
reported in the news that Palestinians were throwing stones and Israeli
settlers were shooting, 'but it is unclear as yet who began'.[3] That is,
the concept of 'resistance' becomes part of the ideologizing structure
of justifying one's own action (or the actions of those with whom the
subject identifies), where the other's action preceding ours is said
to be the cause of – or to have given us cause for – violent action on
our part.

It is why every military force in the world is called a 'defence' force,
governed by a civil ministry of defence that explains what the current
military action is a defence against. Thus a British Falklands war is a
defensive war, sinking the Argentinian warship *General Belgrano* a
defensive action against its hostile change of course, just as bombing
Iraq is but retaliation in defence of an already attacked Kuwait and a
justified response to Saddam Hussein's failure to respond to the UN's
ultimatum. In fact, consulting history we will find that there never has
been an aggressive move in the world, since there always was some
previous action or event considered by one or the other party to have
been the 'cause' for 'retaliation'.

So the question is really which opponent makes this narrative of self, or from whose subjective point of view we regard an action or sequence of actions (that is, history). Since these selves – be they nations or individuals – by definition are 'opponents', each having its 'opposite' and thus its enemy, any action then becomes a form of resistance and self-defence. National history – what we also call revisionism – means developing a narrative of the national self understood as a national-biographic accounting with which the national patient feels emotionally comfortable, in fact, a form of nation-psychoanalysis, 'the creation of a reflexively ordered narrative' enabling nations 'to bring their past "into line" with exigencies of the present, consolidating an emotional story-line with which they feel relatively content'.[4]

For an analysis of *violence*, the violent agent's self-justification for action – the 'reflexively ordered narrative' understood as a 'biographical accounting' with which that agent feels comfortable – is not the issue, is not what determines whether it was violence or not. Most violent men – like most ministries of defence – provide explanations, that is, rationalizations of why they consider their use of violence justified – say, that their wives had been nagging or otherwise getting on their nerves, or that their victims had provoked them beyond endurance (whether through vulnerability or otherwise). In order to understand what violence is and what may be resistance to violence, we need to analyse the actions in question, to see them within their action context, which includes the power relations of that context.

Violence requires a situation where it can be exerted, a power relation that makes its use possible. Counter-violence, however justifiable we may feel it to be, requires a corresponding reversal of the power relations to enable (counter)-violence to take place. Planning an action of counter-violence, even if conceived as an act of resistance, requires constructing a situation in which those carrying out the action will have the necessary power to succeed, that is, to exert violence. It is therefore an act of violence, carried out from a position of power.

A military intervention in Bosnia, as called for by some peace activists and feminists (at least until recently), would not be an act of resistance to war, but an act of aggression with power superior to the power of the Serbian military and paramilitary forces. Similarly, if groups of women in response to incidents of rape decide to beat up men in their neighbourhood, this is less an act of resistance to sexual violence than the construction of a situation in which this group of women will have the power to exert violence against individual men. That is, it is violence, whatever its justification. It is not an act of non-violence simply because men collectively have power over women and because they collectively commit so much violence against women and girls. That is to say, there are different questions involved, namely whether an action – even what we consider an act of resistance or self-defence – is violence, and whether or in what way it is resistance, and resistance to precisely what.

The growing belligerence of identity politics, however, has also brought forth a rhetoric that tends to equate radical resistance with violent resistance. Inversely, one's own violence tends to be presented as non-violence (not really violence) on account of it being resistance. On the 'street' level of movements there is talk of women needing to arm ourselves individually, if not indeed to mount a collective armed struggle, while on the 'respectable' level of national women's politics there are growing numbers advocating that women join their national military, either to acquire adequate training in the art of war or so as not to leave the military exclusively in the hands of men.[5] Analysis of violence and discussion of non-violent means of resistance are becoming increasingly rare, being thought decidedly 'un-radical'. Having identified (that is, personified) the enemy, victory over them has become the 'natural' aim.

Rather than analysing the violent action proposed (from personal violence through to war) and its adequacy as a means to a defined political end, we tend instead to adduce examples – say, of armed liberation struggles in the Third World, the armed uprising of the Warsaw ghetto, or a woman's self-defence in a life-threatening situation – to prove the justifiability of violent self-defence. Far from clarifying the question at hand, namely how we propose to act, why, and to what end, in which situation, such comparisons suggest the self-evident comparability of our own situation (oppression) with the situations (oppressions) in these historical precedents.

Questioning the usefulness of women arming ourselves here and now or of beating up select men in the park thus becomes equivalent to suggesting that the Jews in the Warsaw ghetto should have non-violently awaited their destruction. Such comparisons, however, mean abusing the suffering (and the resistance) of other people in the interests of justifying our own actions. Our situation is alleged to be comparable to that in the examples, the analogy having to stand in for an analysis of our own situation. The proposal to use violence is derived not from an analysis of our situation and a definition of our political aims; rather, violence is the chosen means, for which justification is now being sought.

Similarly, the notion seems to be gaining ground that, as members of oppressed groups, our violence cannot be violence like the violence of the oppressors, just as white women's power within the system of slavery was said to be 'false power', not power 'in the sense' that male tyrants and patriarchal despots have it, and white women's contemporary racism is considered to be not really 'racism' in the sense of 'racism endemic in patriarchy'. In the same way our own violence is thought to be 'not really' violence, in the sense of the violence of those we oppose. Not only does our being – our identity – apparently soften any violence we may exert, it may make us by definition into resisters. Simply by virtue of not belonging to the (chief) oppressors, we seem to constitute some 'kind' of resistance to power.

Resistance, however, like oppression, is not a nebulous climate we vaguely inhabit, move into by coming 'home' to our identity. Much less is it a quality which we have *qua* our (oppressed) identity, so that anything we do by definition becomes 'resistance'. 'There is something in each lesbian', Sarah Hoagland writes, 'that questions the norm at some level . . . That is, there is something within each lesbian of the spirit I consider crucial to the sort of ethical concepts I am interested in working on. It is a certain ability to resist and refocus, and it is this ability in all lesbians which draws me.'[6] The lesbian herself may neither question the norm(s), nor resist or refocus, yet there 'is something within her' that questions the norm (whether she wants it or not). It is an *ability* to resist and refocus, regardless of whether she uses her ability to do so. And there is a spirit crucial to ethical concepts in her – if not like Lévinas's ethics falling on top of us from outside, still pushing through from within.

It is each and every and 'all lesbians' who are blessed with such abilities and spirit – we need not meet or know them individually to know what spirit possesses them and what ethical concepts they are living by. For these are qualities and spirits that come with identity, factors of these 'kinds' of people. Other 'kinds' of people, if they have them at all, have them to a lesser degree, even if they do resist and refocus or question social norms. Perhaps it is something they happen to do, yet not something which they *are* and *have*. In the same way it used to be whites or white men who were blessed with abilities, whether they showed any by using them or not, whereas whatever ability or spirit Black people or women might have shown, it was never, in the eyes of white men, what they really did and what showed what Black people or women could do; it was something they happened to do in spite of what they *are*.[7]

Resistance, I would suggest, does not come with any identity. It is a question of political will and action. It requires the political analysis of systems of oppression through to individual acts of oppression and violence – in terms of agency and its consequences, in terms of agents and beneficiaries and victims – and a corresponding analysis of resistance in terms of actions and their consequences.[8] Only once we know what we are doing, and what our actions actually effect, and what we mean them to achieve, can we begin to act in resistance, knowing what it is resistance to; and only then will we be able to identify and co-operate with those acting for the same political goals.

Resistance to *violence* however cannot consist of violence. Violence may change the direction of violence, invert the roles of violator and victim, but it necessarily affirms the principle of violence, whatever else it may achieve. And it adds new victims to the world – victims of our own making, not to mention more violent perpetrators, whose ranks we have decided to join. While in extremity and under the threat of our lives we may not have any means other than violence to secure our survival, most of us most of the time are not in such situations, though we glibly speak of 'survival'. Instead, we would have ample opportunity in situations of no such threat to challenge the legitimacy of violence and to practise alternatives – above all by deciding not to use violence ourselves.

Notes

Violence and the will to violence

1. As one example amongst many which could be cited, Birgit Rommel-spacher, 'Die Sucht, zu sehr zu lieben', in Roswitha Burgard and Birgit Rommelspacher, eds, *Leideunlust: Der Mythos vom weiblichen Masochismus* (Berlin: Orlanda Verlag, 1989): 'It should be uncontested that those, who as children had especially traumatic experiences and lacked narcissistic confirmation, will later seek to act out their neediness in inadequate ways' (p. 107; my translation).
2. Marc Wadsworth (Anti-Racist Alliance) and Claire Dissington (Anti-Nazi-League), cited in 'To Ban or Not to Ban', *Education Guardian*, 28 September 1993, p. 11.
3. Frank Drieschner, 'Glatzenpflege auf Staatskosten', *Die Zeit* 33 (13 August 1993), p. 50; Gisela Dachs, 'Zur Therapie nach Israel', *Die Zeit* 45 (5 November 1993), p. 7.
4. Rolf Lüdemann, 'Therapie als Gewaltverhältnis', in Peter-Alexis Albrecht and Otto Backes, eds, *Verdeckte Gewalt* (Frankfurt a.M.: Suhrkamp Verlag, 1990), p. 230.
5. Slavenka Drakulić, *Balkan Express: Fragments from the Other Side of War* (London: Hutchinson, 1993), p. 146.
6. Ulrich Beck, *Gegengifte: Die organisierte Unverantwortlichkeit* (Frankfurt a.M.: Suhrkamp Verlag, 1988), p. 11.
7. Sarah Lucia Hoagland, *Lesbian Ethics: Toward New Value* (Palo Alto: Institute of Lesbian Studies, 1988), p. 39.
8. German television, SAT. 1, 'Einspruch', 12 January 1993; see also Eva Quistorp in *Freitag*, 15 January 1993.
9. Swiss television DRS, '10 vor 10', 10 December 1992.
10. *taz*, 3 February 1993, p. 3.
11. Drakulić, *Balkan Express*, p. 146.

Chapter 1 Why the personal is political, and where the private comes from

1. Diane Antonio, for instance, argues for an ethic of care that takes the interests of others (including animals and nature) seriously, on the grounds that this ultimately satisfies a 'moral need' of our own: 'At the same time . . . we would be recognising our own moral need to give respect to non-human animals.' Animals provide us, 'as children provide mothers, with the opportunity to satisfy our needs to "act or forbear acting out of benevolent concern" for living creatures, in order to become self-defined moral beings' ('Women and Wolves: Toward an Ethic of Care Respect', in Carol Adams and Josephine Donovan, eds, *Animals and Women: Feminist Theoretical Explorations* (Durham: Duke University Press, due 1995)). See also Sarah Lucia Hoagland, *Lesbian Ethics: Toward New Value* (Palo Alto, Institute of Lesbian Studies, 1988), where it is similarly a question of 'ethical needs' or 'want[ing] to be ethical, want[ing] to act with integrity' (p. 22), and where the reason for adopting ethical or moral behaviour is to 'avoid de-moralisation' and 'claim our moral agency' (p. 214), i.e. consideration of the consequences of behaviour *for the agent.*
2. Andrea Dworkin, *Right-Wing Women* (London: The Women's Press, 1983), pp. 21, 118. For an analysis of self-interest in relation to apparent selflessness, see also Marilyn Frye, *The Politics of Reality: Essays in Feminist Theory* (Trumansburg, NY: The Crossing Press, 1983), esp. pp. 74–5.
3. Carole Pateman, *The Disorder of Women* (Cambridge: Polity Press, 1989), p. 122.
4. Carole Pateman, *The Sexual Contract* (Cambridge: Polity Press, 1988), p. 10.
5. See Pateman, *The Disorder of Women*, ch. 2; *The Sexual Contract*, ch. 4.
6. Pateman, *Disorder of Women*, p. 122.
7. Pateman, *Sexual Contract*, p. 223.
8. Ibid.
9. See Andrea Dworkin: 'ultimately the law exists to keep men from getting fucked', *Intercourse* (London: Secker & Warburg, 1987), p. 161.
10. Ibid., p. 148.
11. Pateman, *Disorder of Women*, p. 122.
12. Ibid.
13. Ibid.
14. Ibid.
15. Pateman, *Sexual Contract*, p. 216; Lynne Harne, 'Families and Fathers: The Effects of the Children Act 1989', *Rights of Women Bulletin* (Spring 1993), pp. 5–6.

16. Catharine A. MacKinnon, 'Feminism, Marxism, Method, and the State: Toward a Feminist Jurisprudence', *Signs: A Journal of Women in Culture and Society*, vol. 8, no. 4 (1983), pp. 656–7.
17. Ibid., p. 657.

Chapter 2 *Love of foreigners and love of the 'other'*

1. Slavenka Drakulić, *Balkan Express: Fragments from the Other Side of War* (London: Hutchinson, 1993), p. 144.
2. Fania Fénelon, *The Musicians of Auschwitz*, translated from the French by Judith Landry (London: Michael Joseph, 1977), p. 84.
3. Simone de Beauvoir, *The Second Sex*, translated by H. M. Parshley (Harmondsworth: Penguin, 1972), pp. 17, 16.
4. Andrea Dworkin, *Pornography: Men Possessing Women* (London: The Women's Press, 1981), p. 17.
5. I am thinking in particular of the works of Julia Kristeva, Luce Irigaray, Hélène Cixous and others, whose concepts of 'writing with the body', of feminine speech and writing defined through the metaphors of the female body, have been particularly influential in re-biologizing women. Of course, the phenomenon of 'French feminism' has long ceased to be an exclusively French affair, but has become a fixed part of Western 'academic feminism'.
6. A. Sivanandan, 'Introduction', *Race and Class: A Journal for Black and Third World Liberation*, vol. 35, no. 1 (July–September 1993), p. v. See also the discussion about 'multiculturalism' on American university campuses in *Tikkun: A Bimonthly Jewish Critique of Politics, Culture & Society*, vol. 6, no. 4 (1991), pp. 35–57.
7. There has been an explosion of German books on 'the foreign', the 'strange', 'foreigners' and 'strangers', 'foreign women' etc. (*Das Fremde, die Fremden, Fremde Frauen*), while university syllabuses abound with seminars about 'the known and the unknown', 'the strange and the familiar' (*Das Fremde und das Eigene*) and the like.
8. See e.g. Liz Kelly, *Surviving Sexual Violence* (Cambridge: Polity Press, 1988), esp. chs 4 and 5.
9. The following is based on the writings of prominent and influential German feminists; the translations are my own. Christa Wichterich, 'Ganz nah und ganz fern: Bilder–Begegnungen–Bedenkzeit' (Very Close and Very Far: Images – Encounters – Time for Reflection), in *beiträge zur feministischen theorie und praxis* 27 (1990), p. 9.
10. Ibid.
11. Ibid., p. 10.
12. Ibid., p. 11.

13. Ibid.
14. Ibid.
15. Ibid.
16. Ibid.
17. Ibid.
18. Ibid.
19. Ibid., p. 12.
20. Ibid., p. 14.
21. Ibid., pp. 12–13.
22. Ibid., p. 13.
23. Ibid.
24. 'Die Würde des Menschen ist unantastbar', first article of the German constitution.
25. Christina Thürmer-Rohr, 'Weiße Frauen und Rassismus' (White Women and Racism), *taz*, 8 January 1993, p. 13.
26. Ibid.
27. Ibid., p. 12.
28. Ibid., p. 13.
29. Ibid.
30. Ibid.
31. Dagmar Schultz, 'Kein Ort nur für uns allein: Weiße Frauen auf dem Weg zu Bündnissen' (No Place Just of Our Own: White Women on the Way to Coalitions), in Ika Hügel et al., eds, *Entfernte Verbindungen: Rassismus, Antisemitismus, Klassenunterdrückung* (Berlin: Orlanda Verlag, 1993), pp. 176–7. See also Sarah Lucia Hoagland, *Lesbian Ethics: Toward New Value* (Palo Alto: Institute of Lesbian Studies, 1988), where the need for 'others' in general is posed in these terms: 'our need for others . . . who have the capacity to help us expand' (p. 241).
32. Schultz, 'Kein Ort', p. 177.
33. Ibid.

Chapter 3 Personal communication behaviour is political

1. bell hooks, *Talking Back: Thinking Feminist, Thinking Black* (London: Sheba Feminist Publishers, 1989), p. 179.
2. Alice Walker, *In Search of Our Mothers' Gardens: Womanist Prose* (London: The Women's Press, 1984), p. xi.
3. Toni Morrison, cited in bell hooks, *Feminist Theory: From Margin to Centre* (Boston: South End Press, 1984), p. 50.
4. Combahee River Collective, 'A Black Feminist Statement', in Cherríe Moraga and Gloria Anzaldúa, eds, *This Bridge Called My Back: Writings by Radical Women of Color* (New York: Kitchen Table: Women of Color Press, 1981), p. 213.

5. Walker, *In Search of Our Mothers' Gardens*, p. xi.
6. Ibid., p. xii.
7. Ibid.
8. hooks, *Talking Back*, p. 180.
9. Ibid., p. 182.
10. Madhu Kishwar, 'Why I do not Call Myself a Feminist', *Manushi* 6 (November–December 1990), p. 7.
11. Catharine A. MacKinnon, 'Feminism, Marxism, Method, and the State: An Agenda for Theory', *Signs: A Journal of Women in Culture and Society*, vol. 7, no. 3 (1982), pp. 537–8; Catharine A. MacKinnon, *Toward a Feminist Theory of the State* (Cambridge, Mass.: Harvard University Press, 1989), pp. 97, 121.
12. Maria Mies, *Patriarchy and Accumulation on a World Scale: Women in the International Division of Labour* (London: Zed Press, 1986), p. 11.
13. Dagmar Schultz, 'Unterschiede zwischen Frauen – ein kritischer Blick auf den Umgang mit "den Anderen" in der feministischen Forschung weißer Frauen', *beiträge zur feministischen theorie und praxis* 27 (1990), p. 46; my translation.
14. Ibid.
15. Chandra Talpade Mohanti, 'Under Western Eyes: Feminist Scholarship and Colonial Discourses', in Chandra Talpade Mohanti, Ann Russo and Lourdes Torres, eds, *Third World Women and the Politics of Feminism* (Bloomington: Indiana University Press, 1991).
16. Cf. bell hooks, 'to gloria, who is she: on using a pseudonym', in *Talking Back*, pp. 160–6.
17. hooks, *Feminist Theory*, p. 14.
18. Ibid.
19. Ibid., p. 15.
20. Ibid., p. 15.
21. Ibid., p. 14.
22. Ibid., p. 15.
23. Ibid.

Chapter 4 *Is the political psychological?*

1. Deborah Cameron, *Feminism and Linguistic Theory* (London: Macmillan Press, 1985), p. 117.
2. Cf. also, for instance, the pornography debate in Britain, which similarly suffers from the practice that the anti-pornography feminists' criticisms are merely being paraphrased, as discussed by Joan Scanlon and Liz

Kelly, 'Lies About Porn and Feminism', *CAP Newsletter: Campaign Against Pornography* (Winter 1993), pp. 4–5.

3. Audre Lorde, 'An Open Letter to Mary Daly', in Cherríe Moraga and Gloria Anzaldúa, eds, *This Bridge Called My Back: Writings by Radical Women of Color* (New York: Kitchen Table: Women of Color Press, 1981), p. 94.

4. Adrienne Rich, 'Disloyal to Civilization: Feminism, Racism, Gynephobia', in Adrienne Rich, *On Lies, Secrets and Silences: Selected Prose 1966–1978* (London: Virago Press, 1979), pp. 281–2.

5. Ibid., pp. 282–3.

6. Ibid., p. 289.

7. Ibid., p. 290.

8. Ibid., p. 288.

9. Ibid., p. 290.

10. Ibid.

11. Ibid., pp. 290–1.

12. Ibid., pp. 298–9.

13. Ibid., p. 299.

14. Ibid., p. 300.

Chapter 5 Psychotherapy, or the legitimation of irresponsibility

1. Nancy Chodorow, *The Reproduction of Mothering: Psychoanalysis and the Sociology of Gender* (Berkeley and Los Angeles: University of California Press, 1978), p. 52.

2. Luise Eichenbaum and Susie Orbach, *Understanding Women* (Harmondsworth: Penguin Books, 1985), p. 11.

3. Ibid., p. 12.

4. Ibid.

5. See Florence Rush, *The Best Kept Secret: Sexual Abuse of Children* (New York: McGraw-Hill Book Company, 1980), esp. ch. 7.

6. Cf. Barbara Ehrenreich and Deirdre English, *For Her Own Good: 150 Years of the Experts' Advice to Women* (London: Pluto Press, 1979), pp. 1–4.

7. Ann H. Jackowitz, 'Anna O./Bertha Pappenheim and Me', in Carol Ascher, Louise DeSalvo and Sara Ruddick, eds, *Between Women: Biographers, Novelists, Critics, Teachers and Artists Write about Their Work on Women* (Boston: Beacon Press, 1984), p. 269.

8. Letter of October 1925, cited in ibid., p. 269.

9. Ibid., pp. 259–60.

10. Chodorow, *The Reproduction of Mothering*, p. 46n.

11. Ibid., ch. 3. For an exception, see Jessica Benjamin, *The Bonds of Love: Psychoanalysis, Feminism, and the Problem of Domination* (New York: Pantheon Books, 1988), p. 248, n. 2.

12. Susan Griffin, *Pornography and Silence: Culture's Revenge against Nature* (London: The Women's Press, 1981), pp. 60–5, 137–40; Marion Bower, 'Daring to Speak Its Name: The Relationship of Women to Pornography', *Feminist Review* 24 (Autumn 1986), pp. 40–53 *passim*. Generally, this theory is known under the name of the Good and the Bad Breast, and is largely indebted to Melanie Klein, as Eichenbaum and Orbach explain in *Understanding Women*, pp. 31–2, n. 13.

13. Cited in Sabeth Buchmann, 'Feminismus und Kunst: Gender Studies', *Zitty* 2 (1993), p. 216.

14. Swantje Köbsell, 'Humangenetik und pränatale Diagnostik: Instrumente der "Neuen Eugenik" ', in Theresia Degener and Swantje Köbsell, *'Hauptsache, es ist gesund?' Weibliche Selbstbestimmung unter humangenetischer Kontrolle* (Hamburg: Konkret Literatur Verlag, 1992), p. 55.

15. Jessica Benjamin, *The Bonds of Love*, p. 16; Nancy Chodorow, *The Reproduction of Mothering*, p. 68.

16. Eichenbaum and Orbach, *Understanding Women*, pp. 13 and 31, n. 13.

17. Ibid., p. 32.

18. Ibid., p. 14.

19. Ibid., p. 32.

20. Joanna Ryan, 'Psychoanalysis and Women Loving Women', in Sue Cartledge and Joanna Ryan, eds, *Sex and Love: New Thoughts on Old Contradictions* (London: The Women's Press, 1983), p. 202.

21. Cited in ibid., p. 201.

22. Ibid.

23. See for example Roswitha Burgard and Birgit Rommelspacher, eds, *Leideunlust: Der Mythos vom weiblichen Masochismus* (Berlin: Orlanda Frauenverlag, 1989).

24. Cited in Ryan, 'Psychoanalysis and Women Loving Women', p. 201.

25. Ibid., p. 202.

26. Eichenbaum and Orbach, *Understanding Women*, p. 31, n. 13.

27. Chodorow, *The Reproduction of Mothering*, p. 211.

28. Eichenbaum and Orbach, *Understanding Women*, p. 34, n. 13; see also p. 14.

29. Lynne Segal, 'Sensual Uncertainty, or Why the Clitoris is not Enough', in Cartledge and Ryan, *Sex and Love*, p. 44.

30. Janice Raymond, *A Passion for Friends: Toward a Philosophy of Female Affection* (London: The Women's Press, 1986), pp. 161–2.

31. Luise Eichenbaum and Susie Orbach, *What Do Women Want?*, first published by Michael Joseph, London, 1983; all page references to the second edition (London: Fontana, 1984), p. 28.

32. Ibid., pp. 28–9.

33. Ibid., p. 29.

34. Ibid.
35. Ibid., p. 32.
36. Ibid., p. 33.
37. Ibid., pp. 33–4.
38. Ibid., e.g. pp. 29–30.
39. Ibid., p. 51.
40. Robin Norwood, *Women Who Love Too Much* (London: Arrow Books, 1986), p. 9.
41. Ibid.
42. Eichenbaum and Orbach, *What Do Women Want?*, p. 34.
43. Ibid., pp. 34–5.
44. Ibid., p. 34.
45. Ibid.
46. Ibid., p. 29.
47. Ibid., p. 33.
48. Ibid.
49. Segal, 'Sensual Uncertainty', p. 44.
50. Chodorow, *The Reproduction of Mothering*, pp. 99ff, 109.
51. Eichenbaum and Orbach, *What Do Women Want?*, p. 29.
52. Anthony Giddens, *The Transformation of Intimacy: Sexuality, Love and Eroticism in Modern Societies* (Cambridge: Polity Press, 1992), p. 108.
53. Lynne Segal, 'Sweet Sorrows, Painful Pleasures: Pornography and the Perils of Heterosexual Desire', in Lynne Segal and Mary McIntosh, eds, *Sex Exposed: Sexuality and the Pornography Debate* (London: Virago Press, 1992), p. 79.
54. Chodorow, *The Reproduction of Mothering*, p. 51.
55. Thomas Kleinspehn, *Der flüchtige Blick: Sehen und Identität in der Kultur der Neuzeit* (Reinbek bei Hamburg: Rowohlt Taschenbuch Verlag, 1989), p. 309.
56. Marilyn Frye, *The Politics of Reality: Essays in Feminist Theory* (Trumansburg, NY: The Crossing Press, 1983), pp. 66–72.

Chapter 6 Ego-psychology, or My relationship and I

1. E.g. Nancy Chodorow, *The Reproduction of Mothering: Psychoanalysis and the Sociology of Gender* (Berkeley and Los Angeles: University of California Press, 1978), p. 67; or Thomas Kleinspehn, *Der flüchtige Blick: Sehen und Identität in der Kultur der Neuzeit* (Reinbek bei Hamburg: Rowohlt Taschenbuch Verlag, 1989), p. 310.
2. Chodorow, *The Reproduction of Mothering*, p. 45.
3. Ibid., pp. 45–6.
4. Ibid., p. 47.

5. Ibid.

6. Ibid., p. 48.

7. Ibid., p. 45.

8. Monica Streit, ' "Mir geht es schlecht – Du gibst mir nicht genug!" – Symbiose, Opfermentalität und Masochismus in Beziehungen zwischen Frauen', in Roswitha Burgard and Birgit Rommelspacher, eds, *Leideunlust: Der Mythos vom weiblichen Masochismus* (Berlin: Orlanda Frauenverlag, 1989), pp. 159, 160, 164, 181.

9. Margrit Brückner, *Die Liebe der Frauen: Über Weiblichkeit und Mißhandlung* (Frankfurt a.M.: Verlag Neue Kritik, 1983), p. 44; my translation.

10. E.g. Marilyn Frye, *The Politics of Reality: Essays in Feminist Theory* (Trumansburg, NY: The Crossing Press, 1983), esp. pp. 52–83.

11. Robin Norwood, *Women Who Love Too Much* (London: Arrow Books, 1986), p. 16.

12. Ibid., p. 74.

13. Ibid., p. 13.

14. Burgard and Rommelspacher, *Leideunlust*, 'Einleitung', pp. 7–8; my translation.

15. Ibid., p. 8.

16. Ibid., p. 9.

17. Norwood, *Women Who Love Too Much*, p. 10.

18. Ibid., p. 11.

19. Ibid., p. 12.

20. Luise Eichenbaum and Susie Orbach, *What Do Women Want?*, first published by Michael Joseph, London, 1983; page reference to the second edn (London: Fontana, 1984), p. 29.

21. Birgit Rommelspacher, 'Der weibliche Masochismus – ein Mythos?', in Burgard and Rommelspacher, *Leideunlust*, p. 38; my translation.

22. Anthony Giddens, *The Transformation of Intimacy: Sexuality, Love and Eroticism in Modern Societies* (Cambridge: Polity Press, 1992), pp. 73ff.

23. Norwood, *Women Who Love Too Much*, p. 3.

24. Janice Raymond, *A Passion for Friends: Toward a Philosophy of Female Affection* (London: The Women's Press, 1986), pp. 155–60.

25. Norwood, *Women Who Love Too Much*, p. 12.

26. Ibid., p. 16.

27. Ibid., p. 14.

28. Ibid., p. 3.

29. Ibid., p. 4.

30. Ibid.

31. Ibid., p. 10.

32. Ibid.
33. Ibid., p. 203.
34. Ibid., p. 1.
35. Ibid., p. 11.
36. Ibid.
37. Ibid., p. 12.
38. Ibid., p. 6.
39. Jessica Benjamin, *The Bonds of Love: Psychoanalysis, Feminism, and the Problem of Domination* (New York: Pantheon Books, 1988), p. 9.
40. Rommelspacher, 'Der weibliche Masochismus', p. 30; my translation.
41. Ibid., p. 31.
42. Ibid., p. 32.
43. Benjamin, *The Bonds of Love*, p. 5.
44. Ibid., p. 218.
45. Doris Janshen, ed., *Sexuelle Gewalt: Die allgegenwärtige Menschenrechtsverletzung* (Frankfurt a.M.: Zweitausendeins, 1991), p. 16. The expression for 'people affected' is 'betroffene Menschen'.
46. Benjamin, *The Bonds of Love*, p. 5.
47. Ibid.
48. Ibid., p. 12.
49. Ibid., pp. 27–8.
50. Ibid., p. 220.
51. Ibid., p. 53.
52. Ibid., p. 18.
53. Ibid., p. 37.
54. Ibid.
55. Ibid.
56. Ibid., p. 38.
57. Ibid., p. 39.
58. Ibid., p. 48.
59. Ibid.
60. Reutlingen Frauen für Frieden/Freie Frauenliste, 'Vergewaltigungen an Frauen und Kindern in Bosnien-Herzegowina', *Blattgold* (January 1993), p. 7.
61. Letter to *The Independent*, 8 January 1993. For an extended analysis, see Susanne Kappeler, 'Massenverrat an den Frauen im ehemaligen Jugoslawien', in Susanne Kappeler, Mira Renka and Melanie Beyer, eds, *Vergewaltigung, Krieg, Nationalismus: Eine feministische Kritik* (Munich: Frauenoffensive, 1994).
62. Benjamin, *The Bonds of Love*, p. 49.
63. Norwood, *Women Who Love Too Much*, p. 15.

Chapter 7 Ego-philosophy, or the battle with reality

1. Petra Kelly, cited in *Blattgold* (January 1993), p. 7.
2. Jessica Benjamin, *The Bonds of Love: Psychoanalysis, Feminism, and the Problem of Domination* (New York: Pantheon Books, 1988), pp. 71–2.
3. Alain Finkielkraut, *La Sagesse de l'amour* (Paris: Éditions Gallimard, 1984), p. 11; my translation of this and the following quotations.
4. Ibid.
5. Ibid., p. 12.
6. Ibid., p. 11.
7. Ibid., p. 12.
8. Ibid., p. 16.
9. Ibid., p. 22.
10. Ibid., p. 19.
11. Ibid.
12. Ibid., p. 20.
13. Ibid., p. 23.
14. Ibid.
15. Ibid., p. 25.
16. Ibid., p. 24.
17. Ibid., p. 22.
18. Ibid., p. 23.
19. Ibid., p. 22.
20. Ibid., p. 25.
21. Ibid.
22. Ibid., p. 26.
23. Ibid., p. 25.
24. Ibid., p. 26.
25. Jean-Paul Sartre, *L'Être et le néant*, cited in Finkielkraut, *La Sagesse de l'amour*, p. 26.
26. Ibid.
27. Sartre, cited in ibid., p. 27.
28. Ibid.
29. Ibid.
30. Ibid., p. 28.
31. Ibid., p. 29.
32. Ibid.
33. Ibid.
34. Ibid.
35. Ibid., pp. 29–30.
36. Emmanuel Lévinas, cited in Finkielkraut, *La Sagesse de l'amour*, p. 30.

37. Ibid.
38. Ibid.
39. Ibid.
40. Ibid.
41. Ibid., pp. 30–1.
42. Ibid., p. 31.
43. Ibid., p. 32.
44. Ibid.
45. Ibid., pp. 32–3.
46. Ibid., p. 33.
47. Ibid.
48. Ibid.
49. Ibid.
50. Ibid.
51. Ibid.
52. Ibid.
53. Ibid., p. 173.
54. Ibid., pp. 186–7.
55. Ibid., p. 142.
56. Ibid., pp. 141–2.
57. Ibid., pp. 142–3.
58. Emmanuel Lévinas, *Ethics and Infinity: Conversations with Philippe Nemo*, translated by Richard A. Cohen (Pittsburgh: Duquesne University Press, 1985), p. 52.

Chapter 8 Sex and the intimate relationship

1. Emmanuel Lévinas, *Ethics and Infinity: Conversations with Philippe Nemo*, translated by Richard A. Cohen (Pittsburgh: Duquesne University Press, 1985), p. 72.
2. Andrea Dworkin, *Intercourse* (London: Secker & Warburg, 1987), p. 148.
3. Alain Finkielkraut, *La Sagesse de l'amour* (Paris: Éditions Gallimard, 1984), p. 26.
4. Lévinas, *Ethics and Infinity*, p. 62.
5. Ibid., p. 65.
6. Ibid.
7. Ibid., pp. 65–6.
8. See for instance Catharine A. MacKinnon, *Toward a Feminist Theory of the State* (Cambridge, Mass.: Harvard University Press, 1989), ch. 7; Andrea Dworkin, *Pornography: Men Possessing Women* (London: The Women's Press 1981); Dworkin, *Intercourse*; Adrienne Rich, 'Compul-

sory Heterosexuality and Lesbian Existence', *Signs: A Journal of Women in Culture and Society*, vol. 5, no. 4 (1980); Sheila Jeffreys, *The Spinster and Her Enemies* (London: Pandora Press, 1985); Sheila Jeffreys, *Anticlimax: A Feminist Perspective on the Sexual Revolution* (London: The Women's Press, 1990); Shulamith Firestone, *The Dialectic of Sex: The Case for Feminist Revolution* (London: The Women's Press, 1979), pp. 139–40.

9. MacKinnon, *Toward a Feminist Theory of the State*, p. 130.

10. Rich, 'Compulsory Heterosexuality'.

11. Anthony Giddens, *The Transformation of Intimacy: Sexuality, Love and Eroticism in Modern Societies* (Cambridge: Polity Press, 1992), p. 175.

12. Sheila Jeffreys, 'Sexology and Antifeminism', in Dorchen Leidholdt and Janice G. Raymond, eds, *The Sexual Liberals and the Attack on Feminism* (New York and Oxford: Pergamon Press, 1990), p. 15.

13. Quoted in Jeffreys, *The Spinster and Her Enemies*, p. 131. Havelock Ellis's text 'Love and Pain', from his *Studies in the Psychology of Sex*, vol. III, first published in 1903, is also reprinted in Sheila Jeffreys, ed., *The Sexuality Debates* (New York and London: Routledge & Kegan Paul, 1987), pp. 505–33. The quotation is from p. 516.

14. Ellis, 'Love and Pain', p. 510.

15. MacKinnon, *Toward a Feminist Theory of the State*, p. 127.

16. Annabel Farraday, 'Lesbian Outlaws', *Trouble & Strife*, 13 (Spring 1988), pp. 11–16.

17. Ibid., pp. 9–10.

18. Ibid., p. 10 and n. 3.

19. Dworkin, *Intercourse*, pp. 152–3, 156.

20. Quoted in Farraday, 'Lesbian Outlaws', p. 15.

21. Liz Kelly, *Surviving Sexual Violence* (Cambridge: Polity Press, 1988), p. 187. See also Liz Kelly, 'Bitter Ironies', *Trouble & Strife* 16 (Summer 1989), p. 17.

22. See for instance Verena Fiegl, *Der Krieg gegen die Frauen: Zum Zusammenhang von Sexismus und Militarismus* (Bielefeld: Tarantel Frauen Verlag, 1990), pp. 139–40, 142 (quotations from Mark Baker, *NAM: The Vietnam War in the Words of the Men and Women Who Fought There* (New York, 1983); Joan Smith, 'Ghost riders in the sky', *New Statesman/Society*, 10 June 1988, pp. 16–18.

23. Dworkin, *Pornography*, p. 30.

24. Carole Pateman, *The Sexual Contract* (Cambridge: Polity Press, 1988), pp. 155, 163–5.

25. Dworkin, *Pornography*, p. 19.

26. Jane Rondot, 'Representations of Child Sexual Abuse, 1860–1910', unpublished Ph.D. thesis, University of East Anglia (1994).

27. Philippine Women's Support Committee, *Filipina-British Marriage Bureaux: A Report* (GLC, no date; research carried out August 1985–April 1986); Susanne Kappeler, 'The International Slave Trade in Women, or: Procurers, Pimps and Punters', *Law and Critique*, vol. 1, no. 2 (1990), esp. pp. 231–2; Susanne Lipka, *Das käufliche Glück in Südostasien: Heiratshandel und Sextourismus* (Münster: Verlag Westfälisches Dampfboot, revised and extended third edn, 1989), pp. 110–11.

28. S. Warren and L. Brandeis, cited in MacKinnon, *Toward a Feminist Theory of the State*, p. 194.

29. Tom Gerety, cited in Catharine A. MacKinnon, 'Feminism, Marxism, Method, and the State: Toward Feminist Jurisprudence', *Signs: A Journal of Women in Culture and Society*, vol. 8, no. 4 (1983), p. 656.

30. Lynne Segal, 'Sweet Sorrows, Painful Pleasures: Pornography and the Perils of Heterosexual Desire', in Lynne Segal and Mary McIntosh, eds, *Sex Exposed: Sexuality and the Pornography Debate* (London: Virago Press, 1992), p. 77.

31. Giddens, *The Transformation of Intimacy*, especially ch. 5, 'Love, Sex and Other Addictions'.

32. Firestone, *The Dialectic of Sex*, pp. 139–40.

33. Giddens, *The Transformation of Intimacy*, p. 2.

34. Ibid., p. 7.

35. Firestone, *The Dialectic of Sex*, pp. 142–3.

Chapter 9 Female desire, or the democratization of violence

1. Eleanor J. Bader, 'Rough Sex', *Spare Rib* (August 1988), p. 39.

2. Ibid.

3. Ibid.

4. Ibid.

5. Lisa Sliwa, 'Angel Heart', *Arena* (Summer 1988), p. 136.

6. E.g. Barbara Lukesch, 'Schafft Frauenpower Männerhass?', *Tages-Anzeiger*, 12 June 1991; Anthony Giddens, *The Transformation of Intimacy: Sexuality, Love and Eroticism in Modern Societies* (Cambridge: Polity Press, 1992), p. 3.

7. Interview with Klaus-Peter Wolf, *taz*, 14 September 1989, p. 3.

8. See ch. 8, n. 24.

9. Ariane Barth, 'Schau mir in die Augen, Kleiner', *Der Spiegel*, 7 January 1991, p. 144.

10. Ibid.

11. Ibid., pp. 144–5.

12. Ibid., p. 145.

13. Ibid.

14. Ibid.
15. Ibid.
16. Ibid.
17. Ibid.
18. Ibid.
19. Ibid., p. 146.
20. Ibid.
21. Ibid.
22. Ibid., p. 147.
23. Ibid.
24. Ibid., pp. 148, 150, 151.
25. Ibid., p. 151.
26. Ibid.
27. Lynne Segal, 'Sweet Sorrows, Painful Pleasures: Pornography and the Perils of Heterosexual Desire', in Lynne Segal and Mary McIntosh, eds, *Sex Exposed: Sexuality and the Pornography Debate* (London: Virago Press, 1992), p. 79.
28. Ibid., p. 88.
29. Ariane Barth, 'Schau mir in die Augen, Kleiner', p. 151.
30. Ibid.
31. Ibid.
32. Ibid.
33. Ibid.
34. Ibid.
35. Ibid.
36. Ibid., p. 152.
37. Ibid.
38. Ibid.
39. Ibid.
40. Ibid., p. 153.
41. Ibid.
42. Ibid.
43. Ibid.
44. Ibid.
45. Cited in Sally Roesch Wagner, 'Pornography and the Sexual Revolution: The Backlash of Sadomasochism', in Robin Ruth Lindon et al., eds, *Against Sadomasochism: A Radical Feminist Analysis* (East Palo Alto: Frog in the Well, 1982), p. 29.
46. Ariane Barth, 'Schau mir in die Augen, Kleiner', p. 153.
47. Ibid.
48. Ibid.
49. Ibid., p. 151.
50. Cited in Wagner, 'Pornography and the Sexual Revolution', p. 30.

Chapter 10 Relationship as trade, or the free market of bodies and services

1. Robin Norwood, *Women Who Love Too Much* (London, Arrow Books, 1986), p. 41.
2. Karl Marx, *Capital*, vol. I, translated by Ben Fowkes (Harmondsworth: Penguin Books, 1976), p. 165.
3. Ibid., p. 178.
4. Karl Marx, *Das Kapital*, vol. I (Frankfurt a.M.: Verlag Marxistische Blätter, 1976), copyright Dietz Verlag Berlin 1947, 1962; p. 99.
5. Marx, *Capital*, p. 133.
6. Ibid., pp. 178–9.
7. Ibid., p. 126.
8. Ibid.
9. Ibid., p. 127.
10. Ibid., p. 125.
11. Luise Eichenbaum and Susie Orbach, *What Do Women Want?*, first published by Michael Joseph, London, 1983; all page references to the second edn (London: Fontana, 1984), pp. 174ff, 203.
12. Ibid., p. 180.
13. Ibid., pp. 183, 203.
14. See ch. 7, n. 3.
15. Norwood, *Women Who Love Too Much*, p. 7.
16. Ibid.
17. Ibid., p. 30.
18. Ibid., p. 28.
19. Ibid.
20. Ibid.
21. Ibid., pp. 31–2.
22. Ibid., p. 33.
23. Ibid.
24. Ibid., p. 36.
25. Ibid., p. 37.
26. Carole Pateman, *The Sexual Contract* (Cambridge: Polity Press, 1988), p. 192.
27. Ibid., p. 193.
28. Ibid., p. 184.
29. Ibid.
30. Ronald Coase, cited in Andreas Hoffmann, 'Der Preis des Marktes', *Die Zeit* 18 (30 April 1993), p. 26.
31. Pateman, *The Sexual Contract*, p. 184.
32. Norwood, *Women Who Love Too Much*, p. 73.

33. Ibid., p. 63.
34. Ibid., pp. 63, 50.
35. Pateman, *The Sexual Contract*, p. 183.
36. Marilyn Frye, *The Politics of Reality: Essays in Feminist Theory* (Trumansburg, NY: The Crossing Press, 1983), pp. 98ff and n. 5.
37. See ch. 5, n. 29.

Chapter 11 Needs, or the legitimation of dominance

1. Carole Pateman, *The Sexual Contract* (Cambridge: Polity Press, 1988), p. 207.
2. Ibid., p. 224. See also Catharine A. MacKinnon, 'Feminism, Marxism, Method, and the State: Toward Feminist Jurisprudence', *Signs* 8 (1983), p. 650; Catharine MacKinnon, *Toward a Feminist Theory of the State* (Cambridge, Mass.: Harvard University Press, 1989), esp. pp. 168, 238; Catharine A. MacKinnon, *Sexual Harassment of Working Women* (New Haven: Yale University Press, 1979), p. 298, n. 8.
3. Pateman, *The Sexual Contract*, p. 230.
4. Personal communication, Charlotte Friedli, Switzerland.
5. Pateman, *The Sexual Contract*, p. 169.
6. Cited in Pateman, *The Sexual Contract*, p. 169.
7. Cited in Pateman, *The Sexual Contract*, p. 170.
8. Ibid.
9. Ibid., p. 173.
10. Ibid., pp. 173–4.
11. Ibid., pp. 231, 200.
12. M. McMurtry, cited in Pateman, *The Sexual Contract*, p. 154.
13. Anthony Giddens, *The Transformation of Intimacy: Sexuality, Love and Eroticism in Modern Societies* (Cambridge: Polity Press, 1992), p. 192.
14. Pateman, *The Sexual Contract*, p. 151.
15. Ibid.
16. Cited in Pateman, *The Sexual Contract*, p. 148.
17. Ibid., p. 145.
18. Ibid., pp. 151, 146.
19. Ibid., p. 150.
20. Marilyn Frye, *The Politics of Reality: Essays in Feminist Theory* (Trumansburg, NY: The Crossing Press, 1983), p. 67.
21. Ibid.
22. Ibid., pp. 59–60.
23. Ibid., p. 23.
24. Ibid., p. 61.
25. Robin Norwood, *Women Who Love Too Much* (London: Arrow Books, 1986), p. 100.

26. Ibid., p. 44.
27. Giddens, *The Transformation of Intimacy*, p. 202.
28. Ibid.
29. E.g. in Norwood, *Women Who Love Too Much*, p. 69.
30. Ibid., pp. 28–9.
31. Ibid., p. 33.
32. Ibid.
33. Ibid.
34. Luise Eichenbaum and Susie Orbach, *What Do Women Want?*, first published by Michael Joseph, London, 1983; page reference to the second edn (London: Fontana, 1984), p. 109.

Chapter 12 Identity, or history turned biology

1. Alain Finkielkraut, *Remembering in Vain: The Klaus Barbie Trials and Crimes Against Humanity*, translated by Roxanne Lapidus with Sima Godfrey (New York: Columbia University Press, 1992), p. 66. As the translation does not always follow the original literally but the exact wording is important to my purposes, I have made my own translations based both on the English translation and the French original, Alain Finkielkraut, *La Mémoire vaine: Du crime contre l'humanité* (Paris, Éditions Gallimard, 1989), p. 111.
2. Karl Marx, *Capital*, vol. I, translated by Ben Fowkes (Harmondsworth: Penguin Books, 1976), p. 137.
3. Robin Norwood, *Women Who Love Too Much* (London: Arrow Books, 1986), p. 33.
4. Marx, *Capital*, pp. 166–7.
5. Swantje Köbsell, 'Humangenetik und pränatale Diagnostik: Instrumente der "Neuen Eugenik" ', in Theresia Degener and Swantje Köbsell, *'Hauptsache, es ist gesund?' Weibliche Selbstbestimmung unter humangenetischer Kontrolle* (Hamburg: Konkret Literatur Verlag, 1992), p. 21. An extended discussion of subjective validation and classification in 'Zoologie und Völkerkunde', in Susanne Kappeler, Mira Renka and Melanie Beyer, eds, *Vergewaltigung, Krieg, Nationalismus* (Munich: Frauen-offensive, 1994).
6. Finkielkraut, *Remembering in Vain*, p. 67.
7. Audre Lorde, 'The Uses of Anger: Women Responding to Racism', in Audre Lorde, *Sister Outsider: Essays and Speeches* (Freedom, CA.: The Crossing Press, 1984), p. 132.
8. Cherríe Moraga, 'Refugees of a World on Fire: Foreword to the Second Edition', in Cherríe Moraga and Gloria Anzaldúa, eds, *This Bridge Called*

My Back: Writings by Radical Women of Color (New York: Kitchen Table: Women of Color Press, 1983), unpaginated preface.

9. Jenny Bourne, 'Homelands of the Mind: Jewish Feminism and Identity Politics', *Race & Class*, vol. 29, no. 1 (Summer 1987); reprinted as *Jewish Feminism and Identity Politics*, Race & Class Pamphlet no. 11.

10. Kathleen Barry, *Female Sexual Slavery* (New York and London: New York University Press, 1979), p. 44.

11. Ibid., p. 45.

12. Ibid.

13. bell hooks, *Feminist Theory: From Margin To Center* (Boston: South End Press, 1984), pp. 43, 45.

14. Barry, *Female Sexual Slavery*, p. 45.

15. Alain Finkielkraut, *Der eingebildete Jude*, translated by Hainer Kober (Frankfurt a.M.: Fischer Taschenbuch Verlag, 1984), preface to this edn, p. 7; my translation from the German edn.

16. Ibid., pp. 7–8.

17. Alain Finkielkraut, *Le Juif imaginaire* (Paris: Éditions du Seuil, 1980), pp. 207–8.

18. Finkielkraut, *Der eingebildete Jude*, p. 7.

19. Ibid., p. 8.

20. Finkielkraut, *Le Juif imaginaire*, p. 208.

21. Ibid.

22. Katalog Bremer Frauenwoche 1991, p. 24; my translation.

23. Sabine Hark, 'Wer spricht, wenn ich: "Ich bin . . ." sage?: Zum Verhält-nis von Identitäten und Bündnispolitik', *Ihrsinn* 2 (1990), p. 44; my translation.

24. Dagmar Schultz, 'Unterschiede zwischen Frauen – ein kritischer Blick auf den Umgang mit "den Anderen" in der feministischen Forschung weißer Frauen', *beiträge zur feministischen theorie und praxis* 27 (1990), p. 45; Dagmar Schultz, 'Kein Ort für uns allein: Weiße Frauen auf dem Weg zu Bündnissen', in Ika Hügel et al., eds, *Entfernte Verbindungen: Rassismus, Antisemitismus, Klassenunterdrückung* (Berlin: Orlanda Verlag, 1993), p. 177.

25. Finkielkraut, *Remembering in Vain*, p. 17; *La Mémoire vaine*, p. 38.

26. Alain Finkielkraut, *The Undoing of Thought*, translated by Dennis O'Keeffe (London and Lexington: The Claridge Press, 1988), p. 79.

27. Stephen Yearly, blurb for the anthology *Men, Sex and Relationships: Writings from 'Achilles Heel'*, ed. Victor J. Seidler (London: Routledge, 1992), in Routledge New Books and Backlist 1993, p. 30.

28. Christina Thürmer-Rohr, 'Weiße Frauen and Rassismus', *taz*, 8 January 1993, p. 12; my translation, as of the following quotations.

29. Schultz, 'Kein Ort', p. 161.
30. Ibid., p. 162.
31. Ibid., pp. 161ff.
32. Ibid., pp. 181–3.
33. Sarah Lucia Hoagland, *Lesbian Ethics: Toward New Value* (Palo Alto: Institute of Lesbian Studies, 1988), p. 5.
34. Ibid., p. 2.
35. Ibid., pp. 1–2.
36. Ibid., p. 2.
37. Ibid., p. 3.
38. Ibid.
39. Ibid.
40. Ibid.
41. Ibid., p. 1.
42. Ibid., p. 3.
43. Ibid., p. 293.
44. Ibid., p. 295.
45. Ibid., p. 293.
46. Ibid., p. 295.
47. Ibid., pp. 295–6.
48. Ibid., p. 293.
49. Ibid., p. 295.
50. Thürmer-Rohr, 'Weiße Frauen und Rassismus', p. 12.
51. Ibid.
52. Ibid.
53. Ibid., p. 13.
54. Ibid., p. 12.
55. Ibid., p. 13.
56. Ibid., p. 12.
57. Ibid.
58. Theo Sommer, 'Die Vergangenheit vergeht nicht', *Die Zeit* 17 (23 April 1993); my translation.
59. Ibid.
60. Ibid.
61. Ibid.
62. Ibid.
63. Norbert Elias, cited in Wolf-Dieter Narr, 'Staatsgewalt und friedsame Gesellschaft: Einige Notizen zu ihrem Verhältnis in der Bundesrepublik', in Peter-Alexis Albrecht and Otto Backes, eds, *Verdeckte Gewalt: 'Plädoyer für eine "Innere Abrüstung"* ' (Frankfurt a.M.: Suhrkamp Verlag, 1990), p. 71; my translation.
64. Norbert Elias, *Studien über die Deutschen: Machtkämpfe und Habitusentwicklung im 19. und 20. Jahrhundert* (Frankfurt a.M.: Suhrkamp Verlag, 1992; first published 1989), pp. 559–60; my translation.

65. Ibid., p. 7.
66. The notion of a social sexual character of women (*Geschlechtscharakter*) is widespread among German feminists. See e.g. Studienschwerpunkt 'Frauenforschung' am Institut für Sozialpädagogik der TU Berlin, eds, *Mittäterschaft und Entdeckungslust* (Berlin: Orlanda Verlag, 1989), esp. p. 87. For a critique see Susanne Kappeler, 'Vom Opfer zur Freiheitskämpferin: Gedanken zur Mittäterschaftsthese und zum Round-Table Gespräch', in the same book.
67. Elias, *Studien*, p. 539.
68. Ibid., p. 540.
69. Ibid.
70. Ibid., p. 401.
71. An extended critique of this analogy and the biologizing of 'culture' can be found in Susanne Kappeler, 'Die Gemeinschaft "Volk" und die Völkergemeinschaft', and 'Zoologie und Völkerkunde', both in Kappeler, Renka and Beyer, eds, *Vergewaltigung, Krieg, Nationalismus:*
72. Elias, *Studien*, p. 10.
73. Ibid., p. 539.
74. See e.g. Finkielkraut, *The Undoing of Thought*, especially part I; Eric Hobsbawm, *Nations and Nationalism since 1780* (Cambridge: Cambridge University Press, 1990), pp. 102ff.
75. Elias, *Studien*, pp. 549–50.
76. Ibid., p. 550.
77. Hannah Arendt, 'Persönliche Verantwortung in der Diktatur', in Hannah Arendt, *Israel, Palästina und der Antisemitismus* (Berlin: Verlag Wagenbach, 1991), p. 19; my translation. A much abbreviated version of this essay appeared in English in *The Listener*, 6 August 1964.
78. Elias, *Studien*, p. 7.
79. Ibid., p. 552.
80. Finkielkraut, *Remembering in Vain*, p. 51; *La Mémoire vaine*, pp. 91–2.
81. Hannah Arendt, cited in Finkielkraut, *Remembering in Vain*, p. 53.
82. Elias, *Studien*, p. 8.
83. Finkielkraut, *Remembering in Vain*, p. 52; *La Mémoire vaine*, p. 93.
84. Ibid., p. 56; *La Mémoire vaine*, p. 98.
85. Ibid.

Resistance and the will to resistance

1. Cynthia Enloe, *Does Khaki Become You? The Militarization of Women's Lives* (London: Pandora Press, 1988; first published in 1983).

2. See also Patricia Williams's discussion of the racist murders of Howard Beach and the so-called Bernhard Goetz murders in the New York underground and their public media justifications, in Patricia J. Williams, *The Alchemy of Race and Rights* (London: Virago Press, 1993), pp. 58–79.
3. German television ARD, 'Tagesschau', 16 May 1994.
4. Anthony Giddens, *The Transformation of Intimacy: Sexuality, Love and Eroticism in Modern Societies* (Cambridge: Polity Press, 1992), p. 31.
5. Discussed e.g. by Cynthia Enloe in 'The Right To Fight: A Feminist Catch-22', *Ms.* 4, no. 1 (July/August 1993), pp. 84–7. Ruth Seifert, in an interview in *taz*, 17 February 1993, argues in favour of women entering the military, as this could perhaps 'break open the social construction of masculinity and femininity'.
6. Sarah Lucia Hoagland, *Lesbian Ethics: Toward New Value* (Palo Alto: Institute of Lesbian Studies, 1988), p. 6.
7. See e.g. Joanna Russ, *How to Suppress Women's Writing* (London: The Women's Press, 1984); Toni Morrison, *Playing in the Dark: Whiteness and the Literary Imagination* (London: Picador, 1993).
8. Women's resistance often seems to disappear when the focus remains (exclusively) on oppression. Thus Adrienne Rich's essay 'Compulsory Heterosexuality and Lesbian Existence' (see ch. 8, n. 8), for example, seems to have been received more as a confirmation of the oppression of lesbians than as a brilliant example of how to read, that is, perceive, the resistance of (heterosexual as well as lesbian) women to compulsory heterosexuality. See also Chandra Talpade Mohanti (cited ch. 3, n. 15).

Index